Religious Schooling in America

Contributors

Thomas C. Hunt

Norlene M. Kunkel

Jon Diefenthaler

Donald Oppewal

Peter P. DeBoer

George R. Knight

James C. Carper

Eduardo Rauch

Charles R. Kniker

James F. Herndon

Donald A. Erikson

RELIGIOUS SCHOOLING
IN AMERICA

Edited by

JAMES C. CARPER
and
THOMAS C. HUNT

Religious Education Press
Birmingham, Alabama

Library of Congress Cataloging in Publication Data

Main entry under title:

Religious schooling in America.

   Includes bibliographical references and index.
   1. Church schools—United States—History. I. Carper, James C. II. Hunt, Thomas C.
LC427.R44 1984   377′.0973   84-1942
ISBN 0-89135-043-8

Religious Education Press, Inc.
1531 Wellington Road
Birmingham, Alabama 35209
10 9 8 7 6 5 4 3 2

Religious Education Press publishes books exclusively in religious education and in areas closely related to religious education. It is committed to enhancing and professionalizing religious education through the publication of serious, significant, and scholarly works.

PUBLISHER TO THE PROFESSION

TO OUR FAMILIES—SPOUSES, PARENTS, CHILDREN, BROTHERS AND SISTERS— WITH GRATITUDE AND LOVE.

Contents

Preface

All too frequently, discussions about formal education have focused on *public* schooling. Private education in general, and religious schooling in particular, have received scant attention from scholars and persons involved in formulating educational policy. Since the late 1970s, however, researchers, policy makers, government officials, families, and the wider public have become increasingly interested in private education and its programs, characteristics, sources of support, and place in the American educational configuration.

There are several reasons for the growing interest in nonpublic education. First, as problems associated with public education have approached "crisis" proportions (witness the outpouring of reports in 1983 warning that America's public schools are "nearing collapse"), there has been a concomitant awakening of interest in private schooling. Americans seem more receptive now than at any other time in recent history to nonpublic options. Public opinion surveys in 1981 and 1982 suggested that a substantial percentage (some polls placed the figure as high as 45 percent) of public school parents would transfer their children to a private school if the financial means were available. Furthermore, the general public seems to be more supportive than ever before of tuition tax credits, vouchers, and similar proposals for enhancing educational choice. Second, James Coleman's widely publicized and vigorously debated report, *Public and Private Schools*, has focused national attention, not only on questions about the educational climate of private schools, but also on a host of important policy questions concerning the role of these schools in American education. Finally, the Reagan Administration's philosophical preference for private choice, and accompanying advocacy of tuition tax credits and vouchers, has drawn considerable attention to nonpublic education.

Much of the current interest in private education is focused on the largest segment of that enterprise—religious schools. These institutions enroll between 85 and 90 percent of the approximately 5.1

million nonpublic school students (K–12), and according to some projections their enrollment will increase throughout the remainder of the decade.

Religious Schooling in America is an attempt to enhance our understanding of this part of the American educational landscape which, until recently, has been often relegated to the periphery of educational inquiry. Pursuant to this goal, the first part of this book is comprised of essays which trace the history of six major religious school movements—Roman Catholic, Lutheran, Calvinist, Seventh-day Adventist, Christian day, and Jewish. Here Thomas C. Hunt and Norlene M. Kunkel, Jon Diefenthaler, Donald Oppewal and Peter P. DeBoer, George R. Knight, James C. Carper, and Eduardo Rauch, respectively, describe the origins of these movements, the cultural and theological forces which have shaped them, and their current status.

Part two of the book consists of essays on three significant contemporary concerns facing religious schools, and to some degree public education as well. Using the "common school ideology" as a point of reference, Charles R. Kniker examines the past and present relationships between public schools and religious schools and assesses the contributions of each to American society. James F. Herndon then reviews the vexing tuition tax credit/voucher question with an emphasis on legal aspects. Finally, Donald A. Erickson comments on the volatile issue of state regulation of nonpublic schools.

The editors hope this collection of essays will provide a deeper understanding of the history of religious schooling in America and useful insights into some of the current issues facing these schools. We believe this book will fill a gap in the literature on private education. But more importantly, we think it will enhance the quality of the current debate over the future shape of American education. It is indeed a crucial discussion because debate about education is, in David Tyack's words, really talk about the "kind of future we want as a society."

JAMES C. CARPER
Mississippi State, Mississippi
THOMAS C. HUNT
Blacksburg, Virginia

Part One

Historical Insights

Chapter 1

Catholic Schools: The Nation's Largest Alternative School System

THOMAS C. HUNT AND NORLENE M. KUNKEL

Catholic schools have played an important part in the history of the nation in general and of education in particular. Their contributions to both the concept and the existence of educational alternatives have been enormous. Quantitatively, they reached their all-time high of 5.6 million pupils (elementary and secondary) in 1965–66,[1] when they constituted 87 percent of nonpublic school enrollment.[2] In the years following 1966 Catholic school enrollment plummeted. By 1978, for instance, Catholic schools enrolled 3,289,000 students, making up 70 percent of nonpublic enrollment.[3] In 1981–82 Catholic school population had declined to 3,094,000, accounting for 64 percent of nonpublic school enrollment.[4]

The contributions of Catholic schools to the country, as well as to the Catholic Church itself, however, surpass mere quantitative measurement. It is the purpose of this essay to attempt to tell, albeit briefly, and in a fashion which fits the rationale of this book, the story of American Catholic schools. (In the process, several topics, such as the impact of the religion clauses of the First Amendment on Catholic schools as interpreted by the Supreme Court of the United States, and the positions taken by Catholics in these legal matters, had to be omitted.) This story has been told at much greater length and in more exact detail in many other places. It also has been subject to a variety of interpretations, which reflect a difference of perspectives. Space permits only the barest mention of these approaches: the institutional, typified by such writers as James A. Burns;[5] and by what has been termed the social, which can be traced, it would seem, to Robert Cross' seminal article in 1965, "The Origins of Catholic Parochial

1

Schools in America," and has been deepened and broadened conceptually by the writings of such authors as James Sanders, Jay Dolan, and James Hennesey, to name but a few.[6]

BEGINNINGS

The country's first Catholic bishop, a former Jesuit, John Carroll, labored diligently on behalf of Catholic education for men and women in the infant nation.[7] In his "Pastoral Letter" of 1792 Carroll instructed Catholic parents in the importance of the lifelong benefits of a Christian education.[8] It was left to the "Pastorals" of the Provincial Councils of Baltimore, however, to emphasize firmly and repeatedly the significance of Catholic schools. For instance, the Pastoral which emanated from the Provincial Council of 1840 called upon Catholic laity to support Catholic schools and complained of the difficulties Catholics were encountering with public schools over issues such as textbooks, Bible-reading, and the very system itself.[9]

New York City was the scene of an early conflict over schooling. Diane Ravitch has described the contentions there as a "great school war."[10] In New York in the 1840s the Catholics, led by their aggressive bishop, John Hughes, sought a portion of the school funds which were under the auspices of the philanthropic, allegedly nonsectarian, Public School Society. Hughes sought these funds after he had scrutinized the Society's schools and their textbooks, and described the situation as "intolerable" for Catholic children.[11] Hughes' efforts were to no avail. Rebuffed, he embarked on establishing a system of separate parochial schools, which would teach the Catholic creed "*in its entirety.*"[12]

Other conflicts erupted between Catholic and public schools during this period, many of which originated from the nativistic, anti-Catholic sentiment which existed in mid-nineteenth century Protestant America. Some of these struggles had been brought about by the immigration of Catholics, which had been influenced by difficulties of several kinds in their European homelands, and by industrialization and the consequent trend toward urbanization (in 1820 less than 8 percent of the nation's residents lived in urban centers [700,000 out of 9 million]; by 1870, 25 percent [10 of 40 million] lived in communities of 2,500 or more).[13] Catholics in the United States, meanwhile, made up approximately 1 per cent of the nation's population in 1800;[14] their numbers have been estimated at 500,000 (out of a total of 12 million) in 1829; by 1884 they numbered more than 8 million.[15]

The drive toward the establishment of the free, universal public school system, spearheaded by Horace Mann in Massachusetts, had begun in the 1830s. Purportedly nonsectarian, it has been termed "pan-Protestant" by many observers. Catholic children frequently encountered bigotry and prejudice in these schools, manifested in a number of ways, as scholars such as Anson Phelps Stokes have attested.[16] It is well to note, however, at this point that the ideal Catholic position on schooling, as articulated by Hughes and other Catholic leaders, did not call for support of a "religiously neutral" public school, but envisioned the entire educational process for Catholic children being under the control of Catholic authorities. This view, often regarded as the traditional or orthodox position, was to be repeated and reinforced by official Catholic pronouncements in the latter nineteenth and early twentieth centuries.[17]

THE LATTER NINETEENTH CENTURY—GROWTH OF THE SYSTEM

Immigration continued unabated, indeed increased, as the nineteenth century progressed. In some parts of the nation the Protestant base for public schooling began to be replaced by "Americanism" or citizenship education, founded on natural moral premises. Moral education in this setting was divorced from religious education (which was seen as the province of home and church) and became identified as being under the aegis of the public school.[18] The trend toward centralization, bureaucratization, and systematization in public schooling, regulated and orchestrated by local school superintendents accompanied, indeed may be said to have directed, this development.[19] Table 1 shows, however, that the sources of immigration changed as the nineteenth century progressed and the twentieth century was ushered in. The data portrayed in Table 1 do not identify the religion of these immigrants. Buetow notes, however, that the Catholic population of the United States experienced an immense growth from 6,143,222 in 1880 to 17,735,553 in 1920.[20]

The interplay of ethnicity and schooling, especially when compounded with religious factors, is both critical and complex. David Tyack, for instance, has pointed out that there were differences within immigrant groups, as well as between them.[21] Marvin Lazerson has written of the importance of the ethnic factor in the development and maintenance of Catholic parish schools.[22] Other authors, such as Sanders and Kuzniewski, have shown how complex the religious-eth-

TABLE 1

AMERICAN IMMIGRATION, 1861–1920

Period	Total	Northwest Europe		South and East Europe	
		Number	Percent	Number	Percent
1861–1870	2,314,824	2,031,624	87.8	33,628	1.4
1871–1880	2,812,191	2,070,373	73.6	201,889	7.2
1881–1890	5,246,613	3,778,633	72.0	958,413	18.3
1891–1900	3,687,564	1,643,492	44.6	1,915,486	51.9
1901–1910	8,795,386	1,910,035	21.7	6,225,981	70.8
1911–1920	5,735,811	997,438	17.4	3,379,126	58.9

SOURCE: R. Freeman Butts and Lawrence A. Cremin, *A History of Education in American Culture* (New York: Holt, Rinehart and Winston, 1953), p. 308.

nic factors are, as well as how different in their outcome they can be within the church itself.[23]

Support for Catholic schools, as evidenced by their declarations in the Provincial Councils of Cincinnati, was particularly noteworthy among German-American Catholics, and especially by the bishops of that nationality. As early as 1855, in the first of such Councils, the bishops singled out for commendation the "excellent German congregations" for their zeal in supporting Catholic schools. The decrees of this same Council exhorted pastors to erect and maintain schools and called on parents to aid their spiritual leaders and enroll their children in these schools.[24]

Support for the System—The Vatican and the Councils of Bishops

Provincial and Plenary Councils alike, as well as a number of individual Catholic bishops, berated the public school system (it was either "Protestant" or "atheistic," "godless" or "infidel") on the one hand, and proposed Catholic schools on the other. (It should be noted at this point that unanimity among Catholics—whether bishop, priest, or layperson—over the necessity or desirability of Catholic schools did not exist at any time.) Vatican pronouncements, while they did not exert as much influence over the lay Catholic as was once believed, forthrightly endorsed the cause of Catholic schools. Papal encyclicals, especially those authored by Pope Leo XIII, promulgated the Catholic position on the rights of the church in the conduct of schooling. Of particular note in this regard was *Sapientiae Christianae* ("On the Chief Duties of Christians as Citizens"), published in January of 1890. (An encyclical, in Catholic teaching, is a letter which the pope sends through the bishops to the Catholics of the world. Its teachings, while not *in se* infallible, call for the internal assent of Catholics.) In this authoritative letter, the Pontiff wrote that parents have "exclusive authority in the education of their children," and have been divinely commanded to exercise this responsibility by choosing schools which imbued their children with the principles of Christian morality, and "absolutely oppose their children frequenting schools where they are exposed to the fatal poison of impiety." Leo cited as most deserving of praise those "Catholics of all nationalities, who, at the expense of much money and more zeal, have erected schools for the education of their children."[25]

Vatican concern over schooling was expressed by other means than direct papal teaching. One of the most important pronouncements was uttered in 1875 by the Congregation of the Propagation of the Faith, the unit of the Curia (what may be termed the pope's cabinet), which had administrative authority over and responsibility for the American Catholic Church, then officially a "mission" country. Responding to a request for assistance from several American bishops, the Congregation issued a papally approved "Instruction" which dealt with the schooling issue in the United States. The document's major points were: a warning of the evils of schooling which was not under the jurisdiction of the Catholic Church, an admonition to Catholic parents of their God-given responsibilities in the education of their children, a call for the establishment and support of Catholic schools wherever possible, and an invocation of the prospect of ecclesiastical sanction against those parents who shunned their moral duty by failing to oversee properly the moral development (the overriding purpose of education) of their children.[26]

The rapidly swelling numbers of Catholics in the United States, many foreign-born, contributed to the contention over educational issues. Briefly, Catholic authorities, for the most part, were not satisfied with either the Protestant-dominated public schools or with what they felt was the secularly oriented school. In 1884, in conjunction with Vatican influence, the Catholic bishops formally set forth their position on schooling in the Third Plenary Council of Baltimore. The bishops, after noting that three agencies—home, state, and church—

contributed to the fostering of civilization through education, proclaimed that to "shut religion out of the school," as was done in public schooling constituted "a more false and pernicious notion" than could be imagined.[27] Pursuant to an exhortation to Catholic pastors and parents to "multiply our schools," and "perfect them,"[28] the assembled prelates concluded and decreed relative to schools:

> I. That near every church a parish school, where one does not yet exist, is to be built and maintained in perpetuum within two years of the promulgation of this council, unless the bishop should decide that because of serious difficulties a delay must be granted. . . . IV. That all Catholic parents are bound to send their children to the parish school, unless it is evident that a sufficient training in religion is given either in their own homes, or in other Catholic schools; or when because of sufficient reason, approved by the bishop, with the precautions and safeguards, it is licit to send them to other schools. What constitutes a Catholic school is left to the decision of the bishop.[29]

The Council's decree did not end the debate within the Catholic Church's hierarchy over Catholic schools. The "liberal" wing, led by Archbishop John Ireland of St. Paul, fought the "conservative" faction, headed by Archbishop Michael Corrigan of New York and Bishop Bernard McQuaid of Rochester (New York). (It is interesting to note that opposition to "liberal" Catholic positions at this period in American history is often identified with German-American bishops. Corrigan and McQuaid, it should be observed, were English-speaking, Irish-American prelates, as was their featured opponent, John Ireland.) Sometimes the struggle was carried out in the pages of the secular public press, and often with ferocity. Even the visit of Pope Leo's personal legate, Archbishop Francis Satolli, failed to end the controversy. It took a letter from the Pope to the American bishops, written at the request of James Cardinal Gibbons, Archbishop of Baltimore, to bring the controversy to an end. In his letter Leo called for Catholic schools to be "most sedulously promoted," leaving to the judgment of the local bishop, "when it is lawful, and when it is unlawful to attend the public schools."[30]

The external and internal struggles over Catholic schools were part of a larger question—the relationship of Catholicism to American society and its institutions. "Liberals," such as John Ireland, favored cooperating with these institutions whenever possible, envisioning the development of harmonious relations between Catholics and their fellow citizens and the acceptance of Catholicism in American life as the result. "Conservatives," on the other hand, sought to remain apart, calling for the church to maintain and control its own institutions, including schools. The issue was complicated by the antiforeign, nativistic spirit prevalent in the nation at this time. Much of this sentiment was directed at Catholics, so many of whom were recent immigrants, who, it was charged, were loyal first to a foreign ruler—the pope—and second to the United States. The desire of these Catholics to retain their ethnic heritage, including their schools, was viewed as evidence of this foreign affiliation.

As with the controversy over schools, the turmoil was not limited to tensions with elements outside the church. The movement spearheaded by Peter Cahensly, which became known as Cahenslyism, opposed the assimilation of Catholics into the mainstream of American life. Among other things, the Cahenslyites sought the establishment of Catholic parishes and dioceses along lines of national origin, rather than by territory, each of which was to be headed by a pastor and bishop respectively of that nationality.[31]

The relationship of Catholicism to American life manifested itself in another, but related, controversy during this period—the alleged heresy of Americanism. Once again Pope Leo XIII intervened to end the strife. On January 22, 1899, he issued the encyclical *Testem Benevolentiae*, addressed to Cardinal Gibbons, in which he condemned the errors of Americanism. The major errors which Leo identified were calling on the Catholic Church to adapt itself to modern civilization, relax its ancient vigor, show indulgence to modern theories and methods, deemphasize religious vows, and give greater scope for the action of the Holy Spirit on the individual soul.[32] The Pope specified that the name Americanism had been attached to these doctrines, and that his condemnation of them by no means implied a condemnation of the characteristics of the American people. American Catholic "liberal" leaders, such as John Ireland, immediately accepted the Pontiff's teachings, simultaneously denying that they ever held the condemned doctrines.[33]

Catholic Educational Policy and the Control of Schooling

The state of Wisconsin was the scene in 1890 of two hard-fought battles which together illustrate late nineteenth and early twentieth century Catholic educational policy as it relates to the relative rights of parent, church, and civil authority in schooling, and to what may be termed the "religiously neutral" public school. The first of these battles involved the ill-fated Bennett Law, which placed church-affiliated schools under civil control and was repealed in 1891 subsequent to a bitter election campaign in 1890. As a result, church-operated schools in Wisconsin were free to function with substantial autonomy.[34] The second struggle was embodied in what has become known as the Edgerton Bible decision, in which the Supreme Court of Wisconsin in 1890 adjudged that devotional Bible-reading, with attendant religious exercises, constituted sectarian instruction and consequently violated the Wisconsin Constitution.[35] This ruling, the first of its kind by a state supreme court, may be said to have presaged subsequent court decisions which reached their climax in *School District of Abington Township v. Schempp*, 374 U.S. 203 (1963), thereby judicially severing traditional Protestant practices from public schooling.

THE FIRST HALF OF THE TWENTIETH CENTURY—A SETTLED SYSTEM

Changing School Attendance Patterns

School attendance statistics at the turn of the century document that schooling occurred predominantly at the elementary level. High schools attracted a small percentage of the 14 to 18 year old age group. In 1898, for instance, of 100 students in educational institutions, ninety-five were in elementary schools, four in secondary, and one in a postsecondary school.[36] Two years later, in 1900, approximately 10 percent of the high school age population was attending high school.[37] (Secondary enrollments reached about 5 million at the end of the 1920s; elementary schools enrolled approximately 97 percent of the 6 to 13 year olds by the 1920s.[38]) The comprehensive high school, as it exists today, is reflected in the *Cardinal Principles Report* of the National Education Association (NEA), issued in 1918.[39] The *Report* shows the evolution in the kinds of activities secondary schools engaged in. Catholic schools underwent similar changes. Prior to 1920 the overwhelming percentage of Catholic school attendance was found in Catholic elementary schools. Table 2 contains data relevant to Catholic elementary school enrollments, which were supported and conducted by Catholic parishes.

Catholic secondary school efforts were directed, in the main, by religious orders. In the years between 1918 and 1958 substantial expansion occurred in Catholic secondary schools which were conducted under the auspices of a single parish, or a combination of parishes

TABLE 2
CATHOLIC PAROCHIAL SCHOOL GROWTH IN THE U.S., 1880–1920

Year	Catholic Population	Parochial Schools	Pupil Enrollment
1880	6,143,222	2,246	405,234
1890	8,277,039	3,194	633,238
1900	10,129,677	3,811	854,523
1910	14,347,027	4,845	1,237,251
1920	17,735,553	5,852	1,701,219

SOURCE: Cited in Harold A. Buetow, *Of Singular Benefit: The Story of U.S. Catholic Education* (New York: The Macmillan Company, 1970), p. 79.

(the so-called central school). (At the end of 1957 there were 1,539 diocesan and parish high schools with 448,408 students; there were 846 private high schools, i.e., owned and operated by religious orders, with 274,355 pupils.)[40]

The Oregon Case

One more serious challenge had to be repelled, however, before the precious autonomy from state control was to be secure. The state of Oregon, attempting to eliminate alleged divisiveness brought about by private schools, and to bring about the desired attributes of American citizenship via public school education, passed a law which required Oregonians between the ages of eight and sixteen to attend public school.[41] The United States Supreme Court denied the state's contentions, held that parents have the right of choice in the schooling of their children, and ruled the legislation unconstitutional under the 14th Amendment.[42]

The "God-Centered" Nature of Catholic Schools—The Encyclical of Pope Pius XI

In 1925 the Catholic Church in general, and Catholic schools in particular, found themselves in a much more secure and prestigious place in the nation than they had occupied in the late nineteenth century. Having survived the overt (and sometimes covert) hostility of Protestant America, the church and its schools were free to conduct their affairs with a substantial measure of autonomy.

In 1929 Pope Pius XI issued his influential encyclical, *Divini Illius Magistri* ("The Christian Education of Youth"), which formed the ideological basis for Catholic schools for more than three decades. Briefly, the Pontiff averred that, for the Catholic, the only "true education" is Catholic education (schooling), which is founded on Christ and his teachings, takes in the "aggregate of human nature," is directed to "man's last end," and is under the control of Catholic authorities.[43] Pope Pius XII, Pius XI's successor, frequently and firmly reaffirmed the educational teaching of his predecessor throughout his lengthy pontificate.[44]

During the years which spanned the reigns of the two Piuses, Catholic schools in the United States by and large sought to imitate their public school counterparts in being "professional" and, to some extent, "American." It was their "God-centeredness," some claimed, which distinguished them from public schools and elevated them to being legitimate religious, supernatural agencies. There was also operative what a number of Catholic bishops had referred to in earlier eras—that the schools were necessary for the preservation of the church, in that they guaranteed an adult Catholic population. Finally, the ethnic factor referred to above remained influential, especially in parishes in urban areas.

Hierarchical Support in Times of Official Agreement

The motto ascribed to the Third Plenary Council of Baltimore in 1884, "Every Catholic child in a Catholic school," was never fulfilled. For instance, in 1884 there were 6,613 Catholic parishes, 2,532 of which had schools. In 1887 there were 6,910 parishes with 2,697 schools.[45] Parallel statistics existed in 1958–59. The noted Jesuit educator, Neil McCluskey, estimated that about one-half of the Catholic elmentary age population was enrolled in Catholic schools. Since Catholic elementary schools enrolled a higher proportion of their age population than did secondary schools (in 1958–59 Catholic elementary enrollment was 4,101,792; Catholic secondary enrollment stood at 810,768), far less than half of the Catholic secondary age group were attending Catholic high schools.[46] In the late nineteenth century some Catholic sources had castigated, on occasion, public schools as "godless."[47] One possible reason for these derogatory appellations was to motivate Catholic parents to send their children to Catholic schools. Individual bishops had visited attendance at public schools with canonical penalties, such as denial of the sacraments, on the children's parents. (This was in accord with the bishops' powers, contained in Canon Law, as well as in other policy documents.[48]) By the 1950s the language used to describe public schools had been toned down. So had, to some extent, the imposition of ecclesiastical sanctions against noncomplying parents. In 1958, though, fifty-five of 104 Catholic dioceses in the country reported they had a statute requiring parents to send their children to Catholic schools. (Nine of the remaining forty-nine had some form of restriction on attendance at public schools.) Of the fifty-five, twelve dioceses had attached a "reserved sin" (reserved to the bishop for forgiveness) to public school attendance. Thirty-eight of the fifty-five required parents to formally apply for permission to send their children to public school.[49]

In 1957 Archbishop (of Milwaukee) Albert G. Meyer, who was then also president of the National Catholic Educational Association (NCEA), praised both the quantity and quality of Catholic elementary and secondary education.[50] Not all agreed with Meyer, however. The well-known Catholic Church historian, John Tracy Ellis, found Catholic schools wanting in their commitment to the intellectual life. Among the reasons for this alleged failure was, in Ellis' view, the overemphasis on the school "as an agency for moral development."[51] His criticism notwithstanding, it would be fair to state that, prior to 1960, the most serious challenges to Catholic schools resided outside the church. The observation of Neil McCluskey, that the Catholic position on schooling had remained substantially the same since 1840, was accurate indeed.[52]

THE SECOND VATICAN COUNCIL—AN AGE OF TURMOIL

In the 1960s Catholic schools came under increasing criticism from *within* the church. The roots of these criticisms may be traced to the Second Vatican Council (Vatican II), which, generally speaking, "opened up" the church to the world. Schooling, or education, was one of the proposed areas of rapprochement with the world. In Vatican II the church fathers' most direct reference to Catholic schools was in *Gravissimum Educationis* ("Declaration on Christian Education"). In this document the bishops declared that "the church's involvement in the field of education is demonstrated especially by the Catholic school." They further stated that the Catholic school was to be "enlivened by the gospel spirit of freedom and charity"; that it prepared the young for this world and for "the advancement of the reign of God"; and reminded parents of their "duty to entrust their children to Catholic schools when and where this is possible."[53]

Concerns of the Hierarchy

The American bishops who served on the Council's education committee expressed several concerns. Among these were: 1) freedom of choice by parents to select the school of their choice for their children, assisted financially by government, and 2) the church must promote both Catholic schools and the other forms of education for those not in Catholic schools, such as the Confraternity of Christian Doctrine.[54] Here the bishops gave voice to a long-standing concern that the widely held view that Catholic schooling was equated with Catholic education had resulted in the neglect of the religious education for Catholics outside the pale of Catholic schools.[55] For instance, in Milwaukee the sum of $1.21 per child was expended for the religious education of Catholic children who attended public schools in 1967–68. Per pupil tuition costs for Catholic secondary-school students ranged into the hundreds of dollars.[56]

The Attack from Within

The "siege" mentality, and the important role played in that posture by the parochial schools, came under heavy criticism from a number of quarters within the Catholic Church in the years which immediately followed Vatican II. The views of several of these critics are briefly presented here. The first of these was Mary Perkins Ryan. She maintained that the age when Catholic schools were necessary to protect the faith of an immigrant minority population, living in a hostile environment, had passed. The schools were therefore, in a sense, anachronistic. Further, the attention placed on the school as the center of parish life detracted from recognizing the primary role that the liturgy and adult education deserved to play in the life of the parish.[57]

A second source of criticism emanated from the authors of *The Perplexed Catholic*, one a non-Catholic layman, the second a Catholic priest. These men chastised the church for neglecting its children not in Catholic schools, an offense more serious because the schools were ineffective in developing a sense of social justice in their pupils.[58]

Several other events contributed in a major way to the turmoil, indeed chaos, within the Catholic Church over its commitment to Catholic schools. The first occurred with the publication of two major studies in 1966 which concluded that Catholic schools were not necessary for the church to survive.[59] These publications were followed a year later by the call from Monsignor James C. Donohue, then director of education of the United States Catholic Conference (USCC), the civil arm of the American bishops, for pairing Catholic innercity and suburban schools and for cooperating with public schools in urban areas, even to sharing facilities. Donohue viewed with alarm the fact that many of the 452 Catholic schools which had closed in 1966–67 were innercity, and he felt the Catholic Church would be guilty of failing to meet Christ's Second Great Commandment ("Love thy neighbor as thyself") if it did not provide schools for the urban poor.[60] The next year he addressed the urban issue again, calling for Catholic education to focus on two aims in the urban ghettos: 1) academic excellence, and 2) the development of a Christian elite, based not on financial status but on the potential of developing Christian virtues.[61] Donohue was responding, at least in part, to the disturbing prospect that Catholic schools, perhaps under financial pressure, were serving as racial "escape valves" in some urban areas as well as abandoning the urban poor in favor of the suburbs.[62]

Parallel in time to the searching critiques uttered by Donohue were the changes in the structure of Catholic schools proposed by the former associate secretary of the NCEA (1957–1964) Monsignor O'Neil C. D'Amour. In his view, altered political and social realities called for separating the pastoral from the professional in Catholic schools and for establishing lay boards with policy-making powers.[63] Following suit, a committee of the NCEA did issue a report in 1967 on the board movement in Catholic schools. This report, while it did not embrace all of D'Amour's far-reaching suggestions, did conclude that lay boards broadened the schools' "base of support" and fostered the "cooperation of the community" on behalf of Catholic schools.[64]

Indecision over the place of Catholic schools in the life of the church even involved members of the American hierarchy. For instance, Cardinal Joseph Ritter, Archbishop of St. Louis, an archdiocese with a heavy commitment to Catholic schools, publicly wondered in 1967 if the church's investment in schools had been a wise one.[65] Bishop Ernest J. Primeau, president of the NCEA, that same year asked Catholic educators why the church was operating its own schools, and wondered if the longtime, but never achieved, goal of "every Catholic child in a Catholic school" was not only impossible but also undesirable?[66]

In this era, as with other periods of Catholic educational history, the schools reflected the milieu within which they existed. The 1960s witnessed the election of John F. Kennedy to the presidency of the United States, the first Catholic to fill that high office. Kennedy's election stands as evidence that the prejudice against Catholics in the United States had diminished. His performance in office demonstrated that a president could be both Catholic and a loyal American, a fact which contributed further to the lessening of bias against Catholics. The leadership displayed by another Catholic John in the 1960s—the immensely popular Pope John XXIII—also contributed to the dispelling of prejudice against Catholics.

In a sense American Catholicism had come of age. Catholic schools, and American Catholics in general, were affected by the sociological changes. James L. Morrison, observing these changes, averred that traditional Catholic emphasis on "religious training," while still important, was "rapidly becoming of secondary importance to an institutional concern . . . for the secular sociocultural context of contemporary American life." He felt that the most significant sociocultural factors associated with the shift were the nearly total assimilation of Catholic ethnic minorities into the mainstream of American life, the incorporation of large numbers of Catholics into the middle class, and the overall deemphasis of the importance of religion in American society.[67]

REGROUPING AND REAPPRAISAL

The criticism of lay and clerical Catholics, combined with the changed atmosphere of the post-Vatican II period and financial pressures, contributed to the beleagured state in which Catholic schools found themselves as the decade of the 1970s commenced. The last section of this essay will consider, albeit briefly, several issues which are of telling importance to Catholic schools today, and in the immediate future.

The Catholic School As "Faith Community"

In 1967, amid the spiritual crisis which Catholic education was enduring and the initial stages of plunging enrollment, the Catholic bishops of this nation, in an official pronouncement entitled "Catholic Schools Are Indispensable," predicted that "not in the too distant future . . . the trials and troubles of the present moment will be seen for what they really are, steps toward a new era for Catholic education."[68] Then, in a pastoral letter to the country's Catholics in 1972,

To Teach As Jesus Did, the bishops proclaimed the church's educational ministry as: 1) to teach doctrine, the message of hope contained in the gospel; 2) to build community, "not simply as a concept to be taught but as a reality to be lived"; and 3) service to all mankind, which emanated from the sense of Christian community.[69] In this pastoral the bishops identified Catholic schools as affording the "fullest and best opportunity to realize the threefold purpose of Christian education among children and young people." It was only in the "unique setting" of a Catholic school that the young could "experience learning and living fully integrated in the light of faith." The curriculum, but even more the teachers, who model an "integrated approach to learning in their private and professional lives," can bring about the "integration of religious truth and values," the bishops said. It was the "integration of religious truth and values with life" which distinguished Catholic schools from other schools, and made them worthy of the support of the Catholic community.[70] Finally, recognizing the malaise which had affected Catholic schools, the bishops urged Catholics to face up to the immense challenges which confronted Catholic schools, and above all, to "avoid a defeatist attitude."[71]

To Teach As Jesus Did sounded a clarion call for Catholic educators. In 1976 the president of the NCEA, John F. Meyers, posing a question which reflected a switch in basic attitudes, asked "how are we different?" from public schools, rather than wondering whether Catholic schools are as good as public schools.[72] The NCEA, attempting to implement the bishops' ideas, conducted workshops for Catholic school superintendents. These programs were organized around the theme of the school as a Christian educational community. The superintendents then held similar meetings for their principals and teachers. The NCEA-sponsored document, *Giving Form to the Vision,* was published to give Catholic educators tangible, concrete assistance to carry out the bishops' message.[73]

One Catholic educator who played a leadership role in the development of the concept of the Catholic school as "faith community" was Michael O'Neill. In 1978, at the time acting dean of the School of Education at the University of San Francisco, O'Neill wrote that recent emphasis on the direction Catholic schools should take was one becoming "more of an alternative, more unique," which could be accomplished by the schools developing as a "faith community."[74] Content, methodology, and intentionality made up the "modern concept of permeation," according to O'Neill.[75] It was intentionality, in his judgment, which was the most critical of the three. He described it as:

> When people in a school share a certain intentionality, a certain pattern or complex of values, understandings, sentiments, hopes, and dreams that deeply conditions everything else that goes on, including the math class, the athletic activities, the dances, coffee breaks in the teachers' lounge, everything.[76]

It is the "collective intentionality" which will not only distinguish the Catholic school from the public school but more importantly will enable the school to do what it does "extremely well" because it will be "based upon the redemptive love of Jesus Christ" and therefore be, in the full sense of the term, "truly Catholic." The presence of teachers or students who do not share the same beliefs does not impair collective intentionality, according to O'Neill. Rather, he believes their presence "in many cases" will "stimulate the other persons in the school to deepen and broaden their own perspective."[77]

Official Catholic sources have provided substantial support for the "faith community" thesis. One of the most influential of these is Pope John Paul II's *Catechesi Tradendae,* in which the Pope maintained that the task of developing a "community of believers" was embodied in the mission of Catholic schools.[78] The *National Catechetical Directory,* issued in 1979 by the American bishops, reinforced this viewpoint. In particular, the bishops focused in their document on the acceptance and living "of the Christian message" and the striving "to instill a Christian spirit in their students" on the part of teachers in Catholic schools as being especially vital.[79]

The Professional Staff—A Vital Issue in the School As "Faith Community." The responsibility for developing the "faith community" falls to a considerable extent on the building principals. The *National Catechetical Directory,* for instance, charges principals with a plethora of faith-related tasks, including the recruitment of teachers who are in agreement with the school's "goals and character." Once appointed, the principals are held accountable for providing opportunities for spiritual growth for these teachers, in addition to fostering "community among faculty and students."[80]

Principals are indeed critical in the instilling of religious principles in Catholic students. But, those persons with the most direct, regular contact with pupils—teachers—are quite likely the most indispensable ingredient if Catholic schools are to be distinct "faith communities" called for today. Catholic authorities traditionally have recognized their importance. So have Catholic educators. One Catholic educator recently spoke to the critical role of teachers in the faith-imbuing process and the consequent care to be exercised in their selection as follows:

> Selection of teachers to ensure this holistic development (whole child) is the single most significant task of the leadership of Catholic education. It is not enough to hire the best math teacher in the country. That teacher must be imbued with a deep faith in God, know how to identify the needs of students, teach them how to "reach" by using the most effective content and methodology, and care about being a learner himself/herself.[81]

The charge of imbuing teachers with the capacity to build faith has become more complex due to their changed origins. Twenty years ago most of the teachers in Catholic schools were members of religious orders. They lived, as well as worked, together in a community. They had been reared in the spirituality of their respective religious orders. Table 3 shows that in the space of the last thirteen years religious teachers have dropped from a total of 94, 983 (when they constituted 56.7 percent of the staff), to the figure of 37,743 (making up 25.8 percent of the staff).[82] The financial ramifications of this change of staff are recognizable to even the casual observer. The spiritual effects, including the building of the "faith community," are not as readily discernible. New means will have to be discovered for the fostering of spirituality in this largely lay professional staff if the schools are to be distinctively Catholic as called for by Catholic leaders.

Lay Teachers and Collective Bargaining—A Question of Social Justice. There is another issue involving lay teachers and their role in Catholic schools which merits mention at this point. It is the issue of the right of these teachers to form associations of their choice which will in turn represent them in bargaining with their employer—in this instance, the Catholic Church (diocese, parish, religious order, or lay school board). This right was first enunciated by Pope Leo XIII in his epochal encyclical *Rerum Novarum* ("On the Condition of Labor"), published in 1891. Leo's teaching has been reaffirmed by Pope Pius XI, by the Second Vatican Council, and by Pope John Paul II, as well as applied by the American hierarchy in several major recent labor-management disputes.[83] Thus the stance taken by some Catholic leaders toward the collective bargaining efforts by lay teachers in

TABLE 3

NUMBER AND PERCENTAGE OF RELIGIOUS AND LAY TEACHERS IN
CATHOLIC SCHOOLS

	1968–69		1978–79		1981–82	
Elementary						
Sisters	63,204	54.7%	28,453	28.9%	23,289	24.0%
Male Religious	1,278	1.1%	502	.5%	577	.6%
Lay Teachers	51,079	44.2%	69,584	70.6%	72,981	75.4%
Total	115,561	100 %	98,539	100 %	96,847	100 %
Secondary						
Sisters	20,428	39.4%	10,616	21.5%	8,738	17.7%
Male Religious	10,073	19.4%	5,880	11.9%	5,139	10.4%
Lay Teachers	21,416	41.2%	32,913	66.6%	35,448	71.9%
Total	51,917	100 %	49,409	100 %	49,325	100 %
All Schools						
Sisters	83,632	49.9%	42,396	28.1%	32,027	21.9%
Male Religious	11,351	6.8%	6,951	4.6%	5,716	3.9%
Lay Teachers	72,495	43.3%	101,301	67.3%	108.429	74.2%
Total	167,428	100 %	150,648	100 %	146,172	100 %

SOURCE: *Catholic Schools in America: Elementary/Secondary*, 1982 ed. (Englewood, Colo.: Fisher Publishing Co., 1982), p. xviii.

Catholic schools, as evidenced in *National Labor Relations Board v. The Catholic Bishop of Chicago et al.*, 99 S. Ct. 1313 (1979), hereafter referred to as *Catholic Bishop*, raised some questions. It is not within the scope of this essay to assess the *legal* arguments involved in the Supreme Court's decision. (The Court denied jurisdiction to the National Labor Relations Board [NLRB] over teachers in church-operated schools.) It is worthwhile to note, however, that Catholic lay teacher-leaders bitterly criticized the involved bishops and pastors on religious grounds. For instance, one lay teacher-leader noted that the teachers only went to the NLRB after the involved Catholic authorities had failed to recognize their rights.[84] Another found the church's position, especially when contrasted with its support of the "farm worker and the southern textile worker" as "wanting in its own vineyard." The words of the bishops themselves in *To Teach As Jesus Did*, which described lay teachers as "full partners in the Catholic educational enterprise," seemed hollow indeed to this teacher-leader.[85] Harold J. T. Isenberg, president of the Federation of Catholic Teachers, then an AFL-CIO affiliate in New York City, called on the bishops to "practice what you preach." He charged that the bishops were using the label of "faith community" as a "shroud" in which to "bury Catholic teacher unionization efforts."[86]

The Court's ruling in *Catholic Bishop* notwithstanding, the position and tactics of some Catholics—bishops, priests, and lay board members—in dealing with lay teachers does not seem to be consistent with the church's long-standing commitment, based on social justice, to the rights of the worker. A new approach to labor-management disputes, involving pastors, parents, parishioners, administrators, and teachers, simultaneously recognizing the rights of each group and the "uniqueness" of the Catholic school, has been called for. This mutual recognition, strengthened by goodwill and the resolve to listen to each other, will result in conflict resolution, according to one Catholic educator.[87] This kind of collaborative approach, which has resulted in "labor peace" in at least one previously troubled spot, Scranton, Pennsylvania, is similar to what the longtime Catholic labor leader, Monsignor George Higgins, advocated in his 1979 Labor Day address. In that speech he called for the formation of a "voluntary substitute for the National Labor Relations Board," which would ensure on the one hand that Catholic teaching on social justice would be observed and on the other take into account the difference between "church-related" and public schools.[88]

Minorities in Catholic Schools—Some Differences of Opinion

Catholic elementary schools of the nineteenth and early twentieth centuries, established and supported by Catholic parishes, were regularly made available to children of the parish with no tuition charge. They can accurately be termed "Catholic common schools." In the 1960s, however, as noted above, some critics, within and without the church, assailed Catholic schools as "racial escape valves." This section of the essay briefly treats the role of Catholic schools in the education of minority students from the late 1960s to the present.

Some concerns. In a line following James Donohue, Matthew Ahmann, at the time executive director of the National Catholic Conference for Interracial Justice, took the church to task in 1968 for what he felt was an inadequate record in the schooling of black Americans.[89] In a sense Ahmann echoed the concern expressed five years earlier that Catholic schools in urban areas were institutions of *de facto* segregation, places where Catholic children were hidden from community realities.[90]

A number of Catholic writers and educators advocated attempts to desegregate Catholic schools.[91] Facing escalating costs of Catholic schooling, Monsignor Edward Hughes, superintendent of schools in the Archdiocese of Philadelphia, feared that the rising costs would result in the "virtual withdrawal from our primary apostolate in the poor and Negro areas."[92] Meanwhile, a Pittsburgh priest, Father Donald McIlvain, leveled the charge that "the Catholic school system is making only feeble efforts at integration of its schools."[93] Responding to concerns such as these, Monsignor Geno C. Baroni, a well-known Catholic priest, wondered whether Catholic secondary schools engendered in their students an understanding of the meaning of the rising black-white crisis in the nation's cities. He made a number of suggestions which called on Catholic authorities to take concrete steps to guarantee that Catholic schools in innercities be integrated. In his judgment such steps would place the church on the side of contributing to the solution of a racial-justice issue.[94]

Efforts to meet the challenges which Catholic education faced in the innercity were expended by church authorities and educators.[95] For instance, several dioceses, among them Baltimore and Milwaukee, provided financial assistance to innercity students and/or schools. Minority students who were not Catholic were among the aid recipients.[96]

The examples above indicate that in the late 1960s Catholic schools were indeed, at least in some areas, attempting to provide schooling for the poverty-bound minority student. As Table 4 shows, Catholic school closings between 1966 and 1968 took place primarily in innercity and rural areas. In the former instance, it should be noted, they followed the massive moves of Catholics from the central cities to the suburbs.

The story changed precious little during the 1970s. On the one hand, some persons, in and out of the church, criticized the Catholic Church for what they felt was an insufficient commitment to schooling the urban poor.[97] On the other side, a number of instances could be cited which document exceptional effort on the part of Catholic dioceses, clergy, and/or religious orders to furnish schooling for innercity youth, regardless of their religious affiliation.

The Current Situation. Conflicting views still exist. Within the last few years, in part spurred by the publication of James S. Coleman's *Public and Private Schools*, debate has been reopened with renewed vigor over the relative impact of public and private high schools on the achieve-

TABLE 4
CATHOLIC SCHOOL CLOSINGS AND OPENINGS, 1966–1968

	Innercity	Suburban	Rural	Total
Secondary school openings:	21	31	8	60
Secondary school closings:	85	37	95	217
Elementary school openings:	48	72	27	147
Elementary school closings:	182	44	194	420

SOURCE: *The National Catholic Reporter*, 4 September 1968, p. 3.

ment of their students. The academic achievement of minority students in Catholic secondary schools was the focus of a study conducted by the Catholic priest-sociologist, Andrew M. Greeley, under the auspices of the National Opinion Research Center. Using data garnered from the longitudinal study, *High School and Beyond,* entitled "Minority Students in Catholic Secondary Schools," Greeley claimed that attendance at Catholic secondary schools benefitted minority students more than attendance at public high schools.[98]

The publication of *Inner-City Private Elementary Schools* in 1982 by the Catholic League for Religious and Civil Rights disproved, in the opinion of its proponents, one of the most pervasive myths of all about Catholic schools—that they are elitist. The study, using a randomly selected sample of sixty-four schools in eight cities, fifty-four of which were Title I recipients, and with a minority population of at least 70 percent, found strong support for these schools by their patrons. Housed in rundown buildings, beset with financial problems, mostly Catholic-operated but with a third of the student body Protestant, these schools have provided a safe environment, emphasized basic learning skills, and fostered moral values in their pupils. According to their supporters, these schools demonstrate the church's commitment to the urban minority poor (56 percent of their enrollment is black; 31 percent Hispanic-American).[99] Meanwhile, some critics of Catholic schools, who contend that in the main these schools cater to the middle and upper classes, persist in their indictments.

The Role of the Laity in the Modern Catholic School

The Influence of O'Neil C. D'Amour. The last section of the body of this essay deals with lay involvement in Catholic schooling, especially as it relates to: 1) the quest for public funds, and 2) governance of

Catholic schools. The growing number of Catholic schools in the second half of the nineteenth century were governed increasingly by clergy or religious orders, occasionally dotted by a reference to the truism that parents were the "primary educators" of their children. This governance pattern was taken for granted in the American Catholic Church until during and shortly after Vatican II. Then, in 1965, O'Neil C. D'Amour advocated altering the administrative structure of Catholic schools to reflect the social and political realities of American life. In the process D'Amour called for the establishment of school boards with real, not advisory, authority. He also recommended strengthening the professional leadership of these schools, deeming pastoral concern as an unacceptable substitute for professional leadership.[100] The "clerical-controlled" schools, as D'Amour termed them, were felt to be anachronistic. In subsequent articles D'Amour developed his model to include diocesan and area boards of education, which, he believed, could be operated in keeping with the provisions of Canon Law.[101]

A glance at the professional literature in the ensuing years reveals the interest in lay school boards which D'Amour had generated.[102] The lay board movement was to receive support from another source—the Diocesan Superintendents of Schools. In their publication, *Voice of the Community*, these educators promulgated a comprehensive plan for establishing school boards which were not merely advisory, but had real jurisdiction, and which included a rationale for their existence (based on Vatican II), as well as guidelines for their establishment and operation.[103]

The seeds of lay participation in Catholic school governance were sown more than a decade before Vatican II, however. A leading spokesman for lay involvement in the governance of Catholic schools, as well in the organization of lay Catholics to participate in the political arena, was the Jesuit political scientist, Virgil C. Blum. He was an early participant in the Citizens for Educational Freedom (CEF), founded in St. Louis by a group of laymen. Space permits only a brief description of this organization. CEF's basic position, which it has consistently advocated, calls for the recognition of the primacy of parent rights in the choice of schooling for children.

From the outset CEF sought to be an interdenominational organization. In 1963, for instance, clergymen of four different faiths were elected to hold office.[104] This effort continued through the 1970s, as evidenced by the election of a Baptist, Robert Baldwin, to the post of director in 1978. That year Baldwin told the CEF convention that "Protestants have come to realize the vital need for Christian education." It appears that this awareness has helped some evangelical and fundamentalist Protestants to overcome their longtime suspicion of Catholicism and join with Catholics to seek financial aid for their schools.[105]

Virgil Blum is the one person who articulated, coherently and consistently, the ideological position of CEF. In one of his many publications, he argued that the chief asset of the state is its youth, in whom the state is to maintain an active interest in their total development. Government's purpose in education is to seek the good of the individual child, which will benefit not only the child but also the common good. Under the 14th Amendment, there can be no discrimination in this task; all must be treated equally. This constitutional right each child has may not be abridged; nor may the civil authority demand that the child surrender his/her freedom of mind or religion as a condition of sharing in the benefits of government. Thus, if government financially subsidizes one form of schooling, e.g., public, and denies that aid to another kind, e.g., nonpublic, its action is arbitrary, unreasonable, and discriminatory. The state is not meeting the constitutional rights of equal protection under the law of students who attend the nonsubsidized schools in these instances. Further, the state, which is required to be neutral to religion, may not shirk its equal protection obligation due to attendance at religiously affiliated schools. Denial of aid because of attendance at a religiously affiliated school would not only make the state hostile to religion, it would also make the students' religion a liability, depriving them of common benefits due them. If this occurred, the state would be guilty of violating the students' mind and religion.[106]

Lay School Boards—Lay Control. Lay involvement in Catholic schooling, as characterized by the CEF, was not limited to fund-raising activities. Witness, for example, the ideas expressed by Stuart Hubbell, president of CEF, in 1967. While in full support of the ideological positions of CEF on the inalienable, God-given rights of parents to direct their children's education, and of government's responsibility to assist them in this educative task, Hubbell also called for the establishment of school boards which would move Catholic schools to excellence as well as provide parents the opportunity to exercise their rights and duties in the education of their children, an opportunity denied them in the Catholic schools of the past.[107] This message was reiterated and expanded nearly a decade later in the work of Andrew Greeley, William C. McReady, and Kathleen McCourt, entitled *Catholic Schools in a Declining Church.* Greeley and his colleagues reported that Catholic schools had the firm support of the Catholic laity. They cited figures which showed that while only 35 percent of parents of school-age children surveyed reported children in parochial schools, 38 percent of the remainder said that no parochial school was available. Further, 89 percent of the respondents rejected the position that "the Catholic school system is no longer needed in modern-day life," and 80 percent said that they would increase their contributions to save a financially troubled parochial school. Seventy-six percent felt the schools should receive financial aid from the federal government.[108] These researchers maintained that their data indicated that Catholic schools were successful in influencing the values of their students. Among the affected value patterns were students who were "more tolerant of others," and "change-oriented and flexible, but secure in both their worldview and their loyalty to past traditions and values."[109] But even more important to this section is the thesis that Greeley advanced in the "Afterword" of this book. The hierarchy, he maintained, should get out of the school business and turn control over to the laity, who were able and willing to run them. Then, and only then, will the Catholic schools be healthy.[110]

THE 1980S AND BEYOND—CHALLENGES TO THE "FAITH COMMUNITY"

Challenges Related to the Control of Schooling

Andrew Greeley's suggestion in 1976 that the Catholic hierarchy abdicate its role in Catholic schooling has not been followed. There is, however, substantially more participation by the laity in determining Catholic educational policy than in times past. This increased lay role may lead to mixed results. On the one hand, it is indeed a fulfillment of the social teaching of the church. On the other hand, lay participation is not necessarily equated with social justice. In a recent lay teacher strike in New York City, for instance, Catholic lay teachers faced a Catholic school board chaired by a layman, Seraphim Maltese, who was also head of the New York State Conservative Party. The teachers did not find Maltese amenable to their position or conciliatory in his approach.[111] It is erroneous to assume that the Catholic laity will be of one mind as to policy and practice regarding Catholic schools. In fact, they may well be less observant of the tenets of Catholic social teaching than their clerical or religious counterparts.

Challenges Related to the Student Population

Several other issues merit mention at this juncture. Catholic schools did experience a severe enrollment decline beginning in 1965. Greeley and his co-authors reported that Catholic high-school enrollment in 1975 approximated its high of one million which it had reached in 1965.[112] Thus, the enrollment decline occurred almost entirely in elementary schools, the "Catholic common schools," most of which were operated by parishes. Several years ago two authors, James L. Morrison and Benjamin J. Hudgkins, suggested that these enrollment figures indicated a pattern which is inconsistent with the Catholic school as "faith community," a notion so prominent in recent Catholic educational teaching. Part of their thesis is that "although the original purpose of Catholic education was to serve religious ends, the contemporary Catholic educational system is primarily secular and specifically oriented to facilitating the social mobility of selected Catholic youth."[113]

Morrison and Hudgkins viewed the shift in emphasis toward secondary education as an indicator that religious training "is rapidly becoming of secondary importance to an institutional concern in preparing at least a segment of Catholic youth" for today's society.[114] Candid in their statements that their data were not obtained from representative public and Catholic senior high schools, nonetheless they opined that Catholic high schools, following many Protestant colleges, may become religious in name only.[115] Increased lay control of Catholic schools via the board movement, bringing about more institutional autonomy, may well present a challenge to the "faith community" model.

Challenges Related to the Professional Staff

Teachers, and their preparation, certainly call for close consideration in the years ahead. As noted earlier in this essay, historically, teachers in Catholic schools were usually members of religious orders. Often they were of the same order and were steeped in the spirituality of that order. Now, with the majority of teachers being lay persons (some not Catholic), Catholic schools are faced with creating new means for developing the kind of spiritual qualities in teachers (and administrators) called for by Catholic leaders which will enable the schools to become "faith communities." There is evidence that Catholic leaders not only are aware of this challenge but also have taken steps to meet it. Witness, for example, the recent (1981 and 1982) documents published by Catholic sources to that end (*The Christian Formation of Catholic Educators* and *The Pre-Service Formation of Teachers for Catholic Schools*).[116]

There is also the issue of collective bargaining on the part of lay teachers in Catholic schools and the response to it by Catholic authorities. As stated earlier in this essay, the Catholic hierarchy must take the lead in establishing guidelines for dealing with lay teachers in accord with the principles of social justice which the church has long championed, if Catholic schools are to be "faith communities" in anything more than name.

Challenges Related to the Uniqueness of the Schools

Those responsible for the conduct of Catholic schooling need to consider seriously all the ramifications of obtaining governmental financial aid for their schools. On the one hand, such aid would enable the church to increase its capability to deliver educational services to a wider community, including those of little or no means. On the other hand, this aid could be accompanied by governmental controls which would lead to a lessening (or cessation) of the efforts to be self-reliant, leading to an ever-increasing dependency. Further, it could also lead to a decrease (or loss) of the religious distinctiveness and/or uniqueness of the schools, rendering the concept of school as "faith community" sterile indeed.

CONCLUSION

Other issues which Catholic schools face today, such as the constitutionality of government financial aid, could be readily identified and elaborated upon. It is time, however, to conclude this essay with a few final observations. Catholic schools in this nation, born in an era of repression and sometimes persecution, established to maintain and cherish the faith of an immigrant, often besieged and impoverished population, have weathered the storm of external assault and internal criticism. In his keynote address at the 1982 NCEA Convention, Alfred McBride, former NCEA president, identified three major challenges which face Catholic schools in the 1980s. The "most basic one," according to McBride, was to "keep Catholic schools Catholic, institutionally, morally, and spiritually." The second was to "increase academic excellence competitively, professionally, and creatively." The third, and final challenge, was to "secure a financial basis for . . .

schools through endowments, development programs, and government aid."[117]

Only the future will reveal whether Catholic schools will meet these and other challenges successfully. One fact is certain, however: the demise of Catholic schools expected and foretold in some quarters a decade or so ago has not occurred.[118] Catholic schools have survived; perhaps due in part to offering parents an atmosphere in which "home and school share a common and explicitly religious understanding of the meaning of life";[119] perhaps because some believe they are "emphasizing responsible learning, but more importantly they are doing so within the gospel context of love, concern, dedication, and justice";[120] perhaps because of other reasons.

In fine, Catholic schools of 1983, still comprising the largest alternative to public schooling in the United States, face a myriad of challenges, different in kind than those of the past. Unlike the late '60s and early '70s, however, Catholic authorities and educators appear to have the verve to address them. Catholic schools are seen as "worth the effort," no longer laboring under the constant cloud of proving their value to the church.[121] Buoyed by this basic attitudinal change, and alive in an age in which cultural pluralism is encouraged, the future for Catholic schools promises to be interesting indeed.

NOTES

1. *U.S. News and World Report,* 18 August 1975, p. 55.
2. *Education Week,* 30 March 1983, p. 14.
3. Michael O'Neill, "Catholic Education: The Largest Alternative System," *Thrust,* 7 May 1978, p. 25.
4. *Education Week,* 30 March 1983, p. 14. It should be noted here that the statistics reported in *Education Week* are taken from reports by the National Catholic Educational Association (NCEA). They differ, due to the manner in which they are collected, from those presented by the *Official Catholic Directory,* compiled by P. J. Kenedy and Sons of New York, which indicated that Catholic school enrollment had increased in 1981–82 by 32,744 to a total of 3,167,371. (See *The Catholic Virginian,* 7 June 1982, p. 3.) It should also be observed that in 1982–83 Catholic schools experienced an unexpected decline of 68,000 students. This 2.2 percent drop was "not anticipated" according to NCEA sources. (See *Education Week,* 30 March 1983, p. 1.)
5. Three illustrations of Burns' writings in this regard are James A. Burns, *The Principles, Origin and Establishment of the Catholic School System in the United States* (New York: Benziger Brothers, 1908); *The Growth and Development of the Catholic School System in the United States* (New York: Benziger Brothers, 1912); and Burns and Bernard J. Kohlbrenner, *A History of Catholic Education in the United States* (New York: Benziger Brothers, 1937).

6. Robert D. Cross, "The Origins of Parochial Schools in America," *American Benedictine Review* 16 (1965):194–209; James W. Sanders, *The Education of an Urban Minority: Catholics in Chicago 1833–1965* (New York: Oxford University Press, 1977); Jay P. Dolan, *The Immigrant Church: New York's Irish and German Catholics: A History of the Roman Catholic Community in the United States* (New York: Oxford University Press, 1981); and James Hennesey, *American Catholics: A History of the Roman Catholic Community in the United States* (New York: Oxford University Press, 1981).

7. Hennesey, *American Catholics: A History of the Roman Catholic Community in the United States*, p. 86.

8. Bishop John Carroll, "Pastoral Letter" (1792), in *Catholic Education in America: A Documentary History*, ed. Neil G. McCluskey (New York: Teachers College Press, 1964), p. 48.

9. "Pastoral Letter," Fourth Provincial Council of Baltimore (1840), in McCluskey, *Catholic Education in America: A Documentary History*, p. 61. A provincial council is made up of the bishops of a certain province or region, e.g., Baltimore, Cincinnati. A plenary council involves all of the bishops of the country. Thus the decrees of a plenary council, subject to Vatican approval, are binding on Catholics throughout the country. Those of provincial councils apply to Catholics within the territory of that province.

10. Diane Ravitch, *The Great School Wars: New York City, 1805–1973* (New York: Basic Books, 1973), pp. 46–76.

11. John Hassard, *Life of Archbishop Hughes* (New York: Arno Press, 1969), pp. 229–31.

12. James A. Burns, *Catholic Education: A Study of Conditions* (New York: Longmans, Green and Co., 1915), p. 15.

13. R. Freeman Butts, *Public Education in the United States: From Revolution to Reform* (New York: Holt, Rinehart and Winston, 1978), p. 95.

14. H. Daniel-Rops, *The Church in an Age of Revolution*, 2 vols. (Garden City, New York: Doubleday and Co., Inc., 1967), 2:173.

15. Harold A. Buetow, *Of Singular Benefit: The Story of U.S. Catholic Education* (New York: The Macmillan Company, 1970), p. 112.

16. Anson Phelps Stokes, *Church and State in the United States*, 2 vols. (New York: Harper Brothers, 1950): 1:827.

17. See, for instance, Pope Pius IX, "Syllabus of Errors" (1864), in *A Free Church in a Free State?* ed. Ernest C. Helmreich (Boston: D. C. Heath and Co., 1964); "Instruction of the Congregation of Propaganda de Fide" (1875), in McCluskey, *Catholic Education in America: A Documentary History;* Pope Leo XIII, *Immortale Dei* ("The Christian Constitution of States") (1885), *The State and the Church*, ed. John A. Ryan (New York: The Macmillan Company, 1922); Pope Leo XIII, *Sapientiae Christianae* (On the Chief Duties of Christians as Citizens") (1890), in *Social Wellsprings*, 2 vols., ed. Joseph Husslein (Milwaukee: Bruce Publishing Co., 1940):1; and Pope Pius XI, *Divini Illius Magistri* ("The Christian Education of Youth") (1929), in *Five Great Encyclicals* (New York: Paulist Press, 1939).

18. Among the leaders in articulating this position was William Torrey Harris. See, for instance, Selwyn K. Troen, *The Public and the Schools: Shaping the St. Louis System, 1838–1920* (Columbia: University of Missouri Press, 1975). Also consult Neil G. McCluskey, *Public Schools and Moral Education: The Influence of Horace Mann, William Torrey Harris, and John Dewey* (Westport,

Conn.: Greenwood Publishers, 1975); and Thomas C. Hunt, "Public Schools and Moral Education: An American Dilemma," *Religious Education* 74 (July–August, 1979): 350–72, for further treatment of this evolution.

19. See, particularly, David B. Tyack, *The One Best System: A History of American Urban Education* (Cambridge, Mass.: Harvard University Press, 1974); and Tyack and Elisabeth Hansot, *Managers of Virtue: Public School Leadership in America, 1820–1980* (New York: Basic Books, 1982).

20. Buetow, *Of Singular Benefit: The Story of U.S. Catholic Education*, p. 179.

21. Tyack, *The One Best System: A History of American Urban Education*, pp. 104–09, 229–55.

22. Marvin Lazerson, "Understanding American Catholic Educational History," *History of Education Quarterly* 17 (Fall 1977): 297–317.

23. See, for example, Sanders, *The Education of an Urban Minority: Catholics in Chicago, 1835–1965*, and Anthony J. Kuzniewski, *Faith and Fatherland: The Polish Church War in Wisconsin, 1896–1918* (Notre Dame, Ind.: University of Notre Dame Press, 1980), for a revealing contrast of the manner in which the Archdioceses of Chicago and Milwaukee respectively handled the ethnic issue in general and the parochial (ethnic) school matter in particular.

24. "Pastoral Letter," First Provincial Council of Cincinnati (1855), in Burns and Kohlbrenner, *The Growth and Development of the Catholic School System in the United States*, p. 138.

25. Pope Leo XIII, *Sapientiae Christianae* ("On the Chief Duties of Christians as Citizens"), in Husslein, *Social Wellsprings*, 1:162.

26. "Instruction of the Congregation of Propaganda de Fide," in McCluskey, *Catholic Education in America: A Documentary History*, pp. 60–61.

27. Ibid., p. 91. For a more thorough treatment of the educational legislation of the American hierarchy consult Bernard Julius Meiring, *Educational Aspects of the Legislation of the Councils of Baltimore 1829–1884* (New York: Arno Press, 1978).

28. Ibid., p. 92.

29. Ibid., p. 94.

30. Cited in Daniel F. Reilly, *The School Controversy, 1891–1893* (New York: Arno Press, 1969), pp. 228–29. Reilly's book tells the story of the struggles between and among the American Catholic bishops and their respective "spokesmen" over the school question. Consult Thomas Bouquillon, *Education—To whom Does It Belong?* (Baltimore: John Murphy and Co., 1891); and Rene I. Holaind, *The Parent First: An Answer to Dr. Bouquillon's Query: Education—To Whom Does It Belong?* (New York: Benziger Brothers, 1891), for the presentation of the "liberal" and "conservative" Catholic positions respectively on the school question.

31. Cahenslyism is treated in a number of sources which deal with American Catholic history. See, particularly, Colman J. Barry, *The Catholic Church and German Americans* (Milwaukee: Bruce Publishing Co., 1953). Cahensly himself was the author of the Lucerne (Switzerland) Memorial in 1890, which he subsequently presented to Pope Leo. The Memorial, which emanated from a meeting of the St. Raphael Society in Lucerne, expressed concern over the loss of Catholic immigrants to the faith. The establishment of national churches in the United States was one of the Memorial's recommendations, designed to protect the immigrant's faith. On this topic consult Gerald Shaughnessy, *Has the Immigrant Kept the Faith?* (New York: Arno Press, 1969).

32. John Tracy Ellis, *American Catholicism* (Chicago: The University of Chicago Press, 1956), pp. 118–19. For a thorough study of the Americanism controversy consult Thomas T. McAvoy, *The Americanism Heresy in Roman Catholicism 1895–1900* (Notre Dame, Ind.: University of Notre Dame Press, 1963). The English text of the encyclical may be found in John Wynne, ed., *The Great Encyclical Letters of Pope Leo XIII* (New York: Benziger Brothers, 1903), pp. 441–53.

33. Thomas T. McAvoy, *A History of the Catholic Church in the United States* (Notre Dame, Ind.: University of Notre Dame Press, 1969), pp. 333–35.

34. For a brief treatment of the Bennett Law controversy see Thomas C. Hunt, "The Bennett Law of 1890: Focus of Conflict between Church and State," *Journal of Church and State* 23 (Winter 1981): 69–94.

35. Consult Thomas C. Hunt, "The Edgerton Bible Decision: The End of an Era," *The Catholic Historical Review*, 67 (October 1981): 589–619, for further information on this issue.

36. Tyack, *The One Best System: A History of American Urban Education*, p. 66.

37. Neil G. McCluskey, *Catholic Viewpoint on Education* (Garden City, N.Y.: Hanover House, 1959), p. 99.

38. Butts, *Public Education in the United States: From Revolution to Reform*, p. 318.

39. For an account of the post-*Cardinal Principles Report* attendance growth of the public high school, see ibid., pp. 318–21, and Edward A. Krug, *The Shaping of the American High School 1920–1941* (Madison: The University of Wisconsin Press, 1972), p. 42.

40. Buetow, *Of Singular Benefit: The Story of U.S. Catholic Education*, p. 225; and McCluskey, *Catholic Viewpoint on Education*, p. 99.

41. Robert L. Church and Michael W. Sedlak, *Education in the United States: An Interpretive History* (New York: The Free Press, 1976), pp. 359–61.

42. *Pierce v. Society of Sisters*, 268 U.S. 510 (1925).

43. Pius XI *Divini Illius Magistri* ("The Christian Education of Youth") in *Five Great Encyclicals*, pp. 37–67.

44. For a sampling of Pope Pius XII's utterances on education, see Vincent A. Yzermans, ed., *Pope Pius XII and Catholic Education* (St. Meinrad, Ind.: Grail Publications, 1957).

45. Burns and Kohlbrenner, *A History of Catholic Education in the United States*, p. 144.

46. McCluskey, *Catholic Viewpoint on Education*, pp. 98–100.

47. See, for instance, Michael J. Müller, *Public School Education* (New York: D. J. Sadler and Co., 1872); and Thomas J. Jenkins, *The Judges of Faith: Christian versus Godless Schools* (Baltimore: John Murphy and Co., 1886).

48. See T. Lincoln Bouscaren and Adam C. Ellis, *Canon Law: A Text and Commentary* (Milwaukee: Bruce Publishing Company, 1951). The most relevant canon is Canon 1374, which instructs parents to send their children to Catholic schools; to avoid "neutral" or "mixed" schools, attendance at such schools legitimate only with the explicit permission of the local bishop, when in his judgment there is no danger of "perversion" of the faith or morals of the students (pp. 704–05). Other canons, such as Canon 1381, which taught that the religious training of the young is subject at all times to the supreme authority of the church, are also pertinent to this point (pp. 707–08).

49. McCluskey, *Catholic Viewpoint on Education*, pp. 116–18.

50. Buetow, *Of Singular Benefit: The Story of U.S. Catholic Education*, p. 276.
51. John Tracy Ellis, *American Catholics and the Intellectual Life* (Chicago: The Heritage Foundation, Inc., 1956), p. 46.
52. McCluskey, *Catholic Viewpoint on Education*, p. 167.
53. "Declaration on Christian Education," in *The Documents of Vatican II*, ed. Walter M. Abbott (New York: America Press, 1966), pp. 637–47.
54. Mark J. Hurley, ed., *Declaration on Christian Education of Vatican Council II* (Glen Rock, N.J.: Paulist Press, 1966), p. 23.
55. See, for example, Vincent P. Lannie, "Church and School Triumphant: The Sources of American Catholic Educational Historiography," *History of Education Quarterly* 16 (Summer 1976): 142.
56. *The National Catholic Reporter*, 24 April 1968, p. 1.
57. Mary Perkins Ryan, *Are Parochial Schools the Answer?* (New York: Guild Press, 1968), pp. 65–67, 115–17.
58. John L. Reedy and James F. Andrews, *The Perplexed Catholic* (Notre Dame, Ind.: Ave Maria Press, 1966), pp. 63–67, 221.
59. Andrew M. Greeley and Peter H. Rossi, *The Education of Catholic Americans* (Chicago: Aldine Publishing Co., 1966); and Reginald A. Neuwein, ed., *Catholic Schools in Action: The Notre Dame Study of Catholic Elementary and Secondary Schools in the United States* (Notre Dame, Ind.: Notre Dame Press, 1966).
60. James C. Donohue, "Catholic Education in Contemporary Society," *National Catholic Educational Association Bulletin* 64 (August 1967): 13–17.
61. Donohue, "New Priorities for Catholic Education," *America*, 13 April 1968, pp. 476–79.
62. See, for example, Peter Schrag, *Village School Downtown* (Boston: Beacon Press, 1967); Matthew Ahmann, "The Church and the Urban Negro," *America*, 10 February 1968, pp. 181–85; "Are Parochial Schools Racial Escape Valves?" *Christian Century*, 26 October 1968, p. 1298; and John P. Sheerin, "Our Segregated Catholic Schools," *Catholic World*, March 1963, pp. 333–34.
63. O'Neil C. D'Amour, "Parochial Schools without Parochialism," *Ave Maria*, 24 April 1965, pp. 12–14; and D'Amour, "Restructuring Patterns of Education," in *What Is Happening to Catholic Education?* ed. C. Albert Koob (Washington, D.C.: National Catholic Educational Association, 1966), pp. 25–37.
64. National Catholic Educational Association, *Voice of the Community: The Board Movement in Catholic Education* (Washington: National Catholic Educational Association, 1967), Preface.
65. *The National Catholic Reporter*, 27 September 1967, p. 5.
66. Ernest J. Primeau, "The Future of Catholic Education," *National Catholic Educational Association Bulletin* 64 (August 1967): 18.
67. James L. Morrison, "Social Change and American Catholicism," an unpublished research paper, University of Notre Dame, p. 9.
68. *Catholic School Journal* 67 (January 1968): 25–27.
69. National Conference of Catholic Bishops, *To Teach As Jesus Did* (Washington, D.C.: United States Catholic Conference, 1973), pp. 1–9.
70. Ibid., pp. 28–29, 31–33.
71. Ibid., p. 34.
72. *The National Catholic Reporter*, 22 October 1976, p. 8.
73. National Catholic Educational Association, *Giving Form to the Vision:*

The Pastoral in Practice (Washington, D.C.: National Catholic Educational Association, 1974).

74. O'Neill, "Catholic Education: The Largest Alternative System," p. 26.

75. O'Neill, "Toward a Modern Concept of Permeation," *Momentum* 10 (May 1979): 48–49.

76. Ibid., p. 49.

77. Ibid., pp. 49–50.

78. Pope John Paul II, "Catechesi Tradendae," *Catholic Standard*, 1 November 1979.

79. National Conference of Catholic Bishops, *Sharing the Light of Faith, National Catechetical Directory for Catholics of the United States* (Washington, D.C.: United States Catholic Conference, Department of Education, 1979), pp. 143–44.

80. Ibid., p. 131.

81. Francette Keilocker, "Curriculum: The Quest for Quality," *Momentum* 9 (December 1978): 40.

82. *Catholic Schools in America: Elementary/Secondary*, 1982 ed. (Englewood, Colo.: Fisher Publishing Co., 1982), p. xviii.

83. Pope Leo XIII, *Rerum Novarum* ("On the Condition of Labor"), in *Five Great Encyclicals*, pp. 1–30; Pope Pius XI, *Quadragesimo Anno* ("Reconstructing the Social Order"), in ibid., pp. 125–67; *Christus Dominus* ("Decree on the Bishops' Pastoral Office in the Church"), in Abbott, *The Documents of Vatican II*, p. 409; *Apostolicam Actuositatem* ("Decree on the Apostolate of the Laity"), in Ibid., p. 510; *Gaudium et Spes* ("Pastoral Constitution on the Church in the Modern World"), in ibid. pp. 277–78. For an account of the support of the seven southern bishops for the Textile Workers Union in the bitter J. P. Stevens strike, see *The National Catholic Reporter*, from 1977 until the strike was settled in 1980. *The National Catholic Reporter* is also a key source for the labor struggle between the Cesar Chavez-led United Farm Workers Union and the California growers. Chavez' union enjoyed substantial support from the Catholic hierarchy of the country.

84. *The New Catholic Encyclopedia*, s. v. "Teachers' Unions, Catholic," by J. J. Reilly.

85. Rita C. Schwartz, "Social Justice for Catholic School Teachers: Trouble in the Vineyard," paper prepared for the 1980 Convention of the National Association of Women Religious, published by the National Association of Catholic School Teachers, Philadelphia, Penn., pp. 1, 3.

86. Harold J. T. Isenberg, "If You Want To Teach: Catholic Teacher Unionization Without the NLRB," *America*, 3 November 1979, pp. 260–62.

87. John J. Augenstein, *A Collaborative Approach to Personnel Relations* (Washington, D.C.: National Catholic Educational Association, 1980), pp. 3–7.

88. *The National Catholic Reporter*, 17 September 1982, p. 6. For a more complete treatment of this topic see Thomas C. Hunt, "Lay Teachers and Collective Bargaining: A Policy Issue for Today's Catholic Schools," a paper presented to the American Educational Studies Association, Nashville, Tenn., 4 November 1982.

89. Ahmann, "The Church and the Urban Negro," p. 81.

90. Sheerin, "Our Segregated Catholic Schools," pp. 333–34.

91. See, for example, Joseph M. Cronin, "Negroes in Catholic Schools: De Facto Segregation?", *Commonweal*, 7 October 1966, p. 15.

92. "Service for Sale: Tapping Pennsylvania's Till," *Commonweal*, 7 June 1968, pp. 350–51.

93. Ibid., p. 351.

94. Geno C. Baroni, "The Inner City: A New Challenge to the Catholic High School," in *Trends and Issues in Catholic Education*, eds. Russell Shaw and Richard J. Hurley (New York: Citizens Press, 1969), pp. 232–46.

95. See, for instance, Robert J. Starratt, "The Parochial Schools in The Inner City," *The National Elementary Principal* 46 (January 1967): 27–33; M. Melathon, "Response to the Challenges of Schools in Disadvantaged Areas," *National Catholic Educational Association Bulletin* 64 (August 1967): 173–79; and Ann M. Wallace, "A New York City Program for Disadvantaged Students," *National Catholic Educational Association Bulletin* 64 (February 1968): 19–26.

96. *Crux of the News*, 7 November 1969, p. 3; and 17 October 1969, p. 3.

97. The Chicago Archdiocese, under the leadership of John Cardinal Cody, constitutes one local church which was under heavy indictment for failure in this matter. *The National Catholic Reporter* is one source for these criticisms.

98. *Catholic Herald Citizen*, 9 July 1981, p. 1.

99. James G. Cibulka, Timothy J. O'Brien, and Donald Zewe, *Inner-City Private Elementary Schools: A Study* (Milwaukee: Marquette University Press, 1982).

100. D'Amour, "Parochial Schools Without Parochialism," pp. 12–14.

101. A sampling of D'Amour's writing in this field includes: "Restructuring Patterns of Education," in Koob, *What Is Happening to Catholic Education?* pp. 25–37; "School Boards of the Future," *America*, 25 September 1965, pp. 316–17; "The Parish School Board," *National Catholic Educational Association Bulletin* 62 (August 1965): 248–49; "Catholic Schools Must Survive," ibid., 65 (November 1968): 3–7; "The 'Control' Structure of Catholic Education," ibid., 63 (August 1966): 267–74; and "Structural Changes in Catholic Schools," *Catholic School Journal* 66 (June 1966): 27–29.

102. A sample of the literature published in Catholic sources on various aspects of the school board movement at this time includes: Olin J. Murdick, "Parish School Board," *America*, 22 January 1966, pp. 132–36; Aloysius F. Lacki, "Pastor's Viewpoint on School Boards," *National Catholic Educational Association Bulletin* 64 (August 1967): 161–63; M. Simeon Wozniak, "School Boards in American Catholic Education," ibid.: 163–65; Ellen Casey, "The Diocesan Board and the Parish Board," ibid.: 97–103; William C. Bruce, "A Few Thoughts on Parish School Boards," *Catholic School Journal* 67 (December 1967): 65; "Some Don'ts for a Parish School Board," ibid., 68 (April 1968): 90; "Advice for New School Board Members," ibid., 65 (October 1965): 27; and Interview with Msgr. J. William Lester, "How a Diocesan Board Upgrades Lay Teachers," ibid., 65 (September 1965): 76–78.

103. National Catholic Educational Association, *Voice of the Community: The Board Movement in Catholic Education*. For a thorough treatment of the ideological and practical issues involved with lay school boards through 1980, see M. Lourdes Sheehan, "A Study of the Functions of School Boards in the Educa-

tional System of the Roman Catholic Church in the United States" (Ed.D. dissertation, Virginia Polytechnic Institute and State University, 1981).

104. Mae Duggan and Martin Duggan, *Educational Freedom* (Milwaukee: Bruce Publishing Co., 1966), p. 204.

105. *The National Catholic Reporter*, 3 November 1978, p. 20.

106. Virgil C. Blum, *Freedom of Choice in Education* (New York: The Paulist Press, 1963), pp. 98–105. Other salient writings on this subject authored by Blum during this period are *Education: Freedom and Competition* (Chicago: Argus Communications, 1967); and *Catholic Education: Survival or Demise?* (Chicago: Argus Communications, 1969).

107. Stuart Hubbell, "Citizens for Educational Freedom in New York: Outlook for the Future," *National Catholic Educational Association Bulletin* 64 (August 1967): 89–91.

108. Andrew M. Greeley, William C. McReady, and Kathleen McCourt, *Catholic Schools in a Declining Church* (Kansas City, Kan.: Sheed and Ward, 1976).

109. Ibid., p. 301.

110. Ibid., pp. 324–25.

111. *The National Catholic Reporter*, 17 September 1982, p. 6; and 1 October 1982, p. 6.

112. Greeley, McCready, and McCourt, *Catholic Schools in a Declining Church*, p. 9.

113. James L. Morrison and Benjamin J. Hudgkins, "Social Changes and Catholic Education," *Education* 98 (March–April 1978): 264.

114. Ibid., p. 276.

115. Ibid., pp. 276–77.

116. Alfred A. McBride, *The Christian Formation of Catholic Educators* (Washington, D.C.: Chief Administrators of Catholic Education, National Catholic Educational Association, 1981); and Russell M. Bleich et al., *The Pre-Service Formation of Teachers for Catholic Schools: In Search of Patterns for the Future* (Washington, D.C.: The Chief Administrators of Catholic Education, The Association of Catholic Colleges and Universities, National Catholic Educational Association, 1982).

117. McBride, "Major Challenges Facing Catholic Education in the 1980s," *Momentum* 13 (December 1982): 10–11.

118. "The Catholic School System: Tales of its Demise 'Highly Exaggerated,'" *The National Catholic Reporter*, 13 August 1982, pp. 11, 17.

119. Thomas F. Sullivan, "Catholic Schools in a Changing Church," in *Religion and Morality in American Schooling*, eds. Thomas C. Hunt and Marilyn M. Maxson (Washington, D.C.: University Press of America, 1981), pp. 72–73.

120. M. Lourdes Sheehan, "Catholic Schools in 1979: A Unique Tradition and Challenging Future," *Review Journal of Philosophy and Social Science* 4 (Winter 1979): 140.

121. See, for example, James C. Donohue, "New Priorities in Catholic Education," *America*, 13 April 1968, pp. 476–79. In this article Donohue estimated that Catholic elementary and secondary schools absorbed at least one-half of the total expenditures of the nation's 153 dioceses and 17,942 parishes. He felt a reordering of priorities was called for.

Chapter 2

Lutheran Schools in America

JON DIEFENTHALER

Lutherans in America have always been thoroughly committed to religious education as a means of bringing up each new generation in the "nurture and admonition of the Lord." Unlike those Protestants sustained by the revivals that swept the eighteenth and nineteenth centuries, they tended to see "conversion" as a learning process rather than a moment of rebirth. Yet not all Lutherans have followed the same educational strategy. Diversity in fact becomes especially apparent when we examine the role of parish elementary schools in their various denominational histories.

One of the earliest of these focuses on those German immigrants of the eighteenth century who affiliated with the Pennsylvania Ministerium and the later General Synod. Henry Melchior Muhlenberg (1711–1787), the acknowledged "father of American Lutheranism," helped to organize parochial schools as well as congregations. Following the Revolutionary War, the eastern seaboard of the United States was dotted with these schools. Congregations in Pennsylvania, Maryland, and Virginia, however, maintained the bulk of them. In 1820, when the number of congregations reached the 700 mark, there were 342 schools. Since the German language of these Lutherans was one of the chief reasons their schools flourished, the transition to English during the three decades prior to the Civil War contributed to their gradual decline. In addition, elements within the General Synod endorsed the emerging public school system. After 1860, therefore, Sunday School and weekday religious schools clearly supplanted the parochial school in most congregations.[1] While numerical growth and twentieth-century mergers helped the General Synod attain the status of the largest denomination of Lutherans, it claims very few parochial schools. In 1982 the nearly three million member Lutheran Church in America listed only 44 of them with an enrollment of 12,698 pupils.[2]

Less clear-cut was the strategy followed by various Scandanavian and newer German immigrant groups of the nineteenth century. Among Norwegian Lutherans, schools became a major denominational issue following the Civil War. Those who saw the public school as "religionless" became staunch advocates of parochial education as the only sure means of achieving pure Christian teaching and discipline. Others, especially Georg Sverdrup (1848–1907), took the position that this alternative perverted the Lutheran doctrine of the two spheres. God, they charged, had vested, not the church, but the state with the responsibility of training children in secular matters.[3] In general, the Swedes and the Danes had considerably less difficulty embracing public education at the elementary level. One of the reasons they established colleges in the Midwest was to train teachers, whom they hoped would fill the classrooms of public schools in their communities. The Germans who helped found the Ohio Synod (1818), the Buffalo Synod (1845), and the Iowa Synod (1854) placed a somewhat higher premium on parochial schools. Yet the actual number of schools maintained by congregations belonging to these Lutheran groups remained comparatively small. Twentieth-century mergers helped to produce the two-and-a-half-million member American Lutheran Church. But in 1982 this denomination had a modest enrollment of 31,284 pupils in 375 schools with 822 teachers. A nearly identical set of statistics was reported by a much smaller denomination of Lutherans (about 400,000 members), namely the Wisconsin Evangelical Lutheran Synod (1850). Far more supportive of parochial education, this fiercely conservative group of Lutherans in 1982 reported 30,833 pupils were being taught by 1,575 teachers in 374 schools.[4]

The most enduring story of Lutheran elementary schools involves the Missouri Synod (1847). First arriving in 1839, these German immigrants proceeded to develop an extensive system of parochial schools. This system continues to thrive. In 1982 the Synod's 2.8 million member congregations supported 1,584 elementary schools, with a total enrollment of 177,171 pupils, 2,560 male and 6,740 female teachers, at an annual cost of $130,591,080, or $737 per pupil. Apart from this, they maintained 61 community high schools staffed by 1,109 teachers for the benefit of 16,493 pupils.[5] Because they are the most numerous, the parish elementary schools of the Missouri Synod will be the focus of this chapter. Only the Wisconsin Synod maintains a comparable network of schools. But this denomination is more restricted both in size and geographical scope.

Insight into the purpose of the Missouri Synod's schools requires an appreciation of its historical development in America. The denomination's immigrant forebears came to the Midwest because they felt their German homeland was inhibiting their freedom to preach and to teach their Christian beliefs. Thus, from its beginning, the Synod considered purity of Lutheran doctrine essential to the life of its congregations and parochial schools an all-important means of insuring the orthodoxy of future generations. The pluralistic environment of America, however, proved to be as threatening to these Lutherans as it was friendly. Missouri's Americanization was more gradual than it was for other immigrant groups. Interestingly, nowhere are the points of resistance to assimilation more evident than in the development of its parochial schools. And as we shall see, this history remains crucial for interpreting their current status.

THE FORMATIVE YEARS

The Lutherans of the Missouri Synod opened their first parochial school as soon as their exodus from Germany began in 1838. "During the voyage," their emigration code stated, "the children shall receive necessary instruction."[6] Their reason for leaving was primarily religious. The charismatic leadership of a Dresden pastor named Martin Stephan (1777–1846) had united them in dissent against the established church of Saxony. Along with other Lutheran and Reformed elements at the time, these Stephanites, as they were sometimes called, were determined to swim against the strong current of rationalism that the Enlightenment had sent streaming into every aspect of German culture. In their estimation, rationalists not only tended to measure all truth with the yardstick of reason but too quickly dismissed such classical Christian teachings as the deity, miracles, and vicarious atonement of Jesus Christ. Rationalist preaching seemed to offer little comfort to the sin-stricken soul because it usually consisted of discussions of current events or homespun advice on matters of health and agriculture. In rationalist churches all religious literature, including hymnals, agendas, and catechisms were being refashioned to conform to the new outlook. Equally dangerous, as the Stephanites saw it, was the amalgamation of German and Reformed congregations, similar to the "union" King Wilhelm III had forged throughout

Prussia in 1817, that was being encouraged in parts of their native Saxony. To them, this practice could only blur the distinctive features of their Lutheran heritage. In protest, therefore, they called for a strong recommitment to the orthodox teachings set forth in the Lutheran confessions.

In Saxony, the battle was joined frequently at the level of the parish school. Such schools were located within the boundaries of local congregations. Acting as representatives of the state, pastors inspected the religious curriculum and examined the teachers employed in the school. Their authority, however, was neither arbitrary nor final. All supervising pastors were responsible to the crown's ecclesiastical council or consistory, known after 1831 as the Ministry of Worship and Public Instruction. As members of a dissenting minority, "confessionalist" pastors who attempted to correct the rationalist errors they perceived in the school's program of instruction ran the risk of being reported to higher authorities. Frequently they were reprimanded. In the case of at least one pastor who joined the Stephanite emigration, his right to supervise the school in his own parish was revoked for a two-year period.[7]

In America these same Germans hoped to find freedom from such restrictions. Scarcely had they arrived in St. Louis via New Orleans in 1839 than they rented a two-story house at twelve dollars a month for the purpose of conducting a school. The first floor of the house was used for a classroom, living quarters for a teacher, and church meetings. The second floor was turned into a parsonage.[8] When the majority of the group left St. Louis and settled along the Mississippi River in Perry County, Missouri, work was begun on a "college" patterned after the *Gymnasium* type of secondary school they had known in Germany. The faculty consisted of four members of the clergy, all of them university graduates. But the school in which all instruction took place was in fact only a one-room cabin, and the ages of the eight boys and three girls in attendance ranged from five to fifteen years.[9]

Tragedy was not an uncommon feature of life for these immigrants. But one in particular dealt a harsh blow to their self-confidence. Shortly after the move to Perry County, Martin Stephan, who by then had assumed the role of "bishop" over the settlement, was accused of adultery and misuse of funds, excommunicated, and exiled to the Illinois side of the Mississippi. For the next two years, guilt and mistrust troubled the relationships between the laity and their pastors. Stability did not return until Carl F. W. Walther (1811–1887) emerged as the new leader. Meanwhile, each individual congregation was left to struggle on its own. None was able to erect another school building until 1841.[10]

A more crucial result of the "Stephan crisis" was the form of polity with which the group chose to restructure its institutions. Placed on the defensive, the clergy were in no position to counter the laity's efforts to reassert Luther's "priesthood of all believers." Walther, in a debate at the Altenburg parish, recognized this and argued persuasively that ultimate authority in the church rested with the local congregation. A pastor's authority was derived from a "divine call" that transferred certain functions of the congregation to him.[11] Lutheran schools in turn became parish schools. Local congregations not only established and financed them but, through their voters assemblies, made all the major decisions regarding their administration and supervision.

A serious casualty of the new arrangement, however, was the Lutheran teacher. Caught between the clergy and the laity, those who taught in the classrooms of Missouri's schools became ecclesiastical nonentities. At the conventions of the Synod and its districts, the franchise was shared by the lay and pastoral delegates from each congregation. Teachers attended such gatherings. But their position remained advisory. Under no circumstances were they permitted to serve as a congregation's lay delegate.[12] In addition, whereas teachers were responsible to the congregations that operated their schools, the congregations were accountable to no one. Under the polity that Walther had first articulated at Altenburg, synodical officials, as well as later superintendents of schools and boards of parish education, functioned in purely advisory capacities. They still lack any real authority to safeguard teacher interests. At times, especially during the early years of the Synod's history, the school's teacher was the pastor of the congregation. But when a full-time teacher assumed the responsibility, he remained subservient to the pastor, whose authority encompassed the spiritual matters of both the church and the school. Congregations did have the right to issue a "call" to teachers. More often, however, they contracted or hired them. At one point, the president of one of the Synod's teachers colleges even suggested that, outside of the religious subjects he taught, a teacher's work was as secular as that of any other jobholder.[13]

Powerless Pedagogues is the apt title of the book in which Stephen A. Schmidt has probed the history of this problem. "Almost a minister," he writes, was the status that Lutheran teachers aspired to attain. Over the course of Missouri's history they thought that they were clergy with an important stake in the ministry of the local congregation. What they became was "almost a hireling." A teacher's job description usually contained such other parish duties as organist, choir director, secretary to the church council, and even custodian. Yet the respect congregations showed to their pastors was seldom accorded to their teachers. Such confusion, Schmidt concludes, only led to a "weakened professional self-image" for which teachers were forced to compensate with "over-dedication."[14]

By the mid-1840s the Saxons in Missouri had drawn closer to several other midwestern congregations. The most notable of these were located in the Saginaw Valley of Michigan and Indiana's Allen County. The genuine concern of Friedrich C. D. Wyneken (1810–1876), a pastor in Ft. Wayne, over the spiritual plight of German immigrants arriving in these areas caused him to seek the help of a German benefactor named J. K. Wilhelm Loehe in sending missionaries to America. In 1846 Loehe also had provided Wilhelm Sihler (1801–1885) with the funds to establish a theological seminary in Ft. Wayne. In addition, the "American Lutheranism" that was sweeping the older synods to the east disturbed these congregations and their pastors. To them, this movement had not only adapted to the "new measures" of revivalism and the Reformed view of holy communion, but had compromised Lutheranism's historic confessions. All of them desired a more conservative affiliation. In 1847, therefore, these congregations were represented in Chicago and participated in the formation of the German Evangelical Lutheran Synod of Missouri, Ohio, and Other States.

THE FIRST TWENTY-FIVE YEARS: 1847–1872

Those who signed the new Synod's constitution in the years that followed its founding learned that membership implied "provision for the Christian education of the children in the congregation."[15] Missouri's goal was in fact a Lutheran school in every congregation. Most often, congregations and schools were founded simultaneously. Sometimes, the school preceded the establishment of the congregation. Where there was evidence of doctrinal confusion or laxity of practice, the school served to reinforce the orthodox Lutheranism to which the Synod stood committed.[16] Congregations were also reminded that the duty of supporting the school rested with every member. To think that it was the concern only of those who were sending their children to the school or that the school was a source of income for the church, was considered not only "erroneous" but "contrary to the spirit of Christ."[17] All in all, the strategy succeeded remarkably during the first twenty-five years of the Synod's history. By 1872 the number of congregations had increased from 12 to 446, and the number of schools from 14 to 472.[18] Furthermore, enrollment stood in excess of 30,000 children.[19]

Contributing to this early success as well was the German model on which the Synod built its system of schooling. In Germany children received their initial elementary education in the required *Volkschule*. The curriculum included a heavy dose of religious instruction that reflected either the Catholic or the Protestant status of the community. For qualified youngsters, the next step was to enroll in the *Gymnasium* for an additional period of at least six years. Those among them who sought careers in medicine, law, or theology, followed a course of study that accented the classical languages of Greek, Latin, and Hebrew. Only after an examination on these and other subjects could they enter one of Germany's prestigious universities.[20] In America Lutheran children were still to be reared theologically knowledgeable and culturally literate. Since public schools were as yet in their infancy, Missouri's congregations often touted their own schools as the better *Volkschule*. "Colleges" such as those founded in Perry County, Ft. Wayne, and other midwestern locales later on, resembled the *Gymnasium* as much in curriculum as language. Financial realities and the pressing demand for more pastors and teachers soon narrowed the focus of the education at these schools and at the Synod's seminaries. A solid general education for all members of the church, however, was the dream of the first generation's leadership.[21]

Especially in urban areas, the school strengthened the Synod's mission to German immigrant groups. When admitted, these "strangers," as they were called, could comprise up to 50 percent of the enrollment.[22] Their presence often led to overcrowded conditions that made both education and discipline difficult. In a school in Ft. Wayne, for instance, five teachers in five classes were expected to instruct 450 pupils.[23] Yet as early as 1850 the Synod's national convention discouraged enrollment restrictions. "A congregation which turns away the children of other confessions," it said, "may bar them from coming to Jesus and will have it upon its conscience if the little ones are taught false doctrine and lost."[24] Similar sentiments were expressed less than a decade later by Friedrich Wyneken. As the Synod's second president, he urged congregations to realize more fully "what important mission work they are performing through their schools for that sector of our German citizens who have fallen prey to unbelief."[25]

The most important consideration, however, was the conservation of Lutheran beliefs and doctrine. Leaders such as Walther did not reject culture. He asserted that a "general education" was as much the business of the church as the state. "The Christian religion," he argued, regarded all "useful arts" and "knowledge" as gifts of God to be used for the service and glorification of God. The church's duty, therefore, was to establish schools in which these gifts might be developed and children learn to serve the church and the state.[26] But intellect and reason were always to be kept in a ministerial relationship to religious truth. Thus, in his address at the cornerstone laying of Concordia Seminary, St. Louis, in 1849, Walther also issued this strong word of caution: "May the arts and sciences never become the idol to which an altar is built, but only the means by which also in this Western country the church is built on the foundation of the apostles and prophets, beautifully ornamented, and bravely and victoriously defended."[27]

For this same reason, all textbooks used in Lutheran schools became a matter of intensive discussion. Few of the catechisms brought from Germany were considered sufficiently orthodox. The Synod finally requested that Walther revise the *Dietrich Catechism*. It regarded the Baltimore edition of *Huebner's Bible History* as too rationalistic and eventually published its own version of this widely used text. During the 1850s synodical committees were authorized to prepare a *Spruchbuch* of verses that children were expected to commit to memory and a German primer. The arithmetic used in most schools was a reprint of Scheidemann's *Aufgaben Sammlung*.[28] McGuffey's readers failed to gain acceptance because they were perceived to contain the moral distortions of Calvinism and Arminianism. Instead, one of the Synod's pastors issued a *Pictorial Primer or First Reader for Parochial Schools*.[29] Its Concordia Publishing House, built in 1869, served as the supplier of all such texts.[30]

In addition the Missouri Synod felt it necessary to train its own teachers. As early as 1855 a Milwaukee conference of pastors and teachers established a seminary for this purpose. In 1857 the Synod took over this school, moved it to Ft. Wayne, and made it a separate teacher-training department within the Ft. Wayne Seminary. This department was relocated as a separate teachers seminary at Addison, Illinois, in 1864. In 1913 the Synod again moved the school to River Forest, Illinois, where it became Concordia Teachers College. Meanwhile, at Seward, Nebraska, in 1894, it had opened a second school, first as a preparatory department for the Addison school, and then in 1906, as a full teacher-training institution, also known as Concordia Teachers College. The orthodoxy of all graduates had to be certified by the faculties of these colleges. With a new position, a teacher could also expect a theological examination from the pastor of the congregation's school.[31]

The immigrant aspirations of these same Lutherans were not ignored in the formation of their schools. Wyneken, for instance, stressed that God intended the children of the Synod's members to become "more than mere hewers of wood and carriers of water for speculators." The church, he emphasized, must also equip them for positions of leadership in local and state governments.[32] Walther supported the establishment of such secondary schools as Immanuel Academy in St. Louis, where pupils might advance themselves toward their future calling in "English as well as German." "Remember," he told parents, "what a class distinction there was in our old fatherland and how oppressive it was. But do not think that such a class distinction will cease automatically in this country. No, if you do not provide your children with a good education, they will in time to come be regarded as uncultured and crude people."[33] Several others, especially Adolph Biewend (1816–1858), a pastor in Ft. Wayne, also promoted the greater use of English in the schools.

In fact, little was done to further the process of Americanization. German remained the language of the classroom as well as the worship service and synodical convention. Most of the curriculum continued to focus on religious training and allowed no more than an hour of English at the end of the school day.[34] The secondary-school movement that Walther had supported soon fell on hard times. Within several years, academies such as Immanuel in St. Louis were forced to close for lack of students and funds. The failure might be attributed, at least in part, to the Synod's success as a confessional church body. Looking back upon the first twenty-five years, Theodore Julius Brohm, (1808–1881), a vice-president of the Synod, could not ignore the remarkable growth of its congregations and schools. What distinguished Missouri from other denominations, he boasted, was the "pure and unadulterated profession of the Lutheran faith." This, he declared, was the "golden chain" that kept the Synod together, the "banner" under which it still gathered, and the "goal" for which it would continue to strive.[35] Walther could only agree. For the future, as he saw it, the best formula was still a school in every congregation. "As all church bodies in America have worked for their own dissolution from the time when they permitted the state to care

for the education of their children," he declared, "so the most careful
cultivation of our parochial schools is and remains, after the public
ministry, the chief means of our preservation and continuation."[36]
During the next fifty years, however, forces operating within and
outside of the Synod made it more difficult for congregations to
sustain this enthusiasm.

THE TIME OF TESTING: 1873–1919

One of these forces was the rising tide of immigration that followed
the close of the Civil War. To meet the spiritual needs of the Germans
especially, the Missouri Synod accelerated its efforts to train new pastors and teachers. Schools continued to prosper along with congregations. Yet the ideal of a school in every congregation started to fade.
By 1897, while the Synod had expanded to nearly 2,000 congregations and 685,000 members, the number of schools had increased to
1,603, with 89,202 children enrolled. Some of these, moreover, were
only part-time agencies.[37]

The newcomers differed from the Stephanite generation of immigrants who had first settled in Missouri. Economic and political rather
than religious reasons had prompted their journey to America. Some
were seeking to avoid military conscription. Others were attracted by
the propaganda of the steamship companies and sought to cash in on
the promised wealth of the New World. Given their experience of the
political unification of their homeland, the Franco-Prussian War, and
the *Kulturkampf* of Bismarck, these Germans were more nationalis-
tic.[38] They also lacked the respect for culture and learning that their
predecessors had demonstrated with their dream of a general education for the laity as well as the clergy. Reared in the *Volkschule*, they
saw no real need for formal training beyond the elementary level.[39]

Equally varied were the attitudes of these immigrants toward
Lutheran schools. Some eschewed them because they wanted their
children to learn English. For them, it was the public school that
seemed to provide a smoother road to success in America. Others saw
Lutheran schools as a means to perpetuate the Germanness of their
heritage and supported them. Under this influence, parochial education soon became the focal point of controversy over language. The
typical pro-German argument was articulated by Heinrich C. Schwann
in 1890. "It is not the English language itself which contains the
danger," he pointed out.

It is the American spirit, the now prevailing American sentiment, that shallow, slick, indifferent, business-tainted spirit in which also spiritual matters are handled in this country; that sentiment which has no knowledge of the real essence of Christianity and therefore deems the maintenance of pure doctrine ridiculous, holds the fight for the one faith to be sheer blasphemy, but seeks salvation in sweet sensations and in much busied workery of all kinds.[40]

From the Synod's earliest years, English had been part of the school curriculum. Congregations were allowed to engage in English work when it became absolutely unavoidable.[41] For the later defenders of the mother tongue, however, the language of America invited doctrinal laxity and a spirit which they labeled as undesirable. Once adopted, it was asserted, English would inevitably cause young people to defect to other denominations.[42]

Supporters of the English language disagreed. To them, inability to understand German was the real source of the defections. Some also argued that English was essential for mission work among non-Germans, while others insisted that the Christian gospel transcended the issue of language. The Lutheran school for them was neither German nor English but an "ecclesiastical institution" belonging to a Christian congregation. For this reason, as they saw it, a language change was only prudent if English was the predominant tongue of the community.[43]

Yet the Synod remained reluctant to follow such reasoned advice. In general opposition to German was more frequently perceived as an assault upon the schools themselves. The Synod's publications were flooded with pro-school arguments. In their defense, superior instruction and discipline were high on the list of advantages. The importance of centering all instruction in the Word of God was another crucial argument. No matter how competent, it was pointed out, public school teachers could not do this. Other arguments focused on the health of congregations and suggested that growth and vitality could be attributed to the establishment of schools.[44] When a synodical mission committee complained that only one subsidized English congregation had a school, the convention of 1896 resolved to "give material support to such English pastors and congregations only as they establish and maintain Christian schools."[45] English-speaking congregations were also suspected of being more favorably disposed toward Sunday Schools. They were attacked for permitting parents to shirk their duty to send their children to a Lutheran day school. Furthermore, pastors were categorized as "school men" and those who did not favor parochial schools.[46]

If the language issue retarded assimilation, the theological outlook of these Lutherans kept their schools on the front lines of resistance to even a pluralistic form of integration into American society. Classroom teachers taught pupils to regard their Lutheran denomination as the true visible church of God on earth. Since all other denominations were shot through, at least to some degree, with doctrinal error, interaction with any of them was discouraged. Lutherans, it was said, worshiped only with Lutherans and conducted mission work for the purpose of making the heathen "Lutheran" rather than nondescriptly Christian. Similarly, the papacy was labeled as the Antichrist and other Lutheran synods ridiculed for being too soft on members of the Masonic Order or for practicing open communion. Such warnings also encompassed the family. Lutheran schools were in fact the church's antidote for marriage to anyone outside the denominational body.[47]

Social attitudes were shaped, at least in part, by Missouri's understanding of the Lutheran doctrine of the two spheres. This view of things divided the spiritual and the temporal into two distinct realms. Temporal institutions served to maintain the peace and order of humankind. The church, on the other hand, was the source of divine grace and the only true guide to salvation. Walther, it seems, could not forget what he and other confessional pastors had suffered in Saxony. His view of the First Amendment to America's Constitution was staunchly Jeffersonian. Religious liberty for him guaranteed separation of church and state.[48] Yet the tendency of this "dualist" approach was to dwell upon the sinful aspects of all things secular. It also helps account for the distance young Lutherans were taught to maintain from the world. In the late nineteenth century, they opposed life insurance on the ground that it turned death, the biblical wages of sin, into a business venture for profit. Some even opposed the use of lightning rods as a sinful attempt to interfere with the will of God. In dealing with the problems of the workingman, they took the side of neither management nor labor. The clergy regularly denounced dancing as a form of worldly lust and pleasure. The theater was decried as immoral and an evil institution by definition. The new insights of the social sciences were blunted with arguments that there had been no fundamental change in humankind. Its most recent members, or so the argument went, were sinners as much as Adam and Eve.[49]

Similar tensions were reflected in the political behavior of these Lutherans. Obedience to God required them to obey the temporal institutions God had ordained for the sake of good order in society and the punishment of its evildoers. But at the same time, observations concerning the political condition of the nation were invariably pessimistic. Often quoted is Wilhelm Sihler's blast at practically every feature of public life in 1876. "Elections are hopelessly corrupt," he wrote.

> One would expect to see the best in men in Congress, patriots, moral men interested in the common good, but alas, God, one sees fanatical party men, political hacks, sophistical demagogs, big talkers, and a dangerous band of political Jesuits who keep in their nets the poor President, ignorant and inexperienced in matters of state, just as Roman Jesuits keep the pope.[50]

The persistence of this attitude, moreover, may be one of the chief reasons modern Lutherans remain so marginally involved in civic affairs.[51]

Even more revealing was Missouri's attitude toward America's public schools of the late nineteenth and early twentieth centuries. While it remained committed to its own school system, the Synod never dismissed public education. The temporal welfare of society required that the state provide public schools and, as citizens, Lutherans were obliged to give them moral and financial support. This was the position set forth as early as 1870 at a meeting of the Western District by Hermann Fick, one of the Synod's pastors. His "Proper Relationship of an Evangelical Lutheran Christian to the Public School System" urged Lutherans to use their influence as citizens to encourage the hiring of public school teachers who showed a "Christian spirit," to prevent the use of textbooks that contradicted the Christian faith, and to help maintain "good outward order."[52] Walther as well as Fick took the side of those who favored the reading of the Bible in public schools. Both saw it as a body of truth that transcended confessional differences. Walther even seems to have believed that the idea of a nonreligious federal Constitution was inconsistent with the Christian elements in the thinking of the founding fathers.[53]

From a spiritual standpoint, however, Lutherans regarded public schools as wholly inadequate. They consistently opposed the teaching of religion in such institutions. Bible reading, Fick maintained, was never an appropriate substitute for the thorough course of religious instruction in a Lutheran school. When formulated by an "unorthodox" teacher, prayers in public school classrooms might also endanger the faith of a Lutheran child. Furthermore, there was nothing to stop subjects such as history and geography from being injected with the "poison of doctrinal error and unbelief."[54]

Reinforcing these criticisms was the compulsory education legislation of the late nineteenth century. Much of the impetus for it had come from such powerful nativist lobbies as the American Protective Association and the Boston Committee of 100. Their goal was the Americanization of immigrant groups of all religious persuasions. In 1889 Wisconsin adopted the Bennett Law and Illinois, the Edwards Law. Similar bills were introduced in South Dakota and Minnesota. In 1894 the New York state legislature also passed a Compulsory Education Act. All such laws contained restrictions that Lutherans of the Missouri Synod could only regard as a threat to the life of their schools. The Bennett Law, for example, stipulated that the local board of education supervise enforcement of compulsory attendance in either a public or a private school and that English be used in the teaching of reading, writing, arithmetic, and United States history.[55] The Edwards Law went a step further. It insisted that all children between the ages of seven and fourteen attend the public school of the area in which they resided for sixteen weeks (at least eight of which were to be consecutive) a year.[56]

In response Lutherans insisted that the laws of the land dared not infringe upon obedience to the ordinances of the spiritual realm. Building their case upon the First Amendment, they argued that the Bennett and Edwards laws proscribed the "free exercise" of their religious profession and worship. In addition, they contended that such laws usurped parental authority over the education of their children. In no way, they also asserted, did the German language diminish the emphasis they placed on good citizenship. Yet they did reaffirm their commitment to provide "the best possible instruction in English."[57] More crucial to the repeal of the legislation in 1891 were the fall elections of the preceding year. Lutherans joined the Roman Catholics of Wisconsin and Illinois to unseat the Republican Party, which supported the Bennett and Edwards laws. In some Lutheran precincts that year, 90 percent voted for candidates of the Democratic Party.[58]

Some Lutheran historians have called these legislative battles over parochial schools a hidden "blessing." They forced the Missouri Synod in particular to reassess its entire system in light of public school standards of education. In their teachers colleges, for instance, it moved both to upgrade the course of study and to lengthen it by an additional year. A wide range of problems was aired at teachers conferences and improvements proposed. In a number of synodical districts steps were taken to establish a central office of school superintendent.[59] Fresh efforts were also made to strengthen the public image of Lutheran schools. In 1904 the Synod saw the world's fair in

St. Louis as one such opportunity. It exhibited the work done by pupils in 265 Lutheran schools in the areas of English and United States history as well as religion and German. The display was well received, as the judges awarded it a gold medal.[60]

Yet Missouri's schools remained on the defensive. After 1900 the public school system in America developed rapidly in numbers and in program offerings. So fervent was the impulse for public education that many citizens questioned the right of parochial schools to exist at all. Lutherans in about a dozen states following the turn of the century were compelled to oppose additional legislation governing attendance guidelines, textbooks, and language used in the schools.[61] During World War I, Lutheranism was identified with Germany. Amid the patriotic hysteria that swept the nation in 1917, pastors in particular were suspected of treason. A few underwent the public humiliation of being beaten or tarred and feathered. Others were forced to kiss the flag, to pledge allegiance, or subscribe to war bonds. Expressly forbidden was the German tongue. Lutheran churches were frequently plastered with signs proclaiming that "God Almighty understands the English language." Some schools were closed. Others were daubed mysteriously with yellow paint. A few were burned. In Nebraska, a Lutheran teacher, Robert T. Meyer, was convicted under the Simian Act (1919) of teaching reading to a ten-year-old boy in the German language. It took a ruling of the United States Supreme Court to reverse the decision and to ease the pressure it had placed on all Lutheran schools.[62]

At the close of World War I, neither the Synod nor its leaders found cause for boasting about their schools. The legislative battles of the 1890s and the improvement of public school systems seem to have moderated the increase in the number of parochial schools and pupils enrolled in them. By 1916 the Synod's membership over the previous two decades had swelled by 50 percent and was fast approaching the million mark. During the same period, however, its schools had experienced less than a 12 percent increase in enrollment. After 1900, moreover, the expansion of part-time agencies seems to have inflated even this figure. Full-time schools were in fact reporting some losses.[63] Just as adverse were the effects of World War I on Missouri's attitude toward America. Its members were deeply hurt by the ugliness and suspicion with which their neighbors had treated them. Vindication of their rights, as we shall see in a moment, came from the highest court of the land during the 1920s. Yet resistance to cultural integration stiffened, and for the next generation, Lutheran schools were again summoned to hold the line.

AMERICANIZATION: 1920–1960

New threats to the legal existence of Lutheran schools surfaced in several states during the "Red Scare" of the early 1920s. In Michigan, the Wayne County Civic League proposed an amendment to the state's constitution requiring all children between the ages of seven and sixteen to attend public schools. Making "One Language, One Flag, and One School" its slogan, the League mustered the signatures necessary for a popular referendum on the amendment. Like the Lutherans, the Roman Catholic and Christian Reformed churches of Michigan also maintained their own school systems. Yet it took a well-organized campaign of handbills, newspaper advertisements, letters, and rallies on the part of all three to defeat the amendment in the fall elections of 1920 by a margin of two to one. In Oregon, a similar referendum passed by a close popular vote in 1922. Behind it Lutheran congregations with parochial schools saw the sinister hand of the Masonic Order and the Ku Klux Klan. The Oregon-Washington District of the Missouri Synod lacked sufficient forces to mount a legal campaign of its own. Fortunately for it, the Society of Sisters of the Holy Names of Jesus and Mary carried the case to the United States Supreme Court, where in 1925 the Oregon law was declared unconstitutional. Crucial to the Court's reasoning in favor of the plaintiff was the *Meyer v. Nebraska* decision of 1923. In both cases, it sought to check the state's power to "standardize" education and to safeguard the freedom of parents and guardians to direct the upbringing of those children under their control. Still another threat, as Missouri saw it, were the various versions of the Smith-Towner Bill (Sterling-Reed and Curtis-Reed) of 1923. In each of these bills the Synod feared that the creation of a Federal Department of Education might place government controls on all educational institutions. Representatives appeared at several congressional hearings for the purpose of testifying against the bill. It was never passed.[64]

Such threats could only accentuate Lutheran mistrust of public education. The twenties were actually a boom period for public schools. Magnificent new structures, often dedicated to the memory of American presidents, dotted the landscape. The most prominent building in many a smaller community was the new high school.[65] For Lutheran advocates of parochial schools, however, the faith of public school patrons was a "blind faith in education." To them, John Dewey's theories had brought "uncertainty disguised as pragmatism," and in the conflict between Christian and pagan worldviews, had clearly placed the public school on the side of the latter.[66] At the same time the Missouri Synod remained sharply opposed to religious instruction in such schools on the ground that only fully Christian teachers could be trusted to dispense it properly. Toward "released time" programs of religious education they remained cautious because the public school was to some degree still connected with them.[67]

At the same time there was evidence of adaptation. By 1921 only 87 out of 1,090 Lutheran schools conducted religious instruction in the German language. In 487 it was in English only, and in 416 it was in both German and English. The change was in fact more rapid in the schools than in the worship services of their congregations.[68] Supervision also took on new importance. The Missouri Synod created the office of superintendent of schools, established a school board, and gave its blessing to an annual conference of district superintendents. Congregations looked increasingly to the Lutheran principal as the chief administrator of school programs and policies. Gradually, the Sunday School became more than an embarrassing stepchild. Full acceptance was bestowed upon it in 1929, when the Synod stood ready to replace its General School Board and its Sunday School Board with one Board of Christian Education.[69] During the 1930s, teachers began to seek additional education at non-Lutheran colleges and graduate schools. The University of Chicago and Northwestern University in particular were the choices of students at Concordia Teachers College in River Forest.[70] Textbooks were still given careful consideration. Yet the older policy of using only "in-house" publications faded. In some cases, textbook publishers agreed to print readers especially edited to conform to the Lutheran outlook. Aside from the field of music and religion, however, textbooks written for public schools were recommended in increasing numbers.[71]

After 1936, as America began to climb out of the depths of the Great Depression, there came a resurgence of parochial schools among Missouri Synod Lutherans. Schools were founded in areas where none had been established. Older congregations enlarged their school programs and erected new buildings. The rising birthrate after World War II accelerated the expansion. The growth was evident in the construction of modern school plants and in the use of modern school equipment in classrooms. It also took the form of concern for more efficient teaching and the accreditation of schools where required. By 1961 the 1,323 schools of the Missouri Synod in North America had an enrollment of 150,440 pupils and were staffed by 5,525 teachers.[72]

Expansion did not alter the purpose for which Lutheran congregations maintained these schools. Families dissatisfied with public education sometimes enrolled their children. Yet Lutheran educators refrained from making excessive claims about the quality of private education. Nor did their congregations seek to use the schools to finance building programs and other projects of the church. In general, Lutheran schools were still the congregation's ministry to the children of its own members. When classrooms became crowded, such children were usually given priority over nonmembers.[73] The charging of tuition was also discouraged. When it was necessary, the charge was to be kept "at the lowest possible figure and gradually reduced."[74] Christian training, moreover, remained the expressed purpose of these schools. This implied not only instruction in Lutheran doctrine, but presentation of all subjects from a Christian point of view.[75]

CURRENT STATUS

Along with all social institutions, Lutheran schools were subjected to rigorous questioning during the 1960s. In fact their value became the issue of Ronald L. Johnstone's *The Effectiveness of Lutheran Elementary and Secondary Schools as Agents of Christian Education* in 1966. Briefly stated, this survey tended to discount the difference between parochial and public school educated Lutheran youth. Far more significant, it suggested, was the strength of the Lutheran family. Parochial and public school educated youth from solidly Lutheran families were remarkably similar in their worship attendance, stewardship, beliefs, willingness to share their faith, and social attitudes. The study also pointed out that while the direct influence of parochial education was more apparent in marginal families, the children of such families were the group least likely to receive it. Hence, it proposed that Lutheran congregations give more attention to their total program of religious training.[76]

Neither the Johnstone report nor spiraling costs of education seem to have dampened Lutheran support and enthusiasm for parochial schools. After a leveling off period in the early 1970s, the number of pupils attending these schools increased at a steady annual rate.[77] In addition, data not published in *Profiles of Lutherans in the U.S.A.* (1982) because it applied to the Missouri Synod rather than all of the major Lutheran denominations appears to confirm this trend. Some 88 percent of the laity and 98 percent of the clergy still believe that compared to public schools, children enrolled in Lutheran schools receive "better" religious training. Moreover, 70 percent and 83 percent of the same groups think that such education provides "better" preparation for future congregational leaders. In general, more members of both groups than not agree that Lutheran schools offer superior academic training and teaching staff. Only with regard to social activities and school facilities do they have significant feelings of inferiority.[78]

Contributing to this trend as well is an important set of changes in the makeup of the pupils attending Lutheran elementary schools. In 1972, 26 percent were classified as non-Lutheran, and of these 5.4 percent were identified as having no church affiliation. By 1982 these figures had climbed steadily to 40.6 percent non-Lutherans, 9.1 percent of whom were unchurched, and with no indication that the trend itself was about to peak out.[79] It would appear, then, that segments of the American people who once considered Lutheran schools too German or too aloof from the cultural mainstream have now found them considerably more attractive. In urban areas especially, non-Lutheran families have come seeking an alternative to public education. The "Christian" aspects of the training offered in Lutheran schools no doubt appeals to certain evangelical Protestants, especially those who believe that America is on the brink of moral bankruptcy. The apparent commitment of Lutheran teachers to discipline and to excellence in education may be another strong factor. Yet what is this new tide of "strangers" really hoping to gain from the parochial schools of the Missouri Synod?

No less important are the questions raised by this new trend for the Lutheran schools themselves and the congregations that maintain them. Does a classroom consisting of many non-Lutheran pupils require adjustments in a curriculum traditionally designed to inculcate sound Lutheran doctrine? How do Lutheran teachers relate to children and families who do not share their allegiance to certain religious beliefs? The sacramental view of Holy Baptism that Lutherans assert would seem to be a very sensitive matter for those Protestants who insist upon a believer's approach to the subject. One suspects that in multidenominational classrooms, the gospel of Jesus and the truths that all Christians hold in common receive more attention. Yet will this new reality also enhance Lutheran acceptance of religious pluralism? In the popular view the Missouri Synod remains the least ecumenical and the most conservative of the larger Lutheran denominations. Its schools are often assessed as agencies that reinforce such attitudes among its members. But is it not possible that consistent interaction with children and parents from other Christian families will reverse this role of the school within its own denomination? It is too early to make any real judgment. Still, the future of Lutheran schools in America seems ripe with new possibilities.

NOTES

1. Walter H. Beck, *Lutheran Elementary Schools in the United States* (St. Louis: Concordia Publishing House, 1939), pp. 25–85.

2. *1983 Yearbook* (Philadelphia: Board of Publication of the Lutheran Church in America, 1983), pp. 523–25.

3. For a recent discussion of the controversy, see James S. Hamre, "Norwegian Immigrants Respond to the Common School: A Case Study of American Values and the Lutheran Tradition," *Church History* 50 (September 1981): 302–15.

4. *Yearbook for 1983* (Waverly, Iowa: American Lutheran Education Association, 1983), pp. 64–65. Data on Wisconsin schools provided by its Board of Parish Education, Milwaukee Wisconsin, 20 December 1983.

5. *1982 Statistical Yearbook* (St. Louis: Concordia Publishing House, 1983), pp. 16–17, 216, 219, 228–29.

6. Walter O. Forster, *Zion on the Mississippi* (St. Louis: Concordia Publishing House, 1953), p. 574.

7. Ibid., p. 80.

8. Forster, *Zion on the Mississippi*, p. 344; and August C. Stellhorn, *Schools of the Lutheran Church-Missouri Synod* (St. Louis: Concordia Publishing House, 1963), pp. 82–83.

9. A. C. Stellhorn, "The Period of Organization, 1838–1847," in *One Hundred Years of Christian Education*, ed. Arthur C. Repp (River Forest, Ill.: Lutheran Education Association, 1947), pp. 17–25.

10. Stellhorn, *Schools of the Lutheran Church—Missouri Synod*, p. 82.

11. Lutherans recognize that "pastor" or "teacher" is an office ordained by God. Hence, for them, a congregational election is more than a human process. Rather, it is one through which God also "calls" someone to fill the office.

12. Stellhorn, *Schools of the Lutheran Church-Missouri Synod*, p. 217.

13. Ibid., pp. 211–12.

14. Stephen A. Schmidt, *Powerless Pedagogues* (River Forest, Ill.: Lutheran Education Association, 1972), pp. 59–67.

15. See *Constitution of the German Evangelical Lutheran Synod of Missouri, Ohio and Other States*, translated by Roy Suelflow, in *Concordia Historical Institute Quarterly* 16 (April 1943): 2–4.

16. Stellhorn, *Schools of the Lutheran Church-Missouri Synod*, pp. 91–92. To illustrate the point, Stellhorn cites the story of Trinity Lutheran Church in Chicago.

17. *Evangelische Lutherische Schulblatt* 4 (September 1868): 2, in *Moving Frontiers*, ed. Carl S. Meyer (St. Louis: Concordia Publishing House, 1964), pp. 368–69.

18. Stellhorn, *Schools of the Lutheran Church-Missouri Synod*, pp. 94–97.

19. Ibid., p. 171.

20. Schmidt, *Powerless Pedagogues*, p. 22.

21. Ibid., p. 74.

22. Stellhorn, "The Period of Organization, 1838–1847," p. 11.

23. Arthur C. Repp, "The Period of Planting," in Repp, *One Hundred Years of Christian Education*, p. 40.

24. *Vierter Synodal Bericht*, 1850, in Stellhorn, *Schools of the Lutheran Church-Missouri Synod*, p. 75.

25. President's Report, *Synodal Bericht*, 1857, in Stellhorn, *Schools of the Lutheran Church-Missouri Synod*, pp. 93–94.

26. *Der Lutheraner*, 1 October 1868, in Stellhorn, *Schools of the Lutheran Church-Missouri Synod*, pp. 114–15.

27. C. F. W. Walther, "Rede bei Gelegenhert der feierlichen Legung des Grundsteins zu den deutsche evang. luth. Collegium," 8 November 1849, in Meyer, *Moving Frontiers*, pp. 224–25.

28. Repp, "The Period of Planting," p. 41.

29. Walter F. Wolbrecht, "The Period of Expansion, 1864–1894," in Repp, *One Hundred Years of Christian Education*, p. 79.

30. Stellhorn, *Schools of the Lutheran Church-Missouri Synod*, p. 79.

31. Ibid., pp. 129–50.

32. President's Report, *Synodal Bericht*, 1857, in Stellhorn, *Schools of the Lutheran Church-Missouri Synod*, p. 94.

33. C. F. W. Walther, "An Eltern, die fuer das Wohl ihrer Kinder besorgt sind," *Der Lutheraner*, 26 July 1859, in Meyer, *Moving Frontiers*, pp. 226–27.

34. Repp, "The Period of Planting, 1847–1864," p. 43.

35. *Der Lutheraner*, 15 July 1872, in Stellhorn, *Schools of the Lutheran Church-Missouri Synod*, pp. 171–72.

36. C. F. W. Walther, "Gemeindeschulen," *Der Lutheraner*, 15 February 1873, in *Letters of C. F. W. Walther: A Selection*, ed. Carl S. Meyer (Philadelphia: Fortress Press, 1969), p. 22.

37. Stellhorn, *Schools of the Lutheran Church-Missouri Synod*, p. 275.

38. Beck, *Lutheran Elementary Schools in the United States*, pp. 161–62.

39. Repp, "The Period of Planting," p. 58.

40. *The Lutheran Witness*, 7 July 1890, in Meyer, *Moving Frontiers*, p. 356.

41. Everette Meier and Herbert T. Mayer, "The Process of Americanization," in Mayer, *Moving Frontiers*, p. 356.

42. Ibid.

43. *Der Lutheraner*, 25 September 1906, in Meyer, *Moving Frontiers*, pp. 361–62.

44. Meier and Mayer, "The Process of Americanization," pp. 369–71.

45. Stellhorn, *Schools of the Lutheran Church-Missouri Synod*, p. 193.

46. Meier and Mayer, "The Process of Americanization," p. 367.

47. Ibid., pp. 362–66.

48. Ibid., p. 352.

49. Ibid., pp. 345–52, 366.

50. See Lewis W. Spitz, *Life in Two Worlds: A Biography of William Sihler* (St. Louis: Concordia Publishing House, 1968), p. 121; and Norman A. Graebner, "Lutherans and Politics," in *The Lutheran Church in North America*, eds. John E. Groh and Robert H. Smith (St. Louis: Clayton Publishing House, 1979), p. 17.

51. Carl F. Reuss, *Profiles of Lutherans in the U.S.A.* (Minneapolis: Augsburg Publishing House, 1982), pp. 57–72. Based on a nationwide sampling of 4,500 lay members and 800 clergy from all the major synods, *Profiles of Lutherans in the U.S.A.* reveals that this family of denominations, to some degree at least, still reflects Sihler's attitude. Lutherans who participated in the survey tended to be optimistic about their own personal future, their family, and their church. They were found, however, to be deeply pessimistic about the national economy and world affairs.

52. Fick's remarks are summarized by Stellhorn in *Schools of the Lutheran Church-Missouri Synod*, pp. 116–18.

53. Wolbrecht, "The Period of Expansion, 1864–1894," p. 121.

54. Stellhorn, *Schools of the Lutheran Church-Missouri Synod*, pp. 117–18.

55. Beck, *Lutheran Elementary Schools in the United States*, pp. 227–29.

56. Meier and Mayer, "The Process of Americanization," p. 372.

57. Stellhorn, *Schools of the Lutheran Church-Missouri Synod*, pp. 235–47.

58. Graebner, "Lutherans in Politics," p. 16.

59. Beck, *Lutheran Elementary Schools in the United States*, pp. 250–70; and John F. Stach, "The Period of Assimilation, 1894–1920," in Repp, *One Hundred Years of Christian Education*, pp. 147–53.

60. Stellhorn, *Schools of the Lutheran Church-Missouri Synod*, pp. 307–10.

61. Beck, *Lutheran Elementary Schools in the United States*, pp. 316–59.

62. Fred W. Meuser, "Facing the Twentieth Century, 1900–1930," in *The Lutherans in North America*, ed. E. Clifford Nelson (Philadelphia: Fortress Press, 1975), pp. 397–99.

63. Stach, "The Period of Assimilation, 1894–1920," p. 144; and Stellhorn, *Schools of the Lutheran Church-Missouri Synod*, p. 275.

64. Beck, *Lutheran Elementary Schools in the United States*, pp. 324–52; Stellhorn, *Schools of the Lutheran Church-Missouri Synod*, pp. 318–20; and Meuser, "Facing the Twentieth Century, 1900–1930," pp. 428–29.

65. L. G. Bickel, "The Period of Integration, 1920–1947," in Repp, *One Hundred Years of Christian Education*, p. 178.

66. Ibid., p. 179.

67. Meuser, "Facing the Twentieth Century, 1900–1930," p. 429.

68. August C. Stellhorn, *History of the Superintendents Conference* (St. Louis: Concordia Publishing House, 1956), pp. 24–25.

69. Stellhorn, *Schools of the Lutheran Church-Missouri Synod*, pp. 381–84.

70. Schmidt, *Powerless Pedagogues*, p. 87.

71. Stellhorn, *Schools of the Lutheran Church-Missouri Synod*, pp. 323–33.

72. Harry G. Coiner, "The Purposes and History of the Lutheran Elementary School," in *Lutheran Elementary Schools in Action*, ed. Victor C. Krause (St. Louis: Concordia Publishing House, 1963), pp. 18–19.

73. Raymond E. Maag, "The Lutheran Elementary School Pupil," in Krause, *Lutheran Elementary Schools in Action*, pp. 54–60.

74. Stellhorn, *Schools of the Lutheran Church-Missouri Synod*, pp. 476–77.

75. See William A. Kramer, *General Course of Study for Lutheran Elementary Schools* (St. Louis: Concordia Publishing House, 1943).

76. Ronald L. Johnstone, *The Effectiveness of Lutheran Elementary and Secondary Schools as Agencies of Christian Education* (St. Louis: Concordia Publishing House, 1966).

77. *1981 Statistical Yearbook*, p. 218.

78. Data made available by John O'Hara, Department of Research and Planning, Lutheran Church-Missouri Synod, 30 September 1982.

79. Data made available by H. James Boldt, Secretary of Schools, Lutheran Church-Missouri Synod, 1 October 1982.

Chapter 3

Calvinist Day Schools: Roots and Branches

DONALD OPPEWAL AND PETER P. DeBOER

The term "Calvinist" is used to distinguish the schools described below from Catholic, Lutheran, Anglican, Baptist, Methodist, and other Protestant denominational or independent church educational efforts. Calvinists in North America do not commonly refer to their schools as Calvinist schools. Instead they call them "Christian schools," a practice begun in the Netherlands, in the nineteenth century. The schools described here are those that arose in the United States in the middle to late nineteenth century. Since 1920 these schools organized themselves into a National Union of Christian Schools. In 1979 the National Union became Christian Schools International. Its headquarters is at Grand Rapids, Michigan. CSI has 382 schools as members, employs 3,844 full-time teachers, and enrolls 74,541 students.[1] As such it constitutes one of the larger groups of Protestant schools in North America.

In the following essay we will describe and analyze briefly some ethnic or cultural influences on these American Calvinist schools, especially their roots in The Netherlands; the ecclesiastical or denominational affiliation of the schools, especially with the Christian Reformed Church in North America; and the biblical or theological grounding of the schools, including some consequences for educational theory, before we present some problems and prospects for the future.

CULTURAL ROOTS: THE NETHERLANDS

While the roots of the Calvinist day schools in America reach back to The Netherlands, their common soil is the religio-philosophical

58

system called Calvinism. Founded by John Calvin in the sixteenth century and given earliest cultural expression in Geneva, Switzerland, Calvinism since then played a crucial role in the spread of the Protestant Reformation to France, The Netherlands, England, Scotland, and America. Although it has assumed different roles in each of these countries, in none of them has it operated simply as a set of specifically doctrinal or liturgical beliefs; it has always found cultural expression and produced an effect upon economics, politics, and education, although not to the same degree in all countries. The fundamental principle upon which the Calvinist system rests is the sovereignty of God in the totality of life.[2] Education being one of the crucial issues in life, it is not surprising that a standard reference work notes that "one of the . . . most permanent influences of Calvinists in Geneva, France, Holland, Scotland, England, and America was their contribution to education."[3]

In Holland, for example, under the influence of Calvinist Geneva, the universities of Leiden (1575), Gronigen (1614), Amsterdam (1630), Utrecht (1636), and others, enjoyed an international reputation. Popular education was decreed by the church and maintained by the state. The Calvinist Synod of Dort (1618–19) resolved that:

> Schools in which the young shall be properly instructed in piety and fundamentals of Christian doctrine shall be instituted not only in cities, but also in towns and country places. . . . The Christian magistry shall be requested that honorable stipends be provided for teachers, and that well-qualified persons may be employed and enabled to devote themselves to that function; and especially that the children of the poor may be gratuitously instructed by them and not be excluded from the benefits of the schools.[4]

Thus, during the sixteenth and seventeenth centuries, during the height of Calvinist influence, the Dutch founded noted universities and made state supported "Christian" elementary education available to the poor as well as the rich.

The Dutch Republic, which began in 1579, ended in 1795 when the Dutch came under French control. When the Dutch established a kingdom called The Netherlands under William I (1815), historic Calvinist creeds were officially recognized, these being the Heidelberg Catechism, the Belgic Confession, and the Canons of Dort. Calvinism was in effect the national religion, and the Reformed Church (now called the Hervormde Kerk) the state church.

Under newly adopted rules for church government, however, pastors in the churches and professors in the universities were permitted to interpret these confessions rather freely.[5] Orthodox Calvinists protested the changes in church doctrine, liturgy, and polity. Some of those wanting to be faithful to the historic creeds labored to restore the Reformed Church to its original purity; others began a movement which culminated in their seceding from the state church in 1834.

Secession and Emigration

The impulse to secede was nourished by religious revivalism then sweeping most of western Europe,[6] and by the urge to create unofficial groups of believers within the official churches who met regularly for prayer, Bible study, and the exercise of piety.[7] It was spearheaded by a small number of pastors committed to the orthodox faith. These pastors suffered molestations, fines, and even imprisonments. The followers were mainly from the lower classes, with little political power. Crop failures and depressed job opportunities only added to the numerous ecclesiastical, political, economic, and educational discriminations of the Dutch government.[8]

While the full story of the persecutions cannot be told, suffice it to say that the Seceders felt the hand of religious persecution from the state. Since the Dutch school system, the state, and the church were intertwined, the Seceders objected, not only to church polity and doctrine, but to educational emphases as well.

One of the reasons for the Secession was the conviction that the schools under the supervision of the state were becoming neutral in matters of religion. The Seceders objected to the educational policies instituted during the period of French influence, policies which remained in effect after the restoration of Dutch independence. These regulations designated only certain portions of the Bible as suitable for classroom use; they also eliminated from the curriculum the teaching of denominational doctrines, specifically the teaching of the Heidelberg Catechism.[9] Further, efforts by the Seceders to achieve state approval for their own church-controlled or parochial schools were repeatedly frustrated by the civil authorities.[10]

What had been one of the chief reasons for the Secession of 1834—the issue of Christian education—became one of several reasons for emigration to the United States. As pastors Brummelkamp and Van Raalte expressed it:

> Especially we would desire, that they, settling [in the U.S.] in the same villages and neighborhoods, may enjoy the privilege of seeing

their little ones educated in a Christian school—a privilege of which we are here [in The Netherlands] entirely deprived, as the instruction given in the state's schools may be called but a mere general moral one, offensive to neither Jew nor Roman Catholic.[11]

Thus the ideal of the Christian school was carried to America by desperately poor groups of immigrants who in The Netherlands had frequently kept their children from attendance at the state schools[12] and who had repeatedly failed to achieve approval for their own church schools, and by their university-educated leader, A. C. Van Raalte, who looked forward with great anticipation to establishing schools.[13] Given the need literally to hack out of the heavily forested wilderness of western Michigan a form of civilized life which, over time, only approximated life in The Netherlands, one should not be surprised to discover compromises with the ideal, especially with the district (public) school offering its attractions as an alternative.[14]

Calvinist Revival

The Calvinist day school movement in America was also enriched by the Calvinist revival begun in the 1870s under the leadership of Abraham Kuyper.[15] For fifty years in The Netherlands Kuyperian Calvinism "addressed every facet of national life . . . and wrote much of its political and cultural agenda."[16]

Fully as orthodox as the Seceders, and as fervent in piety, Kuyper believed that Calvinism was not limited to matters of religion, narrowly defined, but included politics, economics, science, and the like—or in his favorite phrase, "every sphere of life." On the occasion of the founding of the Free University of Amsterdam in 1880, Kuyper enunciated a principle later called "sphere sovereignty," whereby he maintained that the basic spheres of life—such as family, state, church, art, agriculture, science, education—have their own nature or character and are subject to their own laws, laws established by God in the creation itself. Each sphere is subject to the all encompassing sovereignty of God. The spheres are interrelated, yet no sphere had the right to interfere with the sovereignty, under God, of any of the other spheres. Thus, for example, the sphere of academic science, schooling, or education, being a sovereign sphere, had to develop the task assigned to it by God while free of interference from both the state and the church.[17]

Kuyperian Calvinists, unlike the Seceders, did not denounce certain fields of activity (politics, scholarship, art) as inherently "worldly"; rather, the faithful were called to address such areas as legitimate human concerns and to restore them to something of their original perfection rather than turn their backs on them.[18] With such impetus, these Calvinists established, besides the Free University, a nationwide network of Christian elementary and secondary schools which were free of both the state and the church.

Many immigrants settled in the new world full aware of, though not always in agreement with, the "world and life view" of Kuyperian Calvinism.[19] The presence in America of fresh numbers of pastors, professional educators, and influential laypersons on fire with Kuyperian Calvinist ideas not only brought interest and enthusiasm for Christian education, but led to the administrative break between the Christian Reformed Church in North America and the school system. The schools became officially controlled by societies of laypersons, especially parents, rather than controlled by churches through their councils or consistories.[20]

Thus the Calvinist day schools in America find their ethnic and cultural roots in The Netherlands. The soil of Calvinism in The Netherlands in the nineteenth century produced two roots: the Secession of 1834 and Kuyperian Calvinism of the 1870s and beyond. The Seceder root branched into an overwhelming concern for purity of doctrine, a pietism which often took on an anticultural color, and a desire to establish Christian schools controlled by the churches, which would guarantee the survival of the churches and safeguard the faith of the true believer. The Kuyperian Calvinist root branched into a persistent concern for cultural engagement, testing the spirits to see whether they are of God, and seeking to establish the Lordship of Jesus Christ in all areas of life. The Kuyperians established schools controlled by parents and interested laypersons, convinced that neither church nor state controlled education. How these two roots and their branches, with their opposing views on education, became fruitfully fused over time within the shifting and ambiguous relationship that existed for years between the Christian Reformed Church and the Calvinist school system, will now be discussed.

ECCLESIASTICAL ROOTS: THE CHRISTIAN REFORMED CHURCH

The Calvinist day school, transplanted to America from The Netherlands, grew slowly and made little progress for almost forty years. The American version was begun by A. C. Van Raalte, who led the Seceders of 1834 to western Michigan in 1847 and settled at Holland. Other immigrants settled nearby at Zeeland, Graafschap, Vriesland, Overisel, and Drenthe, or in the already established cities of Grand Rapids, Kalamazoo, and Grand Haven. Joined together to form a church union called Classis Holland, the entire classis in 1850 joined the Dutch Reformed Church whose roots in America went back to the seventeenth century.

The union of Classis Holland with the Dutch Reformed Church helped Van Raalte realize part of his educational ideal. For, with the financial aid of the Dutch Reformed Church, Van Raalte was able to establish an academy in 1851, which became Holland Academy under the care of the General Synod of the Dutch Reformed Church. From out of the Academy came Hope College (1866) and in the same year the beginnings of theological education at Hope.[21]

Van Raalte's larger vision included Christian primary schools. His concept of the "task God has laid in our hands" included "the matter of education and the establishment of a Christian Society." He judged that only education could "deliver this people and their confessions from irrelevance."[22] Yet his followers were so poor that, in 1850, they temporarily refused to tax themselves to support even the public school in Holland. Classis Holland, in 1855, did recommend to the Board of Education of the Dutch Reformed Church the need for a church school in Kalamazoo, and a year later did the same for the Second Reformed Church in Grand Rapids. Van Raalte, soon convinced that the local public school was inappropriate for Christians, proposed to his own consistory the organization of a parochial school where the Bible could be used as a textbook, where instruction could be given in the Heidelberg Catechism, and the Dutch language included as one of the subjects of study. But the school, by 1862, died for lack of interest and support.[23]

Thus, except for Holland Academy and Hope College in Holland, Michigan, and parochial schools in Kalamazoo and Grand Rapids, the Seceders associated with Van Raalte in the western wing of the Dutch Reformed Church showed little zeal for the Calvinist school ideal. That ideal, however, did survive within the True Dutch Reformed Church (later called the Christian Reformed Church), born in 1857 when four congregations in western Michigan seceded from the Dutch Reformed Church. Ironically, the little parochial school begun in 1856 in Grand Rapids by the Second Reformed Church became the first of an eventually flourishing line of Christian schools when that congregation, by secession in 1857, became the First Christian Reformed Church of Grand Rapids.

Early Growth Within the Church

The educational significance of the Secession of 1857 which gave birth to the Christian Reformed Church is "that it was made in the same tradition and spirit as the Secession of 1834 in the Netherlands."[24] The few schools that were built were parochial schools aimed, with Dutch as the language of instruction, at transmitting doctrinal awareness and nurturing true faith among the youth to help preserve a small and struggling denomination.

Among a people who for years have enjoyed the reputation of being advocates of Christian schools, the early growth of the church far outran the growth of the Christian schools. Consider this: When the CRC was born, there was but one little Dutch parochial school in a denomination numbering four congregations. In fifteen years the denomination had grown to twenty-five congregations, served by thirteen ministers, yet there was still only this one school in Grand Rapids, Michigan. By 1880 the church had grown to thirty-eight congregations; in that year there were only four "little Dutch schools," two of them in Grand Rapids. By 1900 the denomination had grown to 144 churches served by 101 ministers, yet there were still only about fourteen Christian schools, seven of them in Grand Rapids with its eleven Christian Reformed churches.[25]

One overriding reason for the slow growth was the economic impoverishment of many of the immigrants and their descendants. This, in the absence of effective compulsory attendance legislation, meant that children were early put to useful occupations.[26] Another was the tolerable character of the public schools in the United States, especially those in rural communities where boards of education could employ Christian teachers and permit Bible reading and devotions. Another reason was the judgment of many parents that the Christian schools which did exist often left much to be desired. In addition to their overly narrow aim, the teachers were often untrained, inept, very young, and they came and went in rapid succession.[27]

For its justification of such schools, the CRC in this era referred to Article 21 of the church order of the Synod of Dort which, prior to its revision in 1914, read in part: "Consistories shall see to it that there are good schoolmasters." Part of the Heidelberg Catechism, until revised, read "that the ministry of the gospel and the schools be maintained."[28] On these foundations the church insisted it "had a warrant . . . to establish and maintain day schools to insure her continued existence and vitality."[29] But late in the century Calvinists challenged such justification for parochial schools, with some intriguing results.

The Kuyperian Calvinist Challenge

During the last decade of the nineteenth century, the Kuyperian notion that Christian schools be free from control of both state and church gained ascendancy. The pressure came especially from Christian school principals educated in The Netherlands, who desired to transplant Kuyper's concept of sphere sovereignty to the American scene.[30] Acceptance of the concept entailed at the least a significant shift in the locus of control from the church to parents and other interested supporters. But beyond that the leaders of this new Kuyperian educational movement hoped that by giving Christian education "a roof of its own," instead of existing by the grace of the church, students from churches other than Christian Reformed would be welcome; that "Reformed symbols" such as the Heidelberg Catechism and the like would not be formally taught (though there would be adherence to "undiluted Reformed principles"); and that English would become the language of instruction in the schools.[31] Underneath all this lay the hope that freedom from the church meant freedom for the schools to prosper.

In 1892 the Christian Reformed Synod adopted a resolution encouraging the organization of a national society to promote Christian education.[32] Within weeks a Society for Christian Education on a Reformed Basis was organized,[33] committed to stimulating the establishment of more schools and the expansion of those already existing, as well as the training of young people to be "Reformed teachers" for the schools."[34]

But what can be read as a victory for Kuyperian Calvinism and, theoretically at least, a significant separation of the schools from the control and influence of the church, ought not be so understood. Consider that the newly born Society, in Article One of its constitution, found its basis in "the Holy Scriptures as expressed in the Formulas of Unity of the Reformed Church."[35] Hence there was no open break with a long tradition linking Christian education with church creeds. Neither did the individual schools quickly move to shed their ecclesiastical controls.[36] Nor were Kuyperian principles rigidly argued by the leadership of the Society. The man who softened the impact of such principles more than any other person was Klaas

Kuiper, a pastor in the CRC and the Society's first president. In favor of the Kuyperian ideal of society-controlled education, he refused to raise his opinion to the level of inviolable principle that would make church ownership of schools illegitimate.[37] Further, the Society did not engage in a campaign opposing church involvement in education. Instead, the Society reminded all pastors in the church of their obligation to support Christian education and urged them to organize local chapters of the national Society within their congregations. The Society even went as far as to allow church consistories operating schools to join the Society as corporate bodies.[38]

Thus Kuyperian Calvinism, transplanted to America, did lead to society or parentally controlled schools. But the constitution of the national Society, the justification offered by the Society for the separation of the schools from the churches, and the membership practices of the Society were such as to create, at the outset already, a highly ambiguous relationship between the schools and the CRC. In theory the Calvinist schools were free to develop their own life sphere; in fact, then and for many years after, the Calvinist schools were virtually parochial, perceived as an arm of the church and essential to her life.[39]

This close relationship of the schools to the CRC "has lent a definite denominational coloring to a school system that is not in principle to be limited to that denomination,"[40] and helps explain the character and some of the tensions associated with two vital aspects of the life of the schools: teacher education and Christian Schools International.

SUPPORTING ORGANIZATIONS

Teacher Education Efforts

Since 1900 Calvin College in Grand Rapids, owned and operated by the CRC, has been the major supplier of teachers for the Calvinist day schools, owned and operated by societies of parents and other supporters. For fifty years Calvin had almost no competition in teacher education.[41] Why, one might ask, did not teacher education for the Calvinist schools lodge with a society rather than the church?

Calvin College and Seminary began in 1876 as a theological school to train young men for the ministry. Its curriculum consisted of four years of studies in a literary department followed by three years of professional training in a theological department. In 1894 the Society for Christian Education on a Reformed Basis requested of the Synod its moral support and encouragement for a normal school that would originate with the Society and be under its direct control. The Synod refused to comply.[42] In the same year there were at Synod several requests, including one from the Theological School's Board of Trustees, to separate the literary department from the Theological School. Instead, Synod expanded the potential clientele of the school by declaring that the theological school would now admit "also those who do not look forward to the ministry."[43] The Society then made an effort to organize teacher training on an apprentice model,[44] but with little success. Formal teacher education had to wait until 1900 when the literary department of the theological school was finally expanded into an academy or preparatory school. Here, at the secondary level, under denominational auspices, Christian school teachers were educated in what slowly developed into a fairly distinctive four-year curricular track: the teachers' course. For nearly twenty years, this course of study enrolled—behind the preseminary course—more students than any other at Calvin.[45]

A serious shortage of teachers for the Calvinist schools rose precipitously during the First World War and immediately afterward. To meet that need, several institutions developed within the CRC which threatened the hegemony that Calvin exercised in the field of teacher preparation.

One source of competition was Christian secondary schools. Until about 1915 Calvin's preparatory school was the only secondary school in existence within the CRC. But almost overnight Christian secondary schools sprang up in Michigan, Illinois, Iowa, New Jersey, and elsewhere. With or without a special teachers' course, many of the graduates became teachers in Christian elementary schools.

Another was the rise in 1916 of the Christian Reformed College of Grundy Center, Iowa. At first controlled by Classis East Friesland (a predominantly German-speaking subdivision of the church), Grundy College became a society controlled school in 1920.[46] As a preparatory school and two-year college, Grundy offered teacher education courses until its demise in the early 1930s during the Great Depression.

An even greater potential source of competition for Calvin arose within the city of Grand Rapids itself. In 1918 about three hundred supporters began the Society for Christian Normal Instruction, its birth partly the result of long-standing criticism by Christian school teachers and principals that Calvin's teachers' course was not sufficiently practical.[47] Reflecting the upgrading taking place in normal training in Michigan, this Christian Normal School, begun in 1919, sought mainly to enroll high-school graduates to teach in Christian elementary schools. Unfortunately for the school, few students enrolled. Operations were suspended after only two years.[48]

Meanwhile, responding to the argument that a church-controlled college had no business operating a preparatory school, Calvin began the dismantling of the preparatory school with the concurrent rise of Grand Rapids Christian High School. Calvin as college, intending all along to enlarge its offering in secondary teacher education, approved, by the spring of 1921, plans for a two-year normal program for training elementary school teachers. Within a year Calvin had graduated six secondary education students who qualified for state certification.[49] Concurrent with the phasing out of seniors in the preparatory school teachers' course, Calvin College phased in its new two-year normal course for elementary teachers with the advice and consent of the National Union of Christian Schools, begun in 1920.[50]

The subsequent history of teacher education within the CRC and the Calvinist day schools is largely one of cooperative interaction and continued upgrading. Early on, most of the Christian high schools ceased their teacher education programs.[51] By 1924 Calvin had four-year programs in elementary and secondary teacher education, yet the college maintained a little publicized two-year elementary teacher education program until the middle fifties as a favor to some of the Christian schools. Partly at the request of the National Union, the college offered a full slate of summer courses, mainly aimed at teacher preparation, from the 1950s onward. Much of the theoretical work on behalf of Christian education was developed from out of the college faculty. In the seventies Calvin began a graduate program leading to the Master of Arts in Teaching degree, fulfilling a desire of the National Union for a Christian graduate-level program in teacher education. Thereby graduates from Christian sister colleges can, if they choose, continue their education at Calvin. Presently Calvin counts four schools as "sister" colleges: Dordt, in Sioux Center, Iowa; Trinity Christian in Palos Heights, Illinois; Kings in Edmonton, Alberta; and Redeemer, in Hamilton, Ontario. Unlike Calvin, which is owned and operated by the CRC, these schools are all controlled by societies. Thus far only the first two colleges engage in teacher education programs.

Dordt College, begun in 1955, was a direct response on the part of members of the CRC in the Midwest to a profound teacher shortage. For nearly a decade Dordt graduated teachers from its two-year program, though some of the graduates interested in teaching transferred to Calvin to finish their programs. Beginning in 1964, Dordt established four-year programs, including one in teacher education, which then matched the upgrading that Calvin had also achieved.

Trinity Christian, begun in 1959, continued as a two-year college until 1970. Prior to that many of the graduates of Trinity transferred to Calvin to complete their teacher education. After 1970 most of the students remained at Trinity.

Thus, even though the Calvinist day schools and the sister Christian colleges are controlled by societies, and Calvin College is church owned and operated, there has been fruitful interaction and close cooperation between Calvin and the schools united into a National Union as well as between Calvin and her sister colleges, a harmony which has only reinforced the ties of the CRC as a denomination to the Calvinist schools.

Service Organizations

When the Society for the Promotion of Christian Education on a Reformed Basis came into being, with the endorsement of the Christian Reformed Synod of 1892, it found itself with only a dozen schools and the abstract cause of society-controlled education to "promote." The administrative break between the denominational system and the existing schools left the schools with no formal budgetary support, no national network of communication, no appointed spokesmen for the cause.

It appears that the Society was largely an idea and not a viable alternative to the denominational structure it was to replace. Local school boards and their societies wrestled alone with the specifics of adequate finances, properly trained teachers, and acceptable locations for instruction. As each local society struggled with these, as well as with the goal of providing teacher training and teaching materials, they soon saw that collective efforts were necessary if any progress was to be made. No single school board could hope to provide leadership in these areas in addition to raising funds, staff,and buildings for local school operation. A grassroots movement for bringing together Reformed, Calvinist school societies into some kind of collective cooperation began as early as 1900. As the number of schools across the country grew, school boards in certain areas where schools were more numerous, and where even high schools were contemplated, banded together.

Alliances. These groups were called Alliances, and were formed into the Michigan, the Chicago, the Western, and the Eastern Alliances.[52] The same logic which led to the forming of geographically local Alliances soon persuaded them that only a national organization could adequately cope with common problems. It was the Chicago Alliance which took the initiative to form a national, and not merely a local, organization to serve all the struggling schools dotting the United States. It called the first meeting to which thirty-seven local school associations sent representatives. By 1920 organizational problems had been overcome and a National Union of Christian Schools was born. With its birth the Alliances maintained their identity by eventually becoming constitutive parts of the National Union, and are now called Districts.

National Union. When the Union was organized it became apparent that there were two schools of thought about its purpose. Some looked upon it as an authoritative body which would weld the various local school associations together and establish policy for all schools. The other view was that it was to offer its services, whether these be pension plans or materials for teachers, but did not obligate the local school to adopt any. This latter perception became the prevailing sentiment, leaving school societies with large amounts of local autonomy.

What is significant for the Calvinist school movement is that the Union was a union of laymember school boards, not church officials. It took from 1892 to 1920 to replace a denominational structure with an alternative one, a nonecclesiastical national structure. The reverberations of this action have been many, and not all can be given in this brief summary. Suffice it to say that they have all stemmed from the attempt to maintain a Calvinist-oriented school system, while being neither administratively, nor in funding, nor in its goals a parochial school system. It produced on the American educational scene a citizen- and parent-controlled conception of day school education. It remains today as almost unique in American religious schooling, a system with religious orientation, but not administered by any denomination. This has freed the Calvinist school to be ecumenical in ways not open to the various parochial schools.

The intent to broaden its base of support has over the years caused changes in the Basis article of its bylaws. Each was an attempt to identify more clearly the requirements for voting membership. The changes signal that the principles are both biblical and educational, and that the biblical grounding is in educationally relevant elements.[53]

At its inception the National Union had numerous goals. One was the ambitious goal of establishing a Christian normal school for the training of teachers in member schools. Unable to agree on whether teacher training was a national or local responsibility, it soon became apparent that the National Union could not achieve its goals.[54]

The Union's efforts turned toward cooperation with Calvin College, which is owned and operated by the Christian Reformed denomination. The inability of the early Union to establish its own non-ecclesiastical teacher-training program was a minor failure in implementing theory, but gave it and the schools it represented a well-established college as the main source of training for its teachers. The Union made a financial contribution to the costs of preparing a Christian school principal to take up his duties as director of the Normal Department at Calvin College. It also for many years has provided scholarships and grants to prospective teachers who attended Calvin or the several other Reformed Colleges which have been established since 1955.

In 1922, only two years after its founding, the Union succeeded in translating another of its purposes into reality. That, as Article 4 of its Bylaws expressed it, was "establishing and maintaining of a teachers' and School Boards' Magazine." First called *Christian School Magazine* it soon became more popular and less professional in its content and was named *Christian Home and School*. While for some years it attempted to speak to both parent and professional educator concerns, with various special departments variously called "Teacher's Exchange" and "The Teacher's Bookself," it was chiefly a monthly periodical for the parent and school board member.

The National Union took seriously its initial goal of assisting the classroom teacher in being professional and in implementing the distinctives of the Calvinist school. It did so in at least three areas: assistance in forming professional organizations, assistance in founding a journal for them, and in publishing textbooks and teaching materials. Each of them merits a brief description.

The Union went far beyond recruiting teachers for its schools by offering scholarships and awards for teacher preparation and providing pension plans. It was the National Union, acting in concert with the Calvin College Education Department, that provided both personnel and some funding for meetings to help teachers organize as a professional group. While slow to organize, teacher associations, with more or less activity, soon dotted the geographical landscape. The present list covers two pages in the national directory. Plans have been made for a national Calvinist teacher organization, but none has yet appeared. In encouraging such associations the Union was motivated by a desire for professional growth of its teachers.

The second area of influence and support was a professional educators journal. Recognizing that the Union's own *Christian Home and School* was chiefly a board member and parent magazine, it gave both personnel and funding for a professional educator's magazine. Acting in concert with Calvin College, it subsidized and founded in 1961 the quarterly *Christian Educators Journal* and appointed a member of the Calvin Education Department as its first editor. The Midwest Christian Teacher's Association soon joined, and presently a dozen teacher associations, Christian colleges, and other service organizations are official members. While for many years the *Journal's* masthead declared it to be a medium for the Calvinist school movement, it later expressed an ecumenical outreach by changing the key word to "Protestant." In its statement of purpose it now speaks of being a channel of communication for educators committed to the idea of evangelical Christian schools. These two activities of the National Union indicate that as a school board organization it was sincerely interested in professionalizing the teachers in the Calvinist school movement, and this interest went far beyond the design of pension plans or suggestions for the upgrading of teacher salaries.

A third area in an early version of its constitution was called "encouraging the publication of literature of a pedagogic nature."[55] While the Union has also published promotional materials and studies of the philosophy of the school movement it has expended considerable amounts of its budget on classroom materials, such as textbooks, curriculum guides, and resource units. Early interest in Bible materials and hymnbooks for classroom use soon expanded into history textbooks, civics and social studies texts, and literature anthologies.

Since 1967 it has had a full-time administrator of a Curriculum Department, plus a number of part-time consultants who work on a contract basis to produce teaching materials in science, music, language arts, and physical education, just to name a few. These materials reflect a determined effort to integrate religious outlook and a given curriculum area. Working with a limited budget, compared to commercial publishing houses, it has not yet produced materials for all grade levels or in all curricular areas. Efforts so far have shown a commitment to counter the secularizing effect in commercial texts with a Christian view of life and learning. Such extensive concern with production of Christian materials has been one of the early distinctives of the Calvinist school movement, a concern which was matched only recently by other Christian groups sponsoring schools. The description of this national school board organization would not be complete without noting a recent change in its name and scope of concern, a change from National Union of Christian Schools to Christian Schools International in 1979.[56]

Christian Schools International. Since the early fifties waves of immigrants from The Netherlands to Canada produced a parallel school movement there. Since the geographic/political differences produced unique needs, in everything from ways to raise money to curriculum materials that are specific to the Canadian context, it eventually was evident to all that if Canadian Calvinist schools were full members their concerns had to be administratively recognized. So the "National" became "International" not only in the name but in everything from Board of Trustees representation to curriculum materials. Such a move from focus on the United States to the broader North American continent produced some strains, both ideological and otherwise, but the commonalities appear to be greater than the differences, and the Canadian contingent is rapidly being assimilated into the CSI system.

The movement promises to become even more international in the future, with affiliations being made with Reformed groups in places as far apart as Australia and Ireland. The National Union of Associations for Christian Parent Controlled Schools in Australia, as an affiliate member representing twenty-three schools across that continent, seems to be the most significant on the international horizon.

BIBLICAL/THEOLOGICAL GROUNDING

As the previous sections have indicated the Calvinist school movement has both ethnic and denominational roots. These have weakened in their influence on the particulars of the ownership and operation of these schools. What has not been altered throughout its one-hundred-and-thirty-year history is its grounding in biblical/theological principles as seen in Calvinist perspective. While motivations of individual supporters have been varied, and while the perceptions of the movement have been understood in various ways by fellow Protestants and other supporters of religious schooling, the leaders and spokesmen have over the years forged a web of interrelated doctrines which provide the religious foundations of the movement, and which have endured through its trials, both economic and ideological. This section will elaborate upon terminology introduced earlier, point to the theological literature available, and indicate more fully its connection with the educational distinctives of the Calvinist school.

The case for the Calvinist school does not rest on any presumed or real deficiencies in the isolated practices of the American public school. It does not exist because of a protest against any specific public school practices relating to its handling of religion or its curricular content affecting values education. It does not reside simply in an immigrant mentality or a desire for social isolation. The Calvinist school is a protest movement only in the sense that its theology provides it with educational positions on key questions that make the very conception of a religiously neutral, government-sponsored educational system pedagogically problematic if not impermissible.

At least three interrelated educational positions are undergirded by Calvinist theology. The first is that the locus of educational authority is neither in the church nor the state but resides in the family. This has led to the founding and propagation of schools owned and operated by societies of like-minded parents and citizens. The second is that the proper relation between education and religion is not that of neutrality toward all, nor simple indoctrination in one, but the integration of a religious worldview into all curriculum content. This has led to serious attempts to produce textbooks and other teaching materials in numerous curriculum areas which incorporate this religious outlook. The third is that the aim of such education is neither evangelization for church membership nor neutral value-free information giving, but preparing the learner for living a Christian lifestyle in contemporary society.

The literature supporting these three distinctives of the Calvinist day-school movement uses various terminology and slogans to reflect them and cannot be reproduced here in detail. It is the position on the three questions of locus of educational authority, aim of education, and curricular integration which joins Calvinists, and not the specifics of rhetoric.

Sovereignty of God and Social Spheres

The most pervasive, but also most abstract, of these is the doctrine of the sovereignty of God.[57] Perhaps it is the taproot among other roots. Whatever else this doctrine has meant for soteriology, for education and the schools it has meant that schools express not merely a secular concern. Calvinists see politics, business, and also education as embraced in the Christian's calling to apply this understanding to all areas of life. Thus educational policy and practice are derived from this worldview, in which the sovereignty of God is the fundamental principle.

A second doctrine, derived from this taproot, and more directly decisive in shaping educational policy is that of sphere sovereignty.[58] According to this view numerous social spheres, or institutions, operate within their own areas, with what are called creation ordinances governing each. None is subordinate to others, or under its control. For our purposes here it is important to note that academics, or schools, are one of the spheres, and this renders both the parochial, church-owned school, and the public, state-owned school a violation of such sphere sovereignty. Although often viewed by others as a parochial school, because of its past ties with the Christian Reformed Church, the Calvinist school idea is that schools are owned and operated by groups of citizen-parents. The locus of educational authority, therefore, is neither the state, nor the church, but the parent community. This doctrine has been influential in affecting both aims of education and curriculum, but it has done so by means of determining the question of ownership and control.

Covenant

Another related doctrine which aided Calvinists to choose parentally controlled schools is that of the covenant.[59] While this doctrine, the terminology of which at least is unique to Calvinism, has many ramifications, the effect of it on the conception of schooling is that God uses the institution of the family to carry forward the Kingdom of God.[60] The family in this concept is not the biological family but the total spiritual community of adults who provide funds and support for education.

These two biblically related doctrines, sphere sovereignty and covenant, have provided the basis for this distinctive system of schools on the question of locus authority. This basic position has then enabled this system to articulate goals of education and curriculum directions which separate it from both secular state education and from other Christian systems of parochial schools, with their pervasive church extension emphasis. Were these the only theoretical foundations for the Calvinist school there would be only negative positions on goals and curriculum, identifying them as being neither institutional church nor state goals and curriculum.

General and Special Revelation

Another peculiarly Reformed and Calvinist doctrine is that of commitment to *both* general revelation and special revelation. This "two book" theory of the sources of knowledge identifies the Bible as one book and the book of nature or creation as the other. The two are held to be in tension and interpenetration with each other, with no basic dichotomy between the sacred and the secular, between Scripture and nature as sources of truth.[61] Both emanating from one sovereign God, both are trustworthy sources of truth.

For aims and curriculum this theory has carved out for the Calvinist day school both areas of cooperation with the Christian church and areas of specialization. The distinction between church education and day-school education is that the church as institution is the expert in interpreting special revelation, with the school offering its leadership in interpreting general revelation. Through Christian teachers trained in the investigations of history, science, and psychology, among others, the aims of the school are cultural involvement and transformation, and not mastery of church doctrine or evangelization. This legitimizes a liberal arts curriculum as a means for discovering creation ordinances, with the aid and direction of the Bible. Community membership becomes more prominent than church membership in the goal. In the curriculum Bible study becomes one among many academic areas for exploration, with biblical insights related to each, but occupying neither a higher nor a lower status in the curriculum than other areas of investigation to discover God's truth.

Cultural Mandate

The doctrine of general and special revelation in its impact on the school is enhanced by the related concept of cultural mandate. Rooted in the Genesis command to till the soil, exercise dominion over creation, and to shape society, it provides for the school an aim which distinguishes it from the merely secular goals of the public school and the denominational goals of parochial schools. This training in community membership, as workers in the world of politics, business, and art, is in the literature of the movement characterized as living the Christian life in contemporary society, and is one of the expressions of the cultural mandate.[62]

This school task of helping young Christians to exercise cultural dominion rather than seeking cultural isolation has important consequences for the curriculum, and the Calvinist school movement has followed through on its rhetoric about goals by translating them into textbooks and other teaching materials.[63] These materials reveal a serious attempt to integrate, rather than keep separate, a religious outlook with curricular raw material.

Such integration has taken two forms. One form consists of adding to descriptive material, whether in science or civics, some interpretation or evaluation as seen in religious or biblical perspective. In a civics text for junior high, for example, the description of alternative forms of government, e.g., monarchy and oligarchy, is followed by evaluation and assessment of democracy in the light of bibilical principles and passages.[64] Another and more recent form of integration is that of reorganizing curricular materials so that they cut across the disciplines, integrating them in new ways so as to focus on some area charged with values where the Calvinist faith has a bearing. Two such areas are health education and technology.[65] The first of these correlates aspects of biology, physical education, and biblical materials, with a focus on human sexuality broadly considered. The second, on technology, correlates health and science materials with a focus on responsible Christian stewardship of resources. These are but brief examples of how the Calvinist doctrines of cultural mandate, and of general and special revelation, have given theological direction to curriculum, and have distinguished publishing efforts from other Protestant groups also involved in publishing Christian teaching materials.

Theoreticians of the Calvinist schools have not always articulated these connections between the network of peculiarly Calvinist doctrines given above and educational policy, nor have they limited themselves to the above doctrines. Treatises on goals of education, for example, have drawn on some of the above, but also have developed a holistic Christian anthropology, as well as used empirical research to articulate what the literature has come to call intellectual, moral (or decisional), and creative learning goals that should characterize Calvinist schools.[66] Others have focused on curriculum and given various justifications.[67] What has been attempted here in brief compass, is a selection of peculiarly Calvinist, Reformed doctrines which characterize its biblical foundations, and which serve to explain, in part, its educational distinctives.

THE FUTURE: PROSPECTS AND PROBLEMS

No movement, either in its past or present form, is as simple or single directional as our description might have indicated. There are always cross currents of thought and practice which serve to dull the distinctives and blur the outlines. To the outside observer or scholar these are valuable chiefly for historical accuracy, but also for predicting future directions. Here we shall highlight just a few of the problematics of the past which will carry forward into the future.

Relation with CRC

The ambiguous relationship between the Christian Reformed denomination and the Calvinist school is one of them. Some have warned of the dangers of parochialism.[68] Most in the school movement have accepted the moral and financial support of the denomination gratefully, while guarding jealously the autonomy of the laymember school board and professional staff.

Disassociation from a denomination, but not from a religious tradition, has opened up new possibilities of educational ecumenism in at least two areas. One is the very practical area of student recruitment and enrollment. Denominational schools, whether Catholic or Protestant, most strongly attract parents affiliated with that church, and in their goals and curriculum often reflect such sectarianism. The Calvinist school theory has the potential of attracting support across denominational lines. The distinctives that attract are less the peculiarities, whether ethnic, creedal, or social class, of any denomination than the more generic features of a Christian view of life and learning. The student population of these schools in the last ten years has changed from a predominantly Dutch, white, middle-class and Christian Reformed population to one that is much more diversified, both denominationally and racially. The urban, and particularly innercity, schools reflect this much more than the rural schools.

There is evidence that this ecumenical outreach is more than a desperate effort to keep schools alive and growing in the face of a declining birthrate. There is serious concern to face the theoretical consequences of this diversity in student population.

A related problem arises when parents of religious affiliation (but of other than Christian Reformed) apply for voting membership in the school society. The Basis article (often Article II) of the constitution of such societies typically states the criteria for membership in terms of a set of Christian beliefs about man, society, and education. Debate over what these touchstone beliefs ought to be has focused on whether these are simply the Christian Reformed ecclesiastical creeds or some more generic beliefs, particularly those that identify the school's educational distinctives.[69]

In the early seventies Christian Schools International altered its

Basis and Principles article, dropping specific reference to denominational creeds and referring instead to "Reformed creedal standards."[70] Both before this change and since, debate over this has continued in both periodicals and at CSI annual conventions.[71] In the early eighties a special task force was appointed to draw up a more comprehensive statement of beliefs, with what to call it constituting one of the challenges of being educationally distinctive without being narrowly denominational. The statement involves, not only a policy of student admission and society membership qualifications, but also the criteria for teachers and administrative staff. Clarification of all of these remains a challenge for the future.

Public Funding

Like all nonpublic schools, adequate funding has always been a problem. Acting in concert with other religiously oriented schools, the Calvinist school movement has in the last two decades aggressively participated in both legislative and litigation efforts to secure its share of the tax dollar allocated to education. These political alliances have succeeded in small ways, like bus rides and loan of textbooks, but failed in efforts to get more than miniscule amounts of tax support. They have been defeated in their efforts by both public referendums and by Supreme Court rulings on legislation.

Efforts for the future are directed at both tax credit mechanisms and the voucher idea. Both promise to be on the agenda of the Calvinist school movement of the future and have received significant treatment in its literature.[72]

Curriculum Integration

A third and final area of problem and prospect in the distinctives of the Calvinist school idea lies in curriculum. The seventies have produced a massive effort to publish distinctive textbooks and teaching materials. Integrating faith and learning into textbooks has proceeded vigorously and rigorously through the efforts of the Curriculum Department of Christian Schools International. What remains to be worked out from theory to practice is the meaning of integration which goes beyond inserting Christian evaluations and interpretations into academic areas. What has emerged in the literature is the concept of cross-disciplinary curriculum making with focus on personal-social problems as the integrating force. The translating of this vision into textbooks remains as one of the agenda items for future development.[73]

This essay on the Calvinist school movement from its inception to the present has depicted both its theoretical roots and its educational branches. The movement promises to endure as one of the significant Protestant efforts to take a Christian vision of life and society seriously in the field of education.

NOTES

1. *Directory 1983–84* (Grand Rapids, Mich.: Christian Schools International, 1983), p. 46.
2. H. Henry Meeter, *Calvinism: An Interpretation of Its Basic Ideas* (Grand Rapids, Mich.: Zondervan, 1939), p. 37.
3. *Cyclopedia of Education*, 1911 ed., s.v. "Calvinists and Education," by Herbert D. Foster.
4. Ibid.
5. Albert Hyma, *Albertus C. Van Raalte and His Dutch Settlements in the United States* (Grand Rapids, Mich.: Eerdmans, 1947), pp. 13–18. See also Gordon J. Spykman, *Pioneer Preacher: Albertus Christian Van Raalte* (Grand Rapids, Mich.: Calvin College and Seminary Library, 1976), p. 13.
6. George Stob, *The Christian Reformed Church and Her Schools* (Ann Arbor, Mich.: University Microfilms, 1974), pp. 23–24.
7. John Bratt, "The Christian Reformed Church in American Culture," *Reformed Journal* 3 (January 1963): 4.
8. One reason for the poverty of the Seceders was the complete lack of government financial aid for ministers' salaries, for the building of churches, or for the needs of the poor—since the "separated ones" had cut themselves off from state church support. See Marian M. Schoolland, *Die Kolonie* (Grand Rapids, Mich.: Christian Reformed Church, 1974), pp. 89–93, for these and other forms of harassment.
9. Herbert J. Brinks, "The Origins of Christian Education in the Christian Reformed Church," (unpublished paper, Heritage Hall, Calvin College, n.d.), pp. 2–3.
10. A. Brummelkamp and A. C. Van Raalte, "Appeal to the Faithful in the United States in North America May 25, 1846," in Henry S. Lucas, *Dutch Immigrant Memoirs and Related Writings* (Assen, Netherlands: Koninklijke Van Gorcum, 1955), p. 17. See also Stob, *The Christian Reformed Church and Her Schools*, p. 26. Brinks, "The Origins of Christian Education in the Christian Reformed Church," p. 3, notes that in The Netherlands it was not until the 1850s that the Seceders were able to establish Christian schools as an alternative to the "neutral" state schools.
11. Brummelkamp and Van Raalte, "Appeal to the Faithful in the United States in North America May 25, 1846," p. 17.
12. Stob, *The Christian Reformed Church and Her Schools*, p. 32.
13. See a letter from A. C. Van Raalte to G. Groen Van Prinsterer, 21 September 1846. Regarding incentives for emigration, Van Raalte wrote: "And the needs of my family and especially the need of school instruction

give me, besides other urgent reasons, keen incentive for this." Cited in Lucas, *Dutch Immigrant Memoirs and Related Writings*, p. 22.

14. Stob, *The Christian Reformed Church and Her Schools*, p. 37.

15. Kuyper was for forty years head of the Anti-Revolutionary political party, a member of the national legislature, and four years prime minister of The Netherlands; author of works in theology, politics, education, science, philosophy; editor of a political daily and religious weekly newspaper; co-founder of and professor at the Free University in Amsterdam; advocate of Christian elementary schools and the Christian labor movement, and much more. See James D. Bratt, *Dutch Calvinism in Modern America: The History of a Conservative Subculture* (Ann Arbor, Mich.: University Microfilms, 1978), pp. 27–71.

16. Ibid., p. 27.

17. Abraham Kuyper, *Souvereinitiet in Eigen Kring* (Amsterdam: J. H. Kruyt, 1880), cited by Stob, *The Christian Reformed Church and Her Schools*, pp. 117–18.

18. Bratt, *Dutch Calvinism in Modern America: The History of a Conservative Subculture*, p. 33, quotes Kuyper: "There is not a single inch on the whole terrain of human existence over which Christ . . . does not exclaim, 'Mine!' "

19. Ibid., p. 27.

20. Donald Oppewal, *The Roots of the Calvinistic Day School Movement* (Grand Rapids, Mich.: Calvin College Monograph Series, 1963), p. 13. According to Henry S. Lucas, *Netherlanders in America* (Ann Arbor, Mich.: University of Michigan Press, 1955), p. 602: "Kuyper's influence was powerful . . . especially in the Christian Reformed Church. . . . The Dutch immigrant's . . .'Christian schools' . . . may be regarded as his most striking contribution to the field of education."

21. According to Stob, *The Christian Reformed Church and Her Schools*, pp. 65–66: "[Van Raalte] conceived the idea of a Christian academy . . . laid it as a challenge on . . . his people, and begged the [Dutch Reformed Church] for assistance. . . . Van Raalte was the chief donor of the grounds . . . of the academy, and the financial agent for . . . soliciting . . . funds . . . and . . . construction of its buildings. This is more remarkable [since] Van Raalte obtained little encouragement from his own people in western Michigan."

22. Ibid., p. 35.

23. Ibid., pp. 45–49.

24. Oppewal, *The Roots of the Calvinistic Day School Movement*, p. 16.

25. Stob, *The Christian Reformed Church and Her Schools*, pp. 97, 129.

26. *Encyclopedia of Education*, 1971 ed., s.v. "Compulsory Attendance," by Peter P. DeBoer.

27. Stob, *The Christian Reformed Church and Her Schools*, pp. 72–76. In the school of the First Christian Reformed Church in Grand Rapids the curriculum consisted of reading, writing, arithmetic, and Psalm singing. The language of instruction was Dutch. The children attended until eight or nine years of age. Thereafter they attended the "English" schools (i.e., public schools). Some of the children who went directly to the public schools went to the First Church school for language instruction during the summer vacation. Neither the first teacher nor his successor were professionally trained. When the first teacher resigned in 1862 to take up farming, his successor was the church janitor who resigned three years later because of inadequate pay.

28. Ibid.

29. Oppewal, *The Roots of the Calvinistic Day School Movement*, p. 17.

30. Stob, *The Christian Reformed Church and Her Schools*, p. 117.

31. See P. R. Holtman in *Grand Rapids DeWachter*, 22 June 1892; and 4 July 1894.

32. Stob, *The Christian Reformed Church and Her Schools*, p. 120.

33. Ibid.

34. Ibid.

35. I.e., the official creeds uniting the Christian Reformed churches: the Belgic Confession, Heidelberg Catechism, and Canons of Dort.

36. Though the national Society was formed already in 1892, by 1905 only nine schools out of twenty were society controlled. Three years later, however, out of twenty-seven schools only four were church controlled. See *Yearbook of the CRC* (Grand Rapids, Mich.: Christian Reformed Church, 1905, 1908). One school (Kelloggsville), organized as late as 1912 as a church-controlled school, became society controlled in 1924. See Stob, *The Christian Reformed Church and Her Schools*, p. 143.

37. He argued that the church as such was not called to own and operate educational institutions; yet if a congregation thought it in the best interest of the children to maintain a school, such an undertaking would manifest the fellowship of the saints. See Henry Zwaanstra, *Reformed Thought and Experience in the New World* (Kampen, Netherlands: J. H. Kok, 1973), p. 139.

38. Ibid., p. 141.

39. Though all supporters would not agree with his assessment, George Stob concludes that though the schools have been good for the church, the obverse is not necessarily true. See Stob, *The Christian Reformed Church and Her Schools*, p. 461.

40. Oppewal, *The Roots of the Calvinistic Day School Movement*, p. 25.

41. In 1955 a society of persons whose church membership *is* limited to the CRC began Dordt College in northwest Iowa; in 1959 a society of persons whose church membership is *not* limited to the CRC began Trinity Christian College just outside Chicago.

42. *Grand Rapids DeWachter*, 19 September 1894. Synod's rejection likely reflected, in large measure, the practical consideration that the Theological School was having sufficient difficulty financially not to risk further diffusion of education effort.

43. *Acts of Synod*, 1894, Art. 48. Some who promoted the separation argued, Kuyperian fashion, that it was not the church's calling to operate a liberal arts school; others simply argued that it was unfair to burden the whole church with the cost of educating somebody else's children. See also Stob, *The Christian Reformed and Her Schools*, p. 223.

44. Zwaanstra, *Reformed Thought and Experience in the New World*, p. 142; and *Grand Rapids DeWachter*, 19 September 1894.

45. Jacob Vanden Bosch, Professor of English, noted that the teachers' course at Calvin was the "principal source whence our free Christian schools from the Atlantic to the Pacific do derive their teachers." See *Banner*, 24 August 1911.

46. *Banner*, 23 December 1920.

47. See, for example, J. L. Zandstra, "Is Calvin College Sufficient for the

Training of Teachers? If Not, What Must be Done?" in *Grand Rapids DeCalvinist*, 28 February 1918.

48. *Minutes, Board of Trustees*, 9 June 1921, Arts. 25 and 27, cited by Stob, *The Christian Reformed Church and Her Schools*, p. 140.

49. *Yearbook* (Grand Rapids, Mich.: Calvin College, 1922–1923), p. 66.

50. *Banner*, 19 April 1923.

51. Western Christian High School at Hull, Iowa, was an exception. It continued the practice until 1955 when Dordt College in Sioux Center, Iowa began as a two-year college.

52. Henry Kuiper, "A National Union of Christian Schools is Born," *Christian Home and School*, April, May, and June, 1954.

53. For a full discussion of the debates over the writing of such an educational creed see the entire issue of *Christian Educators Journal*, April, 1971.

54. See the entire issue of the March, 1970 fiftieth anniversary issue of *Christian Home and School* for the details.

55. *Christian Home and School*, March, 1970, p. 7.

56. Christian Schools International should not be confused with the Association of Christian Schools International (ACSI), a California-based organization founded in 1978, and created to bring together a wide variety of Protestants interested in Christian schools.

57. H. Henry Meeter, *The Basic Ideas of Calvanism*, 5th ed. (Grand Rapids, Mich.: Baker, 1975), p. 32 ff. See also the same claim in H. Henry Meeter, *American Calvinism: A Survey* (Grand Rapids, Mich.: Baker, 1956), p. 6.

58. Meeter, *The Basic Ideas of Calvinism*, chap. 15. For a more theological and historical treatment see Gordon Spykman, "Sphere-Sovereignty in Calvin and the Calvinist Tradition," in *Exploring The Heritage of John Calvin*, ed. David Holwerda (Grand Rapids, Mich.: Baker, 1976), pp. 163–208. For application of this view to a rejection of a statist view of educational control, see Rockne McCarthy et al., *Society, State, and Schools: A Case For Structural and Confessional Pluralism* (Grand Rapids, Mich.: Eerdmans, 1981).

59. For one statement of the necessary connection between the doctrine of the covenant and belief in Christian schools see Louis Berkhof, "Covenant of Grace and Christian Education," in *Fundamentals of Christian Education*, ed. C. Jaarsma (Grand Rapids, Mich.: Eerdmans, 1953), pp. 20–38. See also N. Henry Beversluis, *Toward a Theology of Education* (Grand Rapids, Mich.: Calvin College, 1981), p. 20 ff.

60. For biblical evidence and the organizational chart see "The Organization of the Parental Christian School," a publication of Christian Schools International, Grand Rapids, Mich.

61. Louis Berkhof, *Manual of Reformed Doctrine* (Grand Rapids, Mich.: Eerdmans, 1933), pp. 26–27. See especially p. 31 for the idea of mutual interdependence of the two revelations. See also Donald Oppewal, "Toward a Distinctive Curriculum for Christian Education," *Reformed Journal* 7 (September 1957): 21 ff., for a treatment of the role of general revelation.

62. Nicholas Wolterstorff, *Curriculum: By What Standard?* (Grand Rapids, Mich.: Christian Schools International, 1966), p. 14 ff.

63. For a complete listing of such textbooks and teaching materials see *CSI Publications Catalog 1982–83*, a publication of the Curriculum Department Christian Schools International.

64. The civics text is *Under God*, by William Hendricks (Grand Rapids, Mich.: National Union of Christian Schools and Eerdmans, 1976), pp. 16-17. For the theological explanation of instances such as these see "Culture in the Christian Life," a section in Beversluis' *Toward A Theology of Education*.

65. For health-education texts and teaching materials published by CSI see *Respecting God's Temples*, by Henry Triezenberg et al., 1977; *Toward Christian Maturity-K–6: A Curriculum Guide for Teaching Human Sexuality*, by William Hendricks, 1978; and *God's Temples* (junior high) by William Hendricks, revised 1982. For technology as a curriculum area see *Using God's World* (grades 4–6) by Theodore De Jong et al., 1977. Canadian Calvinists at the Curriculum Development Centre, Toronto, Canada, have also made a contribution to interdisciplinary teaching materials. Its *Joy in Learning: An Integrated Curriculum for the Elementary School* by Arnold De Graaff and Jean Olthuis, revised in 1975, is an instance, and it has published others under the rubric of Transportation.

66. Two noteworthy examples of articulation of Calvinist goals are N. Henry Beversluis, *Christian Philosophy of Education* (Grand Rapids, Mich.: National Union of Christian Schools, 1971); and Nicholas Wolterstorff, *Educating for Responsible Action* (Grand Rapids, Mich.: Christian Schools International and Eerdmans, 1981).

67. Geraldine Steensma and Harro Van Brummelen, eds., *Shaping School Curriculum: A Biblical View* (Terre Haute, Ind.: Signal, 1977), which stresses integrated curriculum; and Henry Triezenberg et al., *Principles to Practice*, rev. ed. (Grand Rapids, Mich.: Christian Schools International, 1979), written by teams of curriculum consultants for numerous curriculum areas.

68. Donald Oppewal, "Parochialism in Christian Schools: Its Perils," *Reformed Journal* 20 (September 1970): 12–14.

69. For one instance of the debate see the entire April 1971 issue of *Christian Educators Journal* in which arguments for an educational creed are presented.

70. See *Christian Educators Journal*, April 1971, which gives an explanation of the change as well as the complete basis article.

71. The 1982 CSI Convention contained a spirited debate over the kind of beliefs undergirding the Calvinist school. A CSI Task Force has distributed widely a document which seeks to identify the present Calvinist consensus, and called "In Their Father's House: A Handbook of Christian Educational Philosophy.

72. Donald Oppewal, "Education Vouchers: The Emerging Coalition," *The Reformed Journal* 31 (February 1981): 18–20. For a more elaborate treatment of funding problems and proposed actions see Rockne McCarthy et al., *Society, State, and Schools: A Case for Structural and Confessional Pluralism*.

73. While a number of sources allude to this new meaning of integration, one which treats it most consistently is Van Brummelen and Steensma, eds., *Shaping School Curriculum: A Biblical View*. See also Jay Adams, *Back to the Blackboard*, Phillipsburg, N.J.: Presbyterian and Reformed, 1982).

Chapter 4

Seventh-Day Adventist Education: A Historical Sketch and Profile

GEORGE R. KNIGHT

In 1982 the Seventh-day Adventist Church operated over 5,000 schools worldwide. In the United States there were 1,106 elementary schools with 51,285 students, 81 secondary schools with 17,290 students, and 9 colleges and 2 universities with 18,393 students. These schools were part of an international system composed of 4,256 elementary schools, 844 secondary schools, and 82 colleges and universities with a total student population of 642,310. These facts indicate a deep commitment to Christian education by a church counting only 609,788 members in the United States and 3,897,814 members in the entire world. This essay traces the development of that commitment with an emphasis on the origin and growth of elementary and secondary education among Adventists in the United States.

Adventists have not always been supporters of formal education. Education, in fact, was the last major institutional development within the denomination—it was preceded by the establishment of a strong publishing work that focused on developing and disseminating gospel literature (1849), a centralized ecclesiastical organization (1863), and a vigorous health-care program (1866).

The author is indebted to Andrews University for providing research funds for the collection of information concerning the history of Adventist education, and to Gilbert Valentine for gathering some of the information used in this chapter. Statistical data, unless otherwise noted, has been provided by the Department of Education and the Department of Statistics and Archives of the General Conference of Seventh-day Adventists, Washington, D.C.

85

Seventh-day Adventism grew out of the widespread interchurch interest in the second coming of Christ in the 1830s and early 1840s that centered around the work of William Miller, a Baptist preacher. The imminence of the return of Christ was the keynote of the Adventist message. By 1845 the group that later became known as Seventh-day Adventists was becoming a visible, although minute, entity.[1]

Religious groups focusing on the nearness of the end of the world have generally not felt much need for educating their children beyond the essential truths of their religious persuasion and the skills needed to earn a living. This was true of the early Christian church, and it was true of early Seventh-day Adventists. Why send children to school, so the logic runs, if the world is soon to end and they will never grow up to use their hard-earned learning? This attitude was widespread among many Adventists. As late as 1862 a church member wrote James White, leader of the incipient denomination and editor of its leading periodical, asking if it was "right and consistent for us who believe with all our hearts in the immediate coming of the Lord, to seek to give our children an education? If so, should we send them to a district or town school, where they learn twice as much evil as good?" White replied that "the fact that Christ is very soon coming is no reason why the mind should not be improved. *A well-disciplined and informed mind can best receive and cherish the sublime truths of the Second Advent.*"[2] His reply is of interest because it indicates a part of the rationale that would later become the foundation for developing an Adventist system of schools.

This query to White is also informative since it shows an early distrust of the public system of education. This distrust was based on a lack of discipline in many of the schools and, more importantly, on the fact that Adventists had a conception of truth and value that was contradicted at times by some of the teachings of the public schools.

ADVENTIST EDUCATIONAL ROOTS: 1853–1891

The problem of where to send their children to school had troubled some Adventist groups so much by the mid-1850s that they decided to try their hand at experimenting with independent Christian schools. The first such endeavor was at Buck's Bridge, New York, where members of the local congregation founded an elementary school in 1853. This one-room school lasted for three years and had a new teacher each year. A similar school was begun in Battle Creek, Michigan, in 1856. This school operated at the headquarters church of the young denomination as a private venture. Although it received semi-official support from the *Review and Herald*, the major Adventist periodical, it only lasted a few years.[3] By the autumn of 1861, however, James White would write that "we have had a thorough trial of a school at Battle Creek, under most favorable circumstances, and have given up, as it failed to meet the expectation of those interested."[4]

These feeble attempts died out in part because of a lack of interest among parents who did not see much need for Adventist schools. Interest in developing Christian elementary schools would, for the most part, lie dormant until the latter years of the 1890s. Meanwhile, the church sought to provide for the religious education of its young people through the pages of *The Youth's Instructor*, a journal founded in 1852. The developing Sabbath School with its weekly lessons also supplemented the family's work in religious instruction.

By 1867 the Adventists in Battle Creek were ready for another attempt at establishing a school. Goodloe Harper Bell, an experienced public school teacher, was hired by the local congregation. This school existed sporadically until 1870 or 1871.[5]

In 1872 the denomination began to more seriously consider the need for a quality school, not so much for elementary children as for older students who needed to be educated to spread the gospel message. It was decided to establish a school at Battle Creek that would be supported formally by the General Conference of Seventh-day Adventists. This school was to be for the children of those at Battle Creek and those "abroad." Its function would be to "thoroughly" acquaint its students, both young and old, "with the teaching of the Bible in reference to those great truths which pertain to this time," and to provide that general knowledge which would enable them to spread the biblical message to the world.[6]

The Battle Creek school opened on 12 June 1872 with twelve students and Bell as their teacher. It was the first "official" Adventist school. By 1873 it had added Sidney Brownsberger as principal, and by the end of 1874 the Battle Creek school had been transformed into Battle Creek College.

Battle Creek College is an important institution in Adventist educational history not only because of its "firstness," but because it received a great deal of attention in terms of policy formation and goal statements.[7] It was for this school that Ellen White, the reforming thought leader among Adventists, penned her first major statement on education, "Proper Education."[8] This document, which was to provide the philosophic undergirding of the proposed school, set forth an educational philosophy that was not congruent with the educational practices of the day, even though it was in tune with the ideas of contemporary reformers. It set forth an educational program emphasizing balance between the mental, physical, and spiritual aspects of man. The exposition included discussion of the differences between the training of animals and the education of human beings, discipline as self-control, the need for a thorough understanding of health, the need for the study of the Bible and the "common branches," and a strong mandate to develop manual training in connection with academic work so that both body and mind could be exercised and young people would be prepared for the practical world. "Proper Education" played down the impractical bookish education of the times which fitted young people to be "educated dunces." On the other hand, it proclaimed:

> Ignorance will not increase the humility or spirituality of any professed follower of Christ. The truths of the divine word can be best appreciated by an intellectual Christian. Christ can be best glorified by those who serve Him intelligently. The great object of education is to enable us to use the powers which God has given us in such a manner as will best represent the religion of the Bible and promote the glory of God.[9]

In essence, "Proper Education" has proven to be a cornerstone in Adventist educational philosophy.

George I. Butler, the president of the church's General Conference, also set forth the purpose of the new school before the entire denomination. "We have," wrote Butler:

> no great respect for that kind of education which is provided in many theological schools. We would not spend years in pouring over heathen mythology and the opinions of the fathers and the commentators, but would rather come directly to the source of true knowledge, God's holy word. It is not so much what men say about it, as what God Himself says that we want to understand. But we want hundreds of our people to take three, six, twelve, eighteen, twenty-four months' schooling, as soon as they can consistently do so.[10]

The founders of Battle Creek College were explicit as to their goals. They wanted to develop a reform institution that would uplift the Bible and manual labor, prepare Christian workers in a short time, and be practical in educating young people for the everyday duties of life rather than schooling them in the esoteric knowledge of the ancient past.

Battle Creek College, in historical perspective, turned out to be a test case for the implementation of these principles. (It should be noted that, even though it bore the name of "college," most of its work in the nineteenth century—like many other American colleges—was on the secondary level.) An evaluation of the institution in terms of its reform goals can be summed up in one word—*failure*. Emmett K. Vande Vere has written that the curriculum of Battle Creek College during the 1870s was a "philosophical betrayal."[11] The school rapidly developed into a liberal arts prep school and college—an institution that built its curriculum around the classical languages and literature, while it almost totally neglected the reform ideals that centered on the curricular primacy of religion and Scripture and the introduction of manual labor as a counterbalance to academic work.[12]

Throughout the 1870s Battle Creek College managed to frustrate the hopes of its founders. By the end of 1881, under a newly appointed president who was not even in verbal agreement with the Adventist philosophy of education, it was headed for disaster. At a meeting in December 1881 the college board and faculty listened to a paper entitled "Our College" which faced the problem head-on. In this paper Ellen White stated in no uncertain terms that the school had failed in meeting its purpose. The study of the arts and sciences was necessary, but "the study of the Scripture should have the first place in our system of education." She continued:

> If a worldly influence is to bear sway in our school, then sell it out to worldlings and let them take the entire control; and those who have invested their means in that institution will establish another school, to be conducted, not upon the plan of popular schools, nor according to the desires of principal and teachers, but upon the plan which God has specified.[13]

During early 1882 the situation steadily deteriorated, and in the summer it was decided to close the school indefinitely.[14] Thus, the first official attempt at formal education by the Adventist denomination collapsed. The school reopened in the autumn of 1883 under more dedicated leadership, but it never managed to displace the centrality of the classics or to fully implement the reform curriculum during the 1880s.

The hard lessons learned at Battle Creek, however, were not lost on the denomination's budding educational mentality. The spring of

1882 saw the opening of two more church-sponsored secondary schools—Healdsburg Academy (later known as Healdsburg College and eventually Pacific Union College) in California,[15] and South Lancaster Academy (later to become Atlantic Union College) in Massachusetts.[16] Even though these schools were founded, respectively, by Brownsberger and Bell, the leading men in the establishment of Battle Creek College in the early 1870s, they made large strides toward implementing the reform curriculum through giving the Bible a larger role, and by making manual labor a vital part of the school program. In some matters, however, they followed the "bad example" of the Battle Creek school.

The 1880s saw a few schools sporadically spring up, and often die, in local churches and conferences. There was, however, no organized coordination of this handful of schools. In 1887 the denomination established an educational department at church headquarters with W. W. Prescott as its first secretary.[17] It was also recommended by church leaders, in 1887 that local church (elementary) schools should be established wherever possible.[18]

In 1888 Prescott called the first Seventh-day Adventist teachers' convention. Thirty teachers from at least five schools attended the meeting. Discussion centered around strategic questions such as how to implement the reform ideas and the need to establish a system of local elementary schools, rather than tactical matters such as teaching methodology. There appears to have been a desire to begin a widespread elementary work, but there was also a cautionary response. The report of the convention noted:

> Concerning church schools, it was the unanimous opinion that great care should be exercised in starting out. A poor Seventh-day Adventist school would be about the poorest thing in the world; and schools should not be established until teachers are well prepared to take charge of them, and the people are ready to support them, both with their sympathies and with their means.[19]

The church was not ready yet for an elementary school movement. Neither had it achieved its educational reform goals by the end of the 1880s. Both of these causes would come onto center stage in the dynamic development of Adventist education in the 1890s and in the early years of the twentieth century.

REFORM: 1891–1903

A major turning point in Adventist educational development was the educational convention held at Harbor Springs, Michigan, in July and August 1891. This six-week convention was attended by over one hundred of the denomination's foremost educators, church administrators, and thought leaders.[20]

At the Harbor Springs convention Prescott, Ellen White, and others called for a revival in Adventist education that would place the denomination's schools on a correct set of Christian principles. The church's basic educational goals were restudied in the light of past failures. In particular, Harbor Springs marked the beginning of the denomination's major assault on the "heathen" classics—an assault that absorbed much reforming energy both inside and outside Adventist education during the nineties. This issue was seen as crucial by Adventist reformers since they were apparently beginning to realize that a curriculum cannot have two focal points. By 1891 it was sensed by the reform leaders that the biblical perspective would never find its proper place in Adventist education as long as the classics and their worldview were central. The recommendations made at Harbor Springs were, in effect, a declaration of all-out war on the traditional secondary and collegiate curriculum.

In addition, at Harbor Springs educational reform was directly linked to the renewed emphasis on the centrality of faith in Christ's righteousness which had been revitalizing the church since the 1888 meetings of its General Conference. As a result, the central place of the Bible and the role of history as seen from the biblical perspective were recommended as the foremost studies in Adventist education.

Prescott and Percy Magan, both reform leaders, would look back on the Harbor Springs convention as the pivotal point in the course of Adventist educational development. From his vantage point in 1893, Prescott wrote:

> The convention ushered in a remarkable change in the history of our educational work. . . . While the general purpose up to that time has been to have a religious element in our schools, yet since that institute, as never before, our work has been *practically* [rather than theoretically] upon that basis, showing itself in courses of study and plans of work as it had not previously.[21]

Prescott's remarks were overly optimistic since the reforms were being fought out at that very time. But the important point is that a reorientation was underway. As such, Harbor Springs should be seen as the first step in the "adventizing" of Seventh-day Adventist education.

The next step in this process began when Ellen White and her son,

W. C. White, sailed for Australia in November 1891. They would remain in Australia until 1900. While there they would have opportunity to work with some of the most responsive of the reform leaders in the Adventist church. One of the most important endeavors of the Adventists in Australia in the 1890s was the founding of the Avondale School for Christian Workers (today known as Avondale College). Australia had the advantage of being beyond the reach of the conservative Adventist leadership in the United States. In addition, it was a new mission field for Seventh-day Adventists. Thus there were no established traditions with which to contend. As a result, several innovations were piloted in Australia during the nineties that would have been much more difficult to experiment with in the United States.[22]

A new type of Adventist school was forged at Avondale. By the end of the century it was being suggested that this school was to be a pattern for Adventist education around the world, since it embodied the major reform elements that were seen as the ideal norm for Adventist education.[23] Because the educational program and ideals of Avondale were to have a continuing impact on Adventist education at all levels in the United States, it is important to briefly look at the experimental paradigm developed there.

Milton Hook, the historian of Avondale's early years, concluded that there were two main goals underlying the Avondale School. The first goal was the conversion and character development of its students. "Higher education" was that which prepared individuals for eternal life. The second goal was the training of denominational workers for Christian service both in the local community and in worldwide mission outreach. These two goals reflect a distinct move away from the academic orientation of Battle Creek College and the schools that came under its influence.

Certain strategies, noted Hook, were developed at Avondale to facilitate the achievement of these goals. Of foremost importance were the following. First, the selection of a rural location for the school. This was done to provide sufficient land for agricultural pursuits, keep young people away from the false excitement of the artificial amusements found in cities, and place young people in contact with the beauties of nature where they could meditate upon the love of the God of nature. Second, the placing of the Bible at the focal point of the curriculum. This included a definite move to teach all subjects within the framework of the biblical worldview. A corollary to the uplifting of the Bible was the removal of the classics and the classical languages from the curriculum. Third, there was a definite initiative taken to weave missionary activities into the school program.

Through missionary activity it was hoped that young people would be imbued with both the concept of service for mankind and the desire to engage in service after graduation. Fourth, there was the development of a strong manual labor program in which every student would participate. Manual labor, it was suggested, would provide the necessary balance between the mental and physical aspects of human nature and thus act as a "recreational" and refreshing activity, provide money for students to attend school, and furnish opportunities for young people to develop practical skills that would help them get along in undeveloped mission fields. Fifth, and last, there was a definite downplaying of the role of games and artificial amusements. The aim of the school was to bring young people face to face with the reality and the needs of a world in turmoil, rather than to provide escapes from that reality. Recreation was to be found in useful employment and service to others rather than in meaningless activity.[24]

These goals, and the strategies developed to implement them, became the normative ideal of Adventist education at all levels. The Avondale experiment had almost immediate repercussions on Adventist education in America and around the world. In regard to Adventist educational development, Avondale, with its emphasis on reform, took the leadership role from Battle Creek College.

Reform was also at the base of the explosion in the number of Adventist schools in the 1890s. The church was in the midst of a major cycle of missionary expansion, and Adventist schools came to be more and more thought of as training institutions to provide workers for this extended work both at home and abroad.

The end of the century saw the curriculum of Adventist secondary and collegiate education undergoing reform as the Bible was increasingly placed at the center, while the classics were rooted out. In addition, new schools were being established on large tracts of land in rural locations. After the turn of the century this movement was extended to long-established schools. Even Battle Creek College sold its property in 1901 and moved near rural Berrien Springs in southwest Michigan where it became Emmanuel Missionary College (now Andrews University).

The experiences of the 1890s had transformed Adventist education at the secondary and collegiate levels. Not only were existing schools and colleges changed, but the decade saw the establishment of many new secondary schools and colleges with substantial preparatory departments.

One of the most exciting developments in Adventist education in the 1890s, however, was the elementary school movement. Up through the middle nineties Adventists had largely neglected elementary education except at locations where they had a college or secondary school. This neglect was reversed by the end of the decade, and Adventists have ever since supported a strong system of local church (elementary) schools.

We earlier noted that there had been a call in 1887 and 1888 to start a system of elementary schools. Nothing much came of these resolutions. In 1897, however, Ellen White challenged the church with a renewed demand for elementary education. She asserted:

> In some countries parents are compelled by law to send their children to school. In these countries, in localities where there is a church, *schools should be established if there are no more than six children to attend.* Work as if you were working for your life to save the children from being drowned in the polluting, corrupting influences of the world.
>
> We are far behind our duty in this important matter. In many places schools should have been in operation years ago.[25]

She also wrote:

> Wherever there are a few Sabbathkeepers, the parents should unite in providing a place for a day school where their children and youth can be instructed. They should employ a Christian teacher who, as a consecrated missionary, shall educate the children in such a way as to lead them to become missionaries. Let teachers be employed who will give a thorough education in the common branches, the Bible being made the foundation and the life of all study.[26]

This counsel was taken to heart by such men as Edward Alexander Sutherland and Percy T. Magan, the reform leaders who would move Battle Creek College into the country in 1901. They developed a normal program for training teachers and did much to stimulate both local congregations and promising young people to get involved in elementary education.[27] The phenomenal growth of Adventist elementary education is reflected in Table 1.

By 1900 the place of the local elementary school was firmly established in Adventist congregations. Table 1 indicates that most of these schools were one-teacher schools. Adventists were taking seriously the counsel that they should establish a school if there were only six students. It should also be realized that the total number of Adventists in the United States was 63,335 in 1900 and 66,294 in 1910. With

TABLE 1

THE GROWTH OF SEVENTH-DAY ADVENTIST ELEMENTARY SCHOOLS
FROM 1880 TO 1910

Year	Number of Schools	Number of Teachers	Enrollment
1880	1	1	15
1885	3	5	125
1890	9	15	350
1895	18	35	895
1900	220	250	5,000
1905	417	466	7,345
1910	594	758	13,357

SOURCE: *Christian Education* 3 (September-October, 1911):14.
NOTE: Table 1 includes some schools outside of the United States.

these numbers in mind one can see that this was a movement that touched a large proportion of Adventist congregations.

The reform in Adventist education and the rapid expansion of Adventist world missions in the 1890s stimulated several other educational developments. One was the internationalization of Adventist education. Schools were started in various parts of Europe, Africa, South America, Asia, Australia, and the Pacific Islands.

A second development was an educational thrust among American blacks in the South. This work was spearheaded by Edson White who built a missionary boat, the *Morning Star,* to work the area around Vicksburg, Mississippi. White's work eventually led to the establishment of the Southern Missionary Society which founded and ran many schools for black children throughout the South. By 1896 the denomination had also opened Oakwood Industrial School (now Oakwood College) near Huntsville, Alabama. This school was similar in many ways to Booker T. Washington's Tuskegee Institute.[28] Emphasis on work and practical skills in education, however, was not restricted to blacks among Adventists. In Adventist education the ideal was work combined with study for students of all races—even for students preparing for professional roles. The education was to be practical as well as intellectual.

A third development was the establishment of a self-supporting branch of Adventist education by Sutherland and Magan. In 1904 they bought a farm near Nashville, Tennessee, and established the Nashville Agricultural and Normal Institute (later to become Madison

College). This was a school that was not supported directly by money from denominational sources. The idea was that in the South, where money was still in short supply, schools could be established where both students and teachers could work at school industries and farming. The income would cover the bulk of their expenses, while allowing the school to operate. A school could be established, therefore, with a minimum of capital in impoverished areas. The school at Madison was connected with a sanitarium. This had become a pattern among Adventists by the turn of the century. Thus Adventist education and mission work early came to have a heavy emphasis on medical service. This, they believed, was modeled on the life of Christ who came healing and teaching as well as preaching. The school at Madison became the mother of a large number of self-supporting elementary and secondary schools throughout the South. Many of these later became official conference institutions or church schools under the control of the denomination. Others still operate today as self-supporting institutions.[29]

The reform movement that began in the 1890s permanently changed the face of Adventist education. Its overall impact was quite healthy. Unfortunately, however, like most reforms it tended to go to extremes. For example, some of the reformers made so much of manual labor that they neglected the intellectual and academic aspects of education. Some Adventist educational institutions during the early years of the twentieth century had more of the quality of labor camps than of schools. Again, some reformers, in their zeal to put the Bible at the center of education, claimed that the Bible should be the only textbook. This issue was so agitated that it found expression as one of the major discussions on the floor of the 1899 General Conference during its worldwide session.[30]

The first decade of the new century would find a gradual withdrawal from the extreme positions taken in the heat of battle and the excitement of change. The period of Adventist educational development from 1903 to 1940 can be characterized as a time of growth and development. It was a period in which the church sought to harmonize the best of the reforms with the best of the old system—it was a time of seeking the mean between two extremes.

GROWTH AND ORGANIZATIONAL DEVELOPMENT: 1903–1940

One of the central features of Adventist education in the first decades of the twentieth century was its rapid and continuous growth. In

1916 the denomination's educational leader, Frederick Griggs, remarked that since 1908 the system had grown at an average of nearly
one thousand additional students each year.[31] This figure takes on
significance when it is realized that church membership itself in the
United States increased by not much more than one thousand per
year during this same period. This educational expansion would continue with rapidity up through the early 1920s when the growth curve
would flatten until the late 1930s.

A second major characteristic of Adventist education in the early
decades of the twentieth century was its retreat from the extremism
that had characterized its development in the late nineties and the
first few years of the new century. By 1904 educational leadership on
the national level had slipped from the hands of the radical reformers, Sutherland and Magan. In their place, Griggs and C. C. Lewis set
forth the more moderate position that was to have a lasting effect on
the church's educational outlook. At the church's 1906 national educational convention, Lewis stated:

> I do not believe that we have passed the [educational] reformation
> itself, and that "so-called reform," as it has been spoken of, is to be
> left behind and dropped out of sight. I believe that a genuine
> reform was begun; and, although mistakes have been made, we are
> profiting by those mistakes and we shall continue to profit by
> them. . . . So instead of dropping the reforms that were started a
> few years ago, I think we should rather be in a position where,
> profiting by the mistakes that have been made, we shall now go
> forward carrying out the true, genuine principles of reform; and
> we shall yet see a system of education built upon these principles
> that will be an honor to God and to the work of this
> denomination.[32]

A third point to note in connection with the educational "excitement" and growth among Adventists in the early years of the new
century was a spate of educational writings which sought to give direction to the rapidly developing system of Adventist education. The
foremost books among these writings were the sixth volume of *Testimonies for the Church* (1900) and *Education* (1903) by Ellen White, *Living Fountains or Broken Cisterns* (1900) by Sutherland, and *The Place of
the Bible in Education* (1903) by A. T. Jones. The periodical literature
in the denomination was enriched by *The Christian Educator* (1897),
The Training School Advocate (1901), *The Educational Messenger* (1905),
and *Christian Education* (1909). This last journal became the official
organ of the General Conference Department of Education. In addi-

tion to these books and periodicals, the educational thrust of the new
century saw the appearance of a number of textbooks for Christian
schools, detailed curriculum guides, and what at times appear to be
verbatim reports of national educational conventions.

A fourth characteristic of Adventist education during the first decades of the twentieth century was a series of highly influential national conventions that helped shape the direction of the development of Adventist education. Full reports of these conventions were
published, and this undoubtedly spread their effectiveness throughout the educational ranks of the denomination.

The changing thrust of these conventions reflects the development
of Adventist education throughout its adolescent stage. The convention reports not only provide insight into the issues discussed, but
they also highlight the personalities of the various participants, since
in many cases they record the formal presentations and the floor
discussions that followed.

The 1900 Conference of Missionary Teachers might best be described as an evangelistic meeting to inspire its participants to create a
church school in every Adventist congregation. Prominently featured
among the discussions were the necessary steps for establishing a
school. The convention also included presentations on, and discussions of, the reforms then being espoused.

By 1903 the emphasis was being placed on administrative organization as the church sought to give some official structure and guidance
to its burgeoning system of schools. One important outgrowth of the
1903 meetings was a series of teachers' manuals that set forth the
curriculum in the light of the denomination's educational philosophy,
gave practical suggestions on how to implement the recommended
curriculum, and standardized the curriculum by grade level up
through grade ten.[33] The 1906 convention focused on refining the
administrative organization, retreating from educational extremes,
firming up the boundaries between the various levels of the educational system, and developing a renewed missionary emphasis.

By the time of the 1910 convention the denomination was ready to
again concentrate on the needs of higher education. The first decade
of the century had been spent in establishing and organizing elementary, intermediate, and secondary schools. In 1910 the convention's
major thrust was aimed at making its training schools of greater service to the denomination as viewed in the context of its worldwide
evangelistic thrust.

The issue of rising educational standards was becoming a major
concern by the time of the 1915 convention. The accreditation of

schools and the certification of teachers were problems that would be at the forefront of denominational controversy and educational endeavors up through the middle 1930s. Pressures concerning these topics came from developments in the public sector of education, but Adventism had early felt the urgency of the problem in connection with its medical school, The College of Medical Evangelists (now Loma Linda University), which had been founded in 1909 and almost immediately had had to weather the storm produced by the Flexner Report.[34] Accreditation and certification were particularly threatening to the conservatives among the Adventist leadership, since these issues meant graduate education for Adventist teachers in "outside" universities. This was feared due to the possibility of the "contamination" of these Adventist teachers who would have a tendency to bring false ideas into the Adventist educational system. The church would seek to solve the problem in part through the establishment of an Adventist graduate school, The Advanced Bible School, at Pacific Union College in California in 1934. The Advanced Bible School operated in California until 1937 when it was moved to the General Conference headquarters at Washington, D.C. where it became the Seventh-day Adventist Theological Seminary. In 1957 the seminary was joined by a newly created graduate school to form Potomac University. In 1960 both the seminary and the graduate school were moved to Berrien Springs, Michigan, where they joined the undergraduate school of Emmanuel Missionary College to form Andrews University.[35] Another attempt to circumnavigate the problems associated with accreditation by state and regional bodies was the establishment of the denomination's own Board of Regents. This was done in 1928 with the hope of being able to avoid accreditation by outside organizations. All this effort was to no avail. Adventists had been caught in a wave of rising standards. Their attempts at internal graduate education were too little and too late, and their move toward internal accreditation did not meet the demands of the professional world. By the early 1930s it was evident to nearly all Adventist leaders that regional accreditation and state certification were necessities if the church was to stay in the business of training its young people for professional roles. By the end of the thirties the accreditation of the denomination's secondary schools and colleges was well under way.[36] This struggle, which had begun by the time of the 1915 convention, had taken two decades to resolve.

The 1923 educational convention would speak to the continuing problem of supplying quality teachers for the denomination's schools. At this convention it was pointed out that three-fourths of the church's elementary teachers had little or no professional training other than what could be gained in short summer courses. In addition, there were not enough teachers. One-third of the teacher force was changing each year. Two hundred and fifty teachers, therefore, were needed annually just to maintain the current number of schools. In addition, two hundred churches had been denied schools due to teacher shortages. Up to 450 teachers were needed each year to meet the demand, but only forty-nine normal graduates had been produced from all church sources in 1922.[37] This was viewed as a crisis. One recommendation growing out of this situation was that more of the denominational academies should offer the first year of normal training. Some academies were already doing this, but 1923 saw a strong push to get more of them involved in teacher training for the elementary schools. The teacher shortage among Adventists, as in other sectors of American education, would remain a problem up through the end of the 1960s. Another concern at the 1923 convention was a renewed emphasis against "the world" and its system of education. Denominational education during the 1920s, under the leadership of W. E. Howell, underwent a conservative cycle. This was probably, in part, a reaction to the perceived threat of accreditation and the fear of curriculum interference and control by a non-Adventist educational power structure. A third emphasis in 1923 was the need for a more practical education to fit the young for missionary service. The church had not lost sight of its mission in the world or the reason for the existence of its schools.

By the time of the 1937 educational convention the Adventist educational system had become well regulated. Its organizational structure had been developed, its curricular stance had solidified, and the denomination was in the process of upgrading its schools at all levels. The machinery was all in place even though it would still take some years to bring about the complete implementation of the upgrading process.[38]

MATURITY AND A PROFILE: 1940–1982

The 1940s found the Adventist church with a major commitment to all levels of Christian education. Like the denomination itself, the Adventist educational endeavor was a unified system with its headquarters in Washington, D.C. At the top of the denomination's educational pyramid was the Department of Education of the General Conference of Seventh-day Adventists. This department provided guidance, counsel, and direction to Adventist schools around the world. Most of the world divisions of the church (e.g., South American Division and Trans Africa Division) also had educational leadership at what might loosely be referred to as the continental level. In North America, however, divisional leadership was handled by the General Conference Department of Education until 1975 when Charles B. Hirsch became director for elementary and secondary education for North America within the General Conference Department of Education.[39] By 1940 the United States was divided into nine (in 1980 this was changed to eight) union conferences, each with its own educational director. It has been at the union conference level that much of the policy-making has taken place for both elementary and secondary schools. At this level the general directives of the General Conference have found a more concrete expression in such forms as curriculum guides and textbook lists. The union director has also become the officer for denominational certification for the teachers within his jurisdiction. Below the union conference director stands the conference (roughly equivalent to state) educational superintendent. He has immediate supervision over all elementary and secondary schools within his territory, and performs many of the same functions as a local superintendent of education in the public schools.

There are many parallels between the organizational structure of the Adventist school system and the structure of traditional public education. At the base stands the eight grade elementary school. Adventists have not developed junior high schools, since the small number of students in each school does not warrant such a division. The denomination, however, has created what they call junior academies. A junior academy is the combination of an eight-grade elementary school with the first two years of high school. These ten-grade schools are a common feature of Adventist education. On the other hand, recent years have seen nine-grade junior academies become more numerous than formerly. The Adventist high school in the United States is still referred to as an academy. All Adventist secondary schools are coeducational, and most of them have state and regional accreditation. Many of these academies are boarding schools. This is a necessity since the denomination's population is sparse in most areas of the country. Where there are sufficient numbers of Adventists, however, they have developed "day" academies. Beyond the high-school level, the Seventh-day Adventist Church in the United States operates nine senior colleges and two universities—Loma Linda University in California which specializes in the medical sciences, and Andrews University in Michigan whose major emphases are theological and educational studies. Both universities are fully accredited as doctoral degree granting institutions.

The growth of elementary and secondary schools among Adventists in the United States has been generally in an upward direction since 1915. Comparative enrollments can be seen in Figure 1. It will be noted from this figure that there have been times of rapid increases as well as periods of enrollment drop-off. The elementary drop-off of the thirties can be attributed in part to the Great Depres-

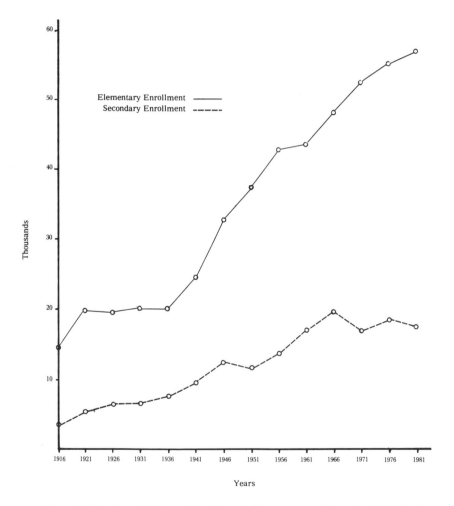

Figure 1. Enrollment in Seventh-day Adventist Elementary and Secondary School in the United States 1916-1981.

sion, while the secondary drop-offs of the sixties and seventies undoubtedly reflect demographic trends.

Even though there has generally been growth in the absolute number of students in Adventist schools, there are some indications that
there may be a decreasing proportion of young people from Adventist homes attending Adventist schools. This is reflected in Figure 2,
which, it should be realized, is only a rough indicator of a problem
since it gives the ratio of students to the entire church membership
rather than the ratio of students to the population of school-age
young people in the church. As a result, it reflects a trend toward
smaller families and may indicate a church with an older constituency.
On the other hand, there are some indications that families are having an increasingly difficult time meeting the ever growing cost of
tuition, and are therefore sending more of their children to public
schools. At any rate, figures of this type are of grave concern to a
church which believes that all of its young people should be in its own
Christian schools.

There are several features of Adventist schools in the United States
that should be noted. First, they have opted, on the basis of their
beliefs, to avoid highly competitive activities. Cooperation rather than
competition, they hold, is more in line with the teachings of Jesus. As
a result, they have avoided interschool athletic competition.

Second, their schools, by and large, are integrated racially. They
have, though, not moved any faster than the public schools on this
matter. Integration in Adventist education has come in the form of
evolution rather than revolution, but it has come. It should be noted,
however, that racial and ethnic groups at times have elected to maintain separate conferences, churches, and schools.[40] This separation
by choice has created racially segregated schools in many areas that
also have integrated schools.

Third, Adventism has developed a curricular stance that is un-
ashamedly based on biblical revelation and looks at science from the
standpoint of creationism. Adventists hold that all truth is essentially
religious, and some contemporary educators such as George Akers
have given great impetus and publicity to the techniques of integrating all subject matter within the context of the worldview of the Bible.
The General Conference Department of Education has been active in
developing textbooks in such areas as science, reading, social studies,
and religion in an attempt to better present the Christian perspective
in every classroom subject. In addition, the North American Division
Curriculum Committee has developed "frameworks" for each subject
discipline taught in the denomination's elementary and secondary

Percentage of Church Membership Enrolled in Adventist Schools

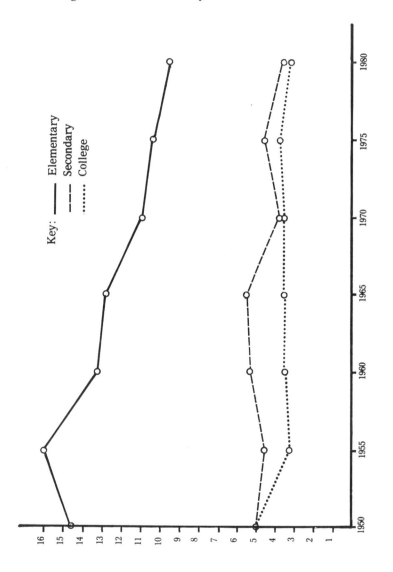

Figure 2. Ratio of Adventist School Population to Church Membership in the United States. (North American Division Summary of Progress, Fourth Quarter, 1980, p. 7.)

schools. The purpose of each framework is to identify the major concepts that need to be taught in each discipline, and to incorporate Seventh-day Adventist principles into each subject area.[41] Thus, when courses are developed on the basis of these frameworks, they can be taught within a Christian frame of reference. The use of these frameworks is therefore a structured way of integrating faith and learning.

Fourth, Adventist schools are small. At the elementary level in 1978–79, for example, 37.6 percent of their schools had one teacher, while 26.1 percent had two teachers, 11.1 percent had three teachers, and only 25.2 percent had four or more teachers.[42] The average enrollment at their senior academies was 248 in 1979. This can be compared to 165 in 1959 and 89 in 1939.[43] The smallness of Adventist schools is due to the fact that the Adventist population is both small and scattered. Teacher-training programs in Adventist colleges are geared to prepare teachers to meet the challenge and opportunities inherent in small schools. Smallness, however, has not had an adverse affect on academic achievement.[44] This, in part, may be explained by the fact that the Adventist student comes from a home where his parents care enough about their children to pay the high cost of tuition, and by the fact that Adventist teachers in small schools generally deal with fewer students than their counterparts in the public sector. For example, the number of students per teacher in Adventist elementary education in 1979 was 14.9. This ratio has some obvious advantages when it comes to individualizing instruction.

A final aspect of Adventist schools that should be noted is their financial support. Adventists have traditionally opposed state aid to religion. As a result, their schools have been largely supported by tuition and church offerings. At the secondary and collegiate levels, students are able to earn a significant portion of their tuition, room, and board by working at school-operated industries. Thus, the Adventist concept of educating the hands as well as the head and heart has had some very pragmatic results.

CONCLUDING REMARKS

Like Roman Catholics in the late nineteenth century and many evangelicals in the 1970s, Adventists early in their history believed that their distinctive needs were not being met by the public schools. As a result, they established an alternative system that would uplift what they considered to be "true education" as viewed from the biblical perspective. The keynote of Adventist education is found in the following quotation:

> Our ideas of education take too narrow and too low a range. There is need of a broader scope, a higher aim. True education means more than the pursual of a certain course of study. It means more than a preparation for the life that now is. It has to do with the whole being, and with the whole period of existence possible to man. It is the harmonious development of the physical, the mental, and the spiritual powers. It prepares the student for the joy of service in this world and for the higher joy of wider service in the world to come.[45]

Adventists have taken the fall of man seriously. As a result, they have uplifted the needs and potential of the student as the center of all education. Ellen White gave direction to Adventist education when she wrote:

> Through sin the divine likeness was marred, and well-nigh obliterated. Man's physical powers were weakened, his mental capacity was lessened, his spiritual vision dimmed. He had become subject to death. Yet the race was not left without hope. By infinite love and mercy the plan of salvation had been devised, and a life of probation was granted. To restore in man the image of his Maker, to bring him back to the perfection in which he was created, to promote the development of body, mind, and soul, that the divine purpose in his creation might be realized—this was to be the work of redemption. This is the object of education, the great object of life.[46]

The realization of the redemptive potential of education has served as a stimulus for the establishment and maintenance of Adventist schools. To Adventists, biblical education is a Christian imperative. It is this vision that underlies their commitment to Christian education.

NOTES

1. Historical accounts of the roots of the Seventh-day Adventist Church are found in P. Gerard Damsteegt, *Foundations of the Seventh-day Adventist Message and Mission* (Grand Rapids, Mich.: William B. Eerdmans, 1977); Francis D. Nichol, *The Midnight Cry* (Washington, D.C.: Review and Herald, 1944); Richard W. Schwarz, *Light Bearers to the Remnant* (Mountain View, Calif.: Pacific Press, 1979); and Arthur Whitefield Spalding, *Origin and History of Seventh-day Adventists*, 4 vols. (Washington, D.C.: *Review and Herald*, 1961–62).

2. "Questions and Answers," *Review and Herald*, 23 December 1862, p. 29.

3. For a discussion of these early educational ventures see E. M. Cadwallader, *A History of Seventh-day Adventist Education*, 4th ed. (Payson, Ariz.: Leaves-of-Autumn Books, 1975), pp. 5–9. It should be noted that, despite its title, Cadwallader's work is not so much a history of Adventist education as it is a series of papers on the history of individual institutions.

4. Editor, *Review and Herald*, 24 September 1861, p. 134.

5. For the most complete study of the life and work of Bell, see Allan Lindsay, "Goodloe Harper Bell: Pioneer Seventh-day Adventist Christian Educator" (Ed.D. dissertation, Andrews University, 1982).

6. School Committee, "The Proposed School," *Review and Herald*, 7 May 1872, p. 168.

7. The History of Battle Creek College is told in Emmett K. Vande Vere, *The Wisdom Seekers* (Nashville: Southern Publishing Assn., 1972).

8. Ellen G. White, *Fundamentals of Christian Education* (Nashville: Southern Publishing Assn., 1923), pp. 15–46.

9. Ibid., pp. 44–45.

10. George I. Butler, "What Use Shall We Make of Our School?" *Review and Herald*, 21 July 1874, p. 45. Cf. John N. Andrews, "Our Proposed School," *Review and Herald*, 1 April 1873, p. 124.

11. Vande Vere, *The Wisdom Seekers*, p. 23.

12. For a discussion of the curricular development of Battle Creek College see George R. Knight, "Battle Creek College: Academic Development and Curriculum Struggles, 1874–1901," Heritage Room, Andrews University, 1979.

13. Ellen G. White, *Testimonies for the Church*, 9 vols. (Mountain View, Calif.: Pacific Press, 1948), 5:25–26.

14. George I. Butler, "Unpleasant Themes: The Closing of Our College," *Review and Herald*, 12 September 1882, p. 586.

15. For the history of the Healdsburg school see Walter C. Utt, *A Mountain, A Pickax, A College* (Angwin, Calif.: The Alumni Assn. of Pacific Union College, 1969).

16. For the history of the South Lancaster school see Myron F. Wehtje, *And There Was Light* (South Lancaster, Mass.: The Atlantic Press, 1982).

17. For the most complete study of the life and work of Prescott, see Gilbert Valentine, "W. W. Prescott: Seventh-day Adventist Educator" (Ph.D. dissertation, Andrews University, 1982).

18. *General Conference Bulletin*, 21 November 1887, pp. 1–2; 25 November 1887, p. 2; and 28 November 1887, p. 4.

19. C. C. Lewis, "Report of Teachers' Institute," *Review and Herald*, 4 September 1888, p. 573.

20. For the most complete account of this convention see Craig S. Willis, "Harbor Springs Institute of 1891: A Turning Point in our Educational Conceptions," Ellen G. White Research Center, Andrews University, 1979.

21. W. W. Prescott, "Report of the Educational Secretary," *General Conference Bulletin*, 23 February 1893, p. 350. See also Percy T. Magan, "The Educational Conference and the Education Reform," *Review and Herald*, 6 August 1901, p. 508.

22. For the most complete account of the Adventist educational experience in Australia and the impact of this experience on Adventist education in

the United States see Milton R. Hook, "The Avondale School and Adventist Educational Goals, 1894–1900" (Ed.D. dissertation, Andrews University, 1978); and Allan G. Lindsay, "The Influence of Ellen White upon the Development of the Seventh-day Adventist School System in Australia, 1891–1900" (M.Ed. thesis, University of Newcastle, 1978).

23. Ellen G. White, *Counsels to Parents, Teachers, and Students Regarding Christian Education* (Mountain View, Calif.: Pacific Press, 1913), pp. 349, 533.

24. Hook, "The Avondale School and Adventist Educational Goals, 1894–1900," pp. 255–94.

25. E. G. White, *Testimonies For the Church*, 6:199 (emphasis supplied). Cf. Letter from Ellen G. White to W. C. White, 5 May 1897.

26. E. G. White, *Testimonies For the Church*, 6:198.

27. The elementary movement among Seventh-day Adventists is discussed in Cadwallader, *A History of Seventh-day Adventist Education*, pp. 285–314; Spalding, *Origin and History of Seventh-day Adventists*, 2:353–71; Lindsay, "The Influence of Ellen White Upon the Development of the Seventh-day Adventist School System in Australia, 1891–1900," pp. 114–29; and Mary Kelly-Little, "Development of the Elementary Schools of Seventh-day Adventists in the United States" (M.A. thesis, University of Washington, 1932).

28. For the origin of Adventist educational work among American blacks in the South see Ronald D. Graybill, *Mission to Black America* (Mountain View, Calif.: Pacific Press, 1971); and Arthur W. Spalding, "Lights and Shades in the Black Belt," Heritage Room, Andrews University, n.d. (mimeographed).

29. For accounts of the self-supporting work among Adventists see Ira Gish and Harry Christman, *Madison: God's Beautiful Farm* (Mountain View, Calif.: Pacific Press, 1979); and William Cruzan Sandborn, "The History of Madison College" (Ed.D. dissertation, George Peabody College for Teachers, 1953).

30. *General Conference Daily Bulletin*, 19 February 1899, pp. 34–36.

31. Frederick Griggs, "Education Problems and Policies," in *Council Proceedings of the Joint Council of the Educational and Missionary Volunteer Departments of the North American Division Conference of Seventh-day Adventists* (Washington, D.C.: Review and Herald, 1915), p. 10.

32. "Story of the Convention," *Central Union Conference Bulletin* II:3 (October 1906): 74–75.

33. E.g., *Teachers' Manual for the Home and School* (Mountain View, Calif.: Pacific Press, [1904]).

34. The accreditation struggle of the College of Medical Evangelists has been told in Merlin L. Neff, *For God and C.M.E.: A Biography of Percy Tilson Magan* (Mountain View, Calif.: Pacific Press, 1964). For the early history of the College of Medical Evangelists see Dores Eugene Robinson, *The Story of Our Health Message* (Nashville: Southern Publishing Association, 1955), pp. 335ff.

35. *Seventh-day Adventist Encyclopedia*, rev. ed., s.v. "Andrews University."

36. For brief accounts on the struggle for accreditation among Adventists see William G. White, Jr., "Another Look at Those Pioneers of Adventist Accreditation," *Focus*, Winter 1978, pp. 10–12; and George R. Knight, "The Accreditation Myth," Heritage Room, Andrews Univesity, 1981.

37. Sarah E. Peck, "Things Most Needed to Make our Normal Work More Efficient and More Productive," in *Proceedings of the Educational and Missionary*

Volunteer Departments of the General Conference of Seventh-day Adventists in World Convention (Washington, D.C.: Review and Herald, 1923), p. 425.

38. Complete sets of the records of these conventions are housed in the Heritage Room at Andrews University and the archives of the General Conference of Seventh-day Adventists in Washington, D.C.

39. Walton J. Brown, comp. *Chronology of Seventh-day Adventist Edcuation*, 2nd ed. (Washington, D.C.: Department of Education, General Conference of Seventh-day Adventists, 1979), p. 209.

40. See Schwarz, *Light Bearers to the Remnant*, pp. 564–78.

41. North American Division Office of Education, *Educational Materials: The Implementation of Seventh-day Adventist Curriculum K–12* (Washington, D.C.: General Conference of Seventh-day Adventists, 1981), p. 4.

42. Minutes of the North American Division Curriculum Committee, 3–6 December 1978. (Mimeographed.)

43. *North American Division: Summary of Progress, Fourth Quarter, 1979* (Washington, D.C.: General Conference of Seventh-day Adventists, 1979), p. 7. "Opening Academy Enrollments: North American Division, 1915–1972," General Conference Department of Education. (Mimeographed.)

44. Jerome Thayer, "Will My Child Suffer Scholastically if He Attends Church School?," *Review and Herald*, 31 August 1978, pp. 11–13.

45. Ellen G. White, *Education* (Mountain View, Calif.: Pacific Press, 1903), p. 13.

46. Ibid., pp. 15–16.

Chapter 5

The Christian Day School

JAMES C. CARPER

For almost two decades American society has been in the throes of a fundamental, and often traumatic, reorientation of its system of belief and institutional structure. As historian William G. McLoughlin has recently suggested: "The ferment of the sixties has begun to produce a new shift in our belief-value system, a transformation of our world-view that may be the most drastic in our history as a nation."[1] Although it is too early to assess the total impact of these years of disenchantment and uncertainty, it appears that there has been a collapse of consensus concerning the basic nature and function of our institutions and the values and traditions undergirding them. Indeed this erosion of consensus may mark a "watershed" in American history. In the words of Henry Steele Commager: "Perhaps the sixties and the seventies are a great divide—the divide of disillusionment."[2]

This disillusionment has been clearly reflected in Americans' dissatisfaction with public education. While systematic schooling has been the object of considerable acrimonious discussion since its inception during the middle decades of the nineteenth century, never before has the criticism been so caustic and sustained. The lay public, commentators of all socio-political persuasions, and many professional educators have scrutinized the public schools and found them wanting by almost any conceivable measure. Evincing the fragmented state of the social order and bewilderment concerning the purposes and outcomes of schooling, charges leveled at the schools have been legion and often contradictory. Public education has been characterized since the 1960s as racist, authoritarian, trendy, academically and socially permissive, irreligious, an agency for social change, an instrument for perpetuating the status quo, and generally unresponsive to both individual and public needs.[3]

Solutions to the perceived school crisis have also been many and

110

varied. Some critics have proposed reforms of the curriculum, while others have advocated alterations of school governance patterns, teacher-education programs, and methods of school finance. Eschewing reform altogether, several scholars have argued that public schooling has outlived its usefulness and should be relegated to the dustbin of history.[4]

Of all the proposed "remedies," one of the most widely discussed has been the free school movement, which emanated originally from the socio-political left. Dedicated to a more "humane" and "liberating" education and opposed to standardization and authoritarian institutions, as many as five hundred of these schools were established independently of the public school system during the late 1960s and early 1970s. Variations of this movement were eventually incorporated within the public system in the form of alternative schools, open campuses, "relevant" curricula, and community control. While much has been written about the successes and failures of the free school movement and related alternative education schemes, one option, the Christian day school, has received scant attention outside the religious press.[5]

THE CHRISTIAN DAY SCHOOL: AN EMERGING ALTERNATIVE

Since the mid-1960s, evangelical Protestants and their churches, few of which are affiliated with mainline Protestant denominations, have been establishing Christian day schools at a phenomenal rate.[6] Several proponents of these institutions have claimed, perhaps with some exaggeration, that Christian schools are being established at the rate of nearly two per day. Not only do these schools currently constitute the most rapidly expanding segment of formal education in the United States, but they also represent the first *widespread* secession from the public school pattern since the establishment of Catholic schools in the nineteenth century.

Protestant-sponsored weekday education is not a contemporary phenomenon. Throughout the nineteenth century most denominations experimented with parochial schooling as an alternative to public education. With few exceptions, their success was limited. By the early twentieth century most mainline denominations had abandoned the religious day school concept.[7] Between 1920 and 1960, however, independent fundamentalist churches and conservative interchurch organizations founded a small number, perhaps 150, of Christian day schools.[8] Until recently, however, the vast majority of evangelical Protestants have shown little interest in such an educational arrangement. Only the Missouri Synod Lutherans, the Seventh-day Adventists, and Christian Reformed groups have maintained a significant number of weekday schools for an extended period of time.

Most evangelical Protestants have supported public schooling since its inception. They approved of early public education because it reflected the Protestant belief-value system of the society and was viewed as an integral part of the crusade to establish a Christian America. According to church historian Robert T. Handy, elementary schools did not need to be under the control of particular denominations because "their role was to prepare young Americans for participation in the broadly Christian civilization toward which all evangelicals were working."[9] While the public school, by means of Bible reading, prayers, teacher example, and the ubiquitous McGuffey readers, emphasized nondenominational evangelical Protestantism, which was tantamount to the American civic faith for the better part of the nineteenth century, the Sunday School stressed the particular tenets of the various denominations. This "parallel institutions" educational arrangement was generally satisfactory to most evangelicals. As William B. Kennedy, an authority on Protestant education, has maintained:

> By 1960 there had emerged a general consensus in American Protestantism that the combination of public and Sunday school teaching would largely take care of the needed religious teaching of the young. In that pattern the public school was primary; the Sunday school was adjunct to it, providing specific religious teaching it could not include.[10]

Much has changed in America since the establishment of this dualistic educational strategy. No longer does evangelical Protestantism influence the society and the public schools as it did in the nineteenth century. The early decades of the twentieth century witnessed its decline as the moving force behind cultural and behavioral patterns. And by the 1960s, the once dominant evangelical strain in American civil religion had been superseded by the more secularistic Enlightenment theme.[11]

Despite this radical alteration of the character of American culture, most Protestants have clung to the myth of the "parallel institutions" educational strategy. The rapid growth of the number of Christian day schools during the past fifteen to twenty years, however, suggests that an increasing number of evangelicals are not only grappling with the consequences of the erosion of Protestantism as a social foundation, but also questioning their historic commitment to public schooling and the dualistic pattern of education.

The term "Christian day school" has been used to describe weekday educational institutions founded since the mid-1960s by either individual evangelical churches or local Christian school societies. These schools are not tied to a denomination per se, as contrasted with Lutheran and Adventist. As is the case with other facets of the Christian school movement, information on sponsorship is difficult to locate. The only reliable source of data is the Association of Christian Schools International, the largest of the Christian school associations. About 70 percent of the approximately 1700 elementary and secondary schools listed in the *1982 Directory* indicated local church sponsorship. The remainder either did not report a sponsoring organization or listed a foundation or society as the governing agency. Schools which do not belong to ACSI, on the other hand, may not follow this pattern.[12]

Christian day schools are diverse in other ways as well. Facilities, for example, range from poorly equipped church basements to modern, multibuilding campuses. While a majority are elementary schools, an increasing number are offering secondary education as well. Though the average number of students per school is probably between 100 and 200, enrollments vary from 10 to over 2,000. Programs of study differ considerably from rudimentary to the most comprehensive available anywhere. A majority of schools follow traditional teaching practices while others utilize, for economic as well as pedagogic reasons, individualized instruction schemes. Some mix healthy doses of pre-1960 "Americanism" with religious education, while others shun this practice. Some Christian day schools are attended by whites only, sometimes because of segregative intent, some are attended by minorities only, while others have integrated student bodies. A militant rejection of any formal state regulation or licensing characterizes some institutions, while others cooperate to varying degrees with state education agencies and officials.[13]

Although these institutions are diverse in many respects, they all profess the centrality of Jesus Christ and the Bible in their educational endeavors. Regardless of the subject matter, a conservative Christian perspective is usually employed. History, for example, is generally approached as the record of God's involvement in human affairs. Though the general theory of evolution receives some attention, science is taught from a creationist perspective, which usually reflects the Genesis account. Moral education, an important aspect of the instructional program, is also biblically based. Students are taught to search the Scriptures as the final authority for value judgments.[14] Summing up the difference between the ethos of the Christian school and that of the public school, Paul A. Kienel, executive director of the Association of Christian Schools International, has asserted:

> Christian schools are Christian institutions where Jesus Christ and the Bible are central in the school curriculum and in the lives of teachers and administrators. This distinction removes us from direct competition with public schools. Although we often compare ourselves academically, we are educational institutions operating on separate philosophical tracks. Ours is Christ-centered education presented in the Christian context. Theirs is man-centered presented within the context of the supremacy of man as opposed to the supremacy of God. Their position is known as secular humanism.[15]

Aside from such statements concerning the beliefs and practices of Christian day schools, little is known about the actual climate or ethos of such institutions and its effect on the education provided. The pervasive religious orientation of these schools, however, may provide the shared sense of mission and common values which recent research suggests are characteristic of "effective" schools.[16]

While there is no doubt that the number of Christian day schools has increased rapidly during the past fifteen to twenty years, and particularly since the mid-1970s, it is almost as difficult to determine precisely their number and student population as it is to assess the nature of the education they offer. The very character of the Christian school movement prohibits an accurate accounting. Some schools are of such a separatist persuasion that they refuse to report enrollment and related figures to state and federal education agencies. For similar reasons others do not affiliate with any of the national associations of Christian schools which are currently the primary sources of data. For example, a 1979 study found that 72 percent of Kentucky and 50 percent of Wisconsin Christian day schools did not belong to any national association.[17] Furthermore, the growth of these schools is so unorganized that exact figures are difficult to obtain.

The variation in estimates of the number of Christian day schools and their enrollment illustrates these problems. Calculations of the number of these institutions founded since the mid-1960s range from 4,000 to as many as 18,000. Enrollment figures for these schools range from 250,000 to over 1,500,000. Based on the best available data, an estimate of between 9,000 and 11,000 schools with a student population of approximately 1,000,000 seems reasonable.[18]

Perhaps the most concrete evidence of the burgeoning Christian day school movement can be seen in the membership figures of the two largest Christian school associations, which provide, among other things, legal counsel, administrative support, and accreditation services to member schools.[19] The Western Association of Christian Schools, which in 1978 merged with two smaller organizations—the National Christian School Education Association and Ohio Association of Christian Schools—to form the Association of Christian Schools International, claimed a membership of 102 schools with an enrollment of 14,659 in 1967. By 1973 the figures were 308 and 39,360 respectively, and in 1983 approximately 1,900 and 270,000. The American Association of Christian Schools, a rival organization of a more separatist nature, was founded in 1972 with eighty schools enrolling 16,000 students. In 1983 the association claimed more than 1,100 schools with a student population in excess of 160,000. Despite the fact that a small number of schools were founded long before they affiliated, these figures testify to the vigor of the movement.[20]

Whether or not this growth pattern will continue is uncertain. But Bruce Cooper, an expert on private school enrollment trends, maintains that the private sector in general, and non-Catholic religious schools in particular, will enjoy substantial growth throughout the 1980s, and perhaps enroll 15 percent of the school-age population by 1990.[21]

REASONS FOR CHRISTIAN DAY SCHOOLS: ALIENATION AND AWAKENING

Why are Christian day schools proliferating? Why are many evangelical Protestants forsaking their historic commitment to public schooling and the "parallel institutions" educational strategy? A number of factors are involved. Some are symbolic of evangelicals' increasing alienation from the American social order. To them the public school exemplifies trends and practices which they deplore in the society at large: widespread uncertainty concerning sources of authority, dissolution of standards, loosening of custom and constraint, waning of evangelicalism as a culture-shaping force, scientism, and government social engineering. Thus when evangelicals, through local churches or societies, establish and support Christian day schools—which in some measure resemble the common school of

nineteenth-century America and emphasize the Bible, moral absolutes, basic subject-matter mastery, discipline, and varying degrees of
separation from state authority and society—they are not only expressing their dissatisfaction with the secular nature of public education, unsatisfactory behavioral and academic standards, and decision
making by groups not accountable to the public, but also disillusionment with the society which sustains the educational enterprise.[22]

While evangelicals have pointed to discipline problems, declining
academic standards, the drug culture, federal meddling, and unresponsive educators as reasons for abandoning the public schools, secularism has disturbed them the most.[23] Although the United States
Supreme Court decisions in 1962 and 1963 which ruled unconstitutional mandatory prayer and devotional Bible reading in tax-sup-
ported schools merely marked the culmination of better than a half-
century long process of "de-Protestantization" of public education,
many evangelical Protestants interpreted the removal of these symbols of the evangelical strain of the American civic faith as "yanking"
God out of the schools.[24] Rather than making the schools "neutral"
on matters related to religion, evangelicals believed that, despite the
intent of the majority of the Court, these decisions contributed to the
establishment of the religion of secular humanism in the public
schools. Such a belief sensitized them to what was being taught in the
schools. So, while these decisions did not cause directly the rapid
growth of Christian day schools, they certainly provoked many conservative Christians to scrutinize public education to a greater extent
than ever before. The result has often been dissatisfaction with the
secular character of the schools which has led many evangelicals either to attempt to restore evangelical symbols and perspectives to
public schooling (e.g., voluntary prayer, Ten Commandments
plaques, and creationism) or to establish Christian educational institutions. As Richard N. Ostling, a staff writer for the religion section of
Time, has observed: "There is little doubt that the rulings produced
anxiety about the climate in public schools that is boosting Protestant
schools many years later."[25]

This anxiety has been evident in recent textbook controversies in,
among other places, West Virginia, New Jersey, California, Texas,
Indiana, and Georgia. Here evangelicals have charged that the exclu-
sion of Christian values and perspectives from public education and
the current orientation of the curriculum has resulted in a *de facto*
establishment of the religion of secular humanism in the public
schools.[26] They have, for instance, often complained that *Man: A
Course of Study,* the well-known, elementary-level social studies curric-

ulum, embodies the tenets of secular humanism. In this course they believe moral absolutes are undermined by an evolutionary framework and situation ethics. Many evangelicals have also seen evidence of secular humanism in moral education schemes which are based on the assumption that values are relative, personal, and situational. Summing up this contention, Charles E. Rice, a professor of law at Notre Dame, has argued:

If the objecting parents are correct in their claim that the public schools are promoting the tenets of a secular religion, it must be on the basis that the nonjudgmental treatment of moral issues without any affirmation of the supernatural is itself an implicit assertion that contradictory moral positions are equally tenable, that there is no objective and binding moral order, that the supernatural is not a necessary factor in the making of moral decisions. It is not unreasonable to describe such teaching as an implicit affirmation of a position that, in its relativism and secularism, is authentically religious. The Christian parents' concern is therefore understandable.[27]

These parents have also been troubled by behavioral sciences texts which imply that a human being is merely a social animal, rather than a unique being created in the image of God, belittle belief in an omniscient and omnipresent Creator and equate the Bible with myth. Social studies texts which ignore the role of Christianity in the American experience have vexed them as well.[28]

Evangelicals have probably been more concerned about public school science courses which present the general theory of evolution as dogma than any other curriculum issue. In recent years an increasing number of evangelical laymen and scientists have questioned the exclusive presentation of the evolutionary explanation of human origins and development. To them such a practice not only burdens the academic freedom and free exercise rights of students who affirm creationism, but it also effectively establishes one of the cardinal tenets of secular humanism, the absolutism of evolution. Until a "neutral" approach which allows for the examination of evidence for evolutionism and creationism is widely adopted, this issue will remain a major source of evangelicals' discontent with public education.[29]

Reflecting many evangelical Protestants' dissatisfaction with the public schools, Floyd Robertson of the National Association of Evangelicals has asserted: "It has become quite obvious to many that this religion of secularism has indeed pervaded our public school system and created an anti-Christian attitude in all too many cases."[30] Based on a survey of factors related to Christian school enrollment, George Ballweg arrived at a similar conclusion. He noted that many Christian families have become alienated from public education because they believe that the schools have turned away from what they "perceived, over the years, to be the traditional standards and values of American society."[31] Although a majority of evangelicals still enroll their children in the public system and continue to wrestle with its secular climate, a growing number are opting for Christian day schools. Like nineteenth-century Roman Catholics who established schools to preserve their religion and culture in an alien environment, a significant number of evangelical Protestants are funding and supporting schools to counter the secularistic influence of society and its institutions on their children.

Awakening, as well as protest and alienation, is involved in the growth of these schools. Though the Christian day school movement emerged primarily as a negative reaction to American society and its educational institutions, it is more than just a "countercultural" phenomenon. The movement has been spurred by what social forecaster John Naisbitt has termed "a revival in religious belief and church attendance," particularly among conservative Protestants.[32]

This recrudescent evangelical consciousness—one manifestation of the spiritual ferment of the past twenty years which William G. McLoughlin has called the "Fourth Great Awakening"—has prompted a growing number of evangelicals to promote Christian education beyond the home and the marginally effective efforts of the Sunday school.[33] Realizing that all education is value oriented and that Christian nurture is a full-time endeavor, evangelicals have increasingly supported schools which embody the biblical beliefs and values of the home and the church. Studies of the reasons parents send their children to such schools point consistently to their desire for a "Christ-centered" or "Bible-centered" academic program.[34] By embracing Christian day schools which complement the worldview of the home and the church, an increasing number of evangelical Protestants believe they have fashioned an educational configuration in which all components are engaged in their conception of the scriptural command to "train up a child in the way he should go."[35]

CRITICISMS AND QUESTIONS

Zeal for these schools is not universal. Some evangelicals have argued that they represent an abdication of Christian social responsibility rather than a manifestation of a reawakened sense of commitment and witness. To these critics the public school is a mission field to be cultivated rather than abandoned. William H. Willimon of Duke University Divinity School enunciated this position in a provocative essay which raised the perennially controverted question of how to be in the world but not of it. He wrote:

> In too many communities, parents who are talented, educated, committed Christians have withdrawn their children (along with their time, talent, and prayers) from the public schools without a thought for their responsibility as their brothers' keeper. Without children in the public schools, they have little interest in the needs of public education. . . . Certainly there is much wrong in today's public schools—mostly the same things that are wrong with our society as a whole. Christian parents have good reason to feel alarmed over many recent developments in public education. But who will improve it? What kind of society will we have if all Christians abandon the public school?[36]

Others have charged that many Christian schools were established primarily to maintain racial segregation. A recent study by David Nevin and Robert E. Bills suggests that racism was an important factor in the founding of some purportedly Christian schools in the South during the late 1960s and early 1970s.[37] Other investigations, however, indicate that these schools are not merely segregation academies. Based on an analysis of Christian day schools in two states, William Lloyd Turner concluded that religious and academic factors rather than racial ones motivated parents to remove their children from public schools. He explained:

> Many authors have charged that these "Christian" schools are only a new type of segregation academy, similar to those that sprang up in the South after passage of the 1964 Civil Rights Act. These "new segregation academies" are said to be adopting a religious guise in order to claim First Amendment guarantees of religious protection and thus escape federal desegregation regulations. But research conducted in early 1979 on fundamentalist schools in Kentucky and Wisconsin disputes this claim and suggests that the factors producing this new wave of fundamentalist schools are more complex than previously supposed. . . .
> The motivation for founding and maintaining nonpublic schools appears to be more than racial prejudice. In recent decades religious influences in American public education have eroded rapidly. Many evangelical Protestants have come to believe that the

public schools now espouse a philosophy that is completely secular, perhaps even antireligious. Hence many conservative Protestants have withdrawn their children from public schools and have established sectarian schools with quite different standards and curricula.[38]

Sociologist Peter Skerry reached the same conclusion after studying Christian day schools in North Carolina. "At least since the late 1960s," he asserted, while pointing out the vigor of the recent evangelical revival, "social and religious conservatism have been on the march. To reduce this conservatism—and the Christian schools that have emerged from it—to racism is simply to ignore two decades of social and cultural upheaval."[39]

Although racism has been a factor in the founding and maintenance of some Christian day schools, the vast majority do not discriminate on the basis of race. Most Christian school associations and spokesmen for the movement condemn racially motivated schooling. In the words of D. Bruce Lockerbie, a respected Christian educator: "The racist stronghold claiming also to be a 'Christian school' is, by definition, an imposter, a fraud. Its reason for being is indefensible by standards of Scripture, the Constitution, . . . or common decency."[40] Besides professing nondiscrimination, an increasing number of these institutions are enrolling minority students, though their proportion of the total student population remains small.[41]

Proponents as well as opponents of Christian day schools have also raised questions concerning the nature and quality of the education provided at some of these institutions. Although there is some evidence that students attending these schools outperform their public school counterparts on standardized tests, several observers have lamented the poor academic standards evident in some schools. Other critics have deplored the "super-patriotism" which characterizes a number of Christian schools. Commentators have also suggested that these schools may shelter students and thus fail to prepare them for life in the "real world."[42]

Regardless of these criticisms, the Christian day school movement continues to flourish. While the recently established schools have yet to attain the stature of the major alternative to public schooling, the Roman Catholic educational enterprise, they are becoming increasingly visible on the educational landscape. Whether or not they ever achieve the status of the Catholic schools will depend to some extent on the resolution of the aforementioned problems and on responses to a number of more critical questions.

Perhaps the most important question facing Christian day schools concerns their present and future relation to state and federal regulatory agencies. Courts in Vermont, Ohio, New Hampshire, Kentucky, North Carolina, North Dakota, Nebraska, Hawaii, Massachusetts, Michigan, and Maine have recently decided cases in which Christian schools have claimed that state-mandated "minimum educational standards" and licensing practices violated their free exercise of religion rights and entailed "excessive entanglement" of state agencies with religious institutions. In the first four instances state supreme courts ruled that detailed and extensive accreditation and teacher certification requirements as applied to Christian schools went beyond the bounds of reasonable regulation and thus unduly burdened free exercise rights. In North Carolina a lower court sustained state accreditation and teacher qualification standards. That decision was, in effect, overturned by legislature action repealing all state regulation of religious schools except for health, safety, attendance reporting, and competency testing requirements. (Vermont, Alabama, and Arizona have also recently deregulated religious schools.)[43] The North Dakota, Nebraska, Hawaii, and Massachusetts Supreme Courts ruled against Christian schools seeking exemption from state licensing on the grounds that the state had a "compelling interest" in providing a quality education for all children. In Michigan, a lower court overturned the state's teacher certification and curriculum standards as applied to a Christian school on the basis of excessive government entanglement with religion and a lack of a "compelling interest" in such requirements. In Maine a federal district court ruled that the state could not close Christian schools which refused to comply with teacher certification and curriculum requirements. The state and the Christian school appealed the Kentucky and Nebraska decisions respectively to the United States Supreme Court. Their appeals, however, were dismissed for lack of a substantial federal question.[44]

Even if efforts are made to reconcile First Amendment rights with state interest in regulating schooling (an issue which also raises questions concerning the very validity of state education regulatory schemes), more litigation of a serious nature seems likely because some Christian educators are asserting that the state has no right to license their schools. As one commentator has noted:

> Although most of the proponents of the Christian school movement agree that the state has a legitimate interest in expecting all children to achieve competency in basic reading, writing, and mathematics skills and requiring safe school facilities, an increasing

number of them are questioning the authority of the state to license or charter Christian schools under any circumstances. As far as they are concerned, such a procedure is tantamount to imposing the state's philosophy and control on an arm of the church. They raise what may become in the near future one of the most profound and litigated questions in the church-state realm: "What right does the state have to license a ministry of the church?"[45]

Besides this fundamental church-state issue, there are other pressing questions which will require time and/or research for answers. To what extent, for example, will the public school system attempt to accommodate disgruntled evangelicals? How much accommodation will be tolerated by the federal courts and secular-minded interest groups such as the American Civil Liberties Union? Will proponents of Christian day schools accept the discredited assumption that schooling is a panacea for all problems? How will graduates of these schools fare in society?[46] Will the initial negative character of the Christian school movement develop into a more positive orientation? How will changes in the national economy affect enrollment patterns? What is the attrition rate of these schools? Will denominations which have taken a strong stand for public education, e.g., Methodists, Baptists, and the United Church of Christ, affirm the value of Christian day schools? What direction will the apparent evangelical awakening take during the next ten years? To what extent, if any, will tuition tax credits or deductions be implemented at the national level?

Regardless of its future status, the Christian day school has emerged as a viable alternative to the public school, and its rapid growth, particularly since the mid-1970s, indicates that a significant number of evangelical Protestants are reconsidering their historic commitment to the "parallel institutions" educational arrangement. It also symbolizes alienation and awakening among evangelicals, represents a reassertion of parental rights, and, most importantly, suggests a crisis in the American civic faith and one of the major vehicles of its transmission, the public school.

NOTES

This is a revised version of an article which appeared in *Educational Forum* 47 (Winter 1983): 135–49.

1. William G. McLoughlin, *Revivals, Awakenings, and Reform: An Essay on Religion and Social Change in America, 1607–1977* (Chicago: University of Chicago Press, 1978), p. 179. For other assessments of the ferment of the 1960s and 1970s, see Robert N. Bellah, *The Broken Covenant: American Civil Religion*

in Time of Trial (New York: Seabury Press, 1975); Christopher Lasch, *The Culture of Narcissism: American Life in an Age of Diminishing Expectations* (New York: Norton, 1978); Richard John Neuhaus, "Educational Diversity in Post-Secular America," *Religious Education* 77 (May–June 1982): 309–20; and William L. O'Neill, *Coming Apart: An Informal History of America in the 1960s* (New York: Quadrangle Books, 1971).

2. "In Quest of Leadership," *Time*, 15 July 1974, p. 23.

3. See, for example, Carl Bereiter, *Must We Educate?* (Englewood Cliffs, N.J.: Prentice Hall, 1973); Harry S. Broudy, *The Real World of the Public Schools* (New York: Harcourt Brace Jovanovich, 1972); R. Freeman Butts, "Assaults on a Great Idea," *The Nation*, 30 April 1973, pp. 553–60; Ronald and Beatrice Gross, eds. *Radical School Reform* (New York: Simon and Schuster, 1969); Robert M. Hutchins, "The Schools Must Stay," *The Center Magazine*, January/February 1973, pp. 12–23; Allan C. Ornstein, "Critics and Criticism of Education," *Educational Forum* 42 (November 1977): 21–30; David Tyack and Elizabeth Hansot, "Conflict and Consensus in American Public Education," *Daedalus* 110 (Summer 1981): 14–23; and Peter Witonski, *What Went Wrong with American Education and How to Make It Right* (New Rochelle, N.Y.: Arlington House, 1973).

4. Seymour W. Itzkoff, *A New Public Education* (New York: David McKay, 1976); and John Martin Rich, *Innovations in Education: Reformers and Their Critics*, 3rd ed. (Boston: Allyn and Bacon, 1980).

5. Lawrence A. Cremin, "The Free School Movement: A Perspective," *Notes on Education* 2 (October 1973): 1–11; Mario Fantini, ed., *Alternative Education* (Garden City, N.J.: Anchor Books, 1976); Allen Graubard, "The Free School Movement," *Harvard Educational Review* 42 (August 1972): 351–73; and David Thornton Moore, "Social Order in an Alternative School," *Teachers College Record* 79 (February 1978): 427–60.

6. Evangelical Protestantism defies precise definition. Though all evangelicals recognize the Bible as the sole rule of faith and practice, believe that the New Testament promises eternal life to those who are "born again," and are committed to spreading the "good news" of Christ's substitutionary atonement for the sins of the human race, they are members of a wide variety of churches and differ in their understanding of these historic doctrines of the Christian faith. Richard Quebedeaux has identified four ideological subgroups of evangelical Protestantism. Ranging from the most conservative on theological and social issues, they are: "Separatist Fundamentalism," "Open Fundamentalism," "Establishment Evangelicalism," and "The New Evangelicalism." Although no systematic research has been done on the question, anecdotal evidence suggests that enthusiasm for Christian schools is greater in the "fundamentalist wing" than in the "evangelical wing." Richard Quebedeaux, *The Young Evangelicals* (New York: Harper & Row, 1974). See also Augustus Cerillo, Jr., "A Survey of Recent Evangelical Social Thought," *Christian Scholar's Review* 5 (1976): 272–80; and Cullen Murphy, "Protestantism and the Evangelicals," *The Wilson Quarterly* 5 (Autumn 1981): 105–16.

7. The efforts of various Protestant denominations to establish parochial schools are described in Francis X. Curran, *The Churches and the Schools: American Protestantism and Popular Elementary Education* (Chicago: Loyola University Press, 1954); Otto F. Kraushaar, *Nonpublic Schools: Patterns of Diversity* (Baltimore: The Johns Hopkins University Press, 1972); Richard Ognibene,

"Catholic and Protestant Education in the Late Nineteenth Century," *Religous Education* 77 (January–February 1982):5–20; and Lewis J. Sherrill, *Presbyterian Parochial Schools, 1846–1870* (New Haven: Yale University Press, 1932).

8. Joseph R. Schultz, "A History of Protestant Christian Day Schools in the United States" (D.R.E. thesis, Southwestern Baptist Theological Seminary, 1954), pp. 208–18; William Lloyd Turner, "Reasons for Enrollment in Religious Schools: A Case Study of Three Recently Established Fundamentalist Schools in Kentucky and Wisconsin" (Ph.D. dissertation, University of Wisconsin, 1979), pp. 42, 159; and "Where Christian Schools Mushroom," *Christian Life* (June 1957), p. 13. Between the 1920s and 1940s, fundamentalists developed several educational institutions, such as radio programs, foreign missions agencies, and Bible schools. With few exceptions, however, fundamentalists and other evangelicals did not perceive the public schools as sufficiently "godless" to warrant a full-blown effort to establish religous day schools. Joel Carpenter, "Fundamentalist Institutions and the Rise of Evangelical Protestantism, 1929–1942," *Church History* 16 (March 1980): 62–75.

9. Robert T. Handy, *A Christian America: Protestant Hopes and Historical Realities* (New York: Oxford Univeristy Press, 1971), p. 102. For similar assessments, see Timothy L. Smith, "Protestant Schooling and American Nationality," *Journal of American History* 53 (March 1967): 679–95; and David Tyack, "The Kingdom of God and the Common School," *Harvard Educational Review* 36 (Fall, 1966): 447–69.

10. William B. Kennedy, *The Shaping of Protestant Education* (New York: Association Press, 1966), p. 27. The role of the Sunday school is also discussed in Robert W. Lynn, *Protestant Strategies in Education* (New York: Association Press, 1964); and Robert W. Lynn and Elliot Wright, *The Big Little School: Two Hundred Years of the Sunday School*, rev. ed. (Birmingham, Ala.: Religious Education Press, 1980).

11. American civil religion comes primarily from a frequently tension-producing fusion of elements of Enlightenment ideology (secular humanism) and the Puritan world view (evangelical Christianity). See Robert D. Linder, "Civil Religion in Historical Perspective: The Reality that Underlies the Concept," *Journal of Church and State* 17 (Autumn 1975): 412–18; and Timothy L. Smith, "Righteousness and Hope: Christian Holiness and the Millennial Vision in America, 1800–1900," *American Quarterly* 31 (Spring 1979): 21–45.

12. Association of Christian Schools International, *1982 Directory* (LaHabra, Calif.: Association of Christian Schools International, 1982).

13. American Association of Christian Schools, *Directory of the American Association of Christian Schools, 1982* (Normal, Ill.: American Association of Christian Schools, 1982); Association of Christian Schools International, *1982 Directory;* B. Drummond Ayres, "Private Schools Provoking Church-State Conflict," *New York Times,* 8 April 1978, sec. A, pp. A1, A23; Joseph Bayly, "How Wide is the Spectrum in Christian Schools?" *Eternity* (September 1980), pp. 24–31; William J. Lanouette, "The Fourth R is Religion," *National Observer,* 15 January 1977, pp. 1, 18; Roy W. Lowrie, Jr., "Christian School Growing Pains," *Eternity* (January 1971), pp. 19–21; Richard Ostling, "Why Protestant Schools Are Booming," *Christian Herald* (July–August 1977), pp. 44–47; Ken Ringle, "D.C. Surburban School Systems Are Swept by Changes—'Christian Schools,'" *Washington Post,* 31 December 1973, sec. B, p.

31; and Elmer Towns, "Have the Public Schools Had It?" *Christian Life* (September 1974), pp. 18–19, 50–51.

14. Joseph Bayly, "Why I'm for Christian Schools," *Christianity Today*, 25 January 1980, pp. 24–27; Daniel Mark Gleason, "A Study of the Christian School Movement" (Ed.D. dissertation, University of North Dakota, 1980), pp. 120–23; Anthony Ramirez, "No-Nonsense Schools Tilt with Bureaucrats," *Wall State Journal*, 7 December 1978, sec. 1, pp. 1, 34; Dorothy W. Rose, "Success Story of Christian Schools," *Good News Broadcaster* (September 1979), pp. 48–50; and George Sweeting, "When the Bible Goes to School," *Moody Monthly* (September 1979), pp. 64–66.

15. Paul A. Kienel, "The Forces Behind the Christian School Movement," *Christian School Comment* (1977), p. 1. For a summary of similar claims, see John C. Holmes, *What Parents Expect of the Christian School* (Santa Fe Springs, Calif.: JoHo Publications, 1983), pp. 30–57.

16. For discussions of recent research on school effectiveness and its policy implications, see Gerald Grant, "The Character of Education and the Education of Character," *Daedalus* 110 (Summer 1981): 135–49; and Arthur G. Powell, "Stalking the Public-Private School Dualism," *Independent School* (February 1982), pp. 17–23.

17. Virginia Davis Nordin and William Lloyd Turner, "More Than Segregation Academies: The Growing Protestant Fundamentalist Schools," *Phi Delta Kappan* (February 1980), p. 392.

18. Ayres, "Private Schools Provoking Church-State Conflict," p. A23; Donald A. Erickson, Richard L. Nault, and Bruce S. Cooper, *Recent Enrollment Trends in U.S. Nonpublic Schools* (Washington, D.C.: National Institute of Education, U.S. Department of Health, Education and Welfare, 1977); Lanouette, "The Fourth R is Religion," p. 1; Gene I. Maeroff, "Private Schools Look to Bright Future," *New York Times Winter Survey of Education*, 4 January 1981, p. 14; Dave Raney, "Public School vs. Christian School," *Moody Monthly* (September 1978), p. 42; and Towns, "Have the Public Schools Had It?" pp. 18–19.

19. The structure and role of these associations are described in Gleason, "A Study of the Christian School Movement," p. 64; and Fred Wilson, "Why Are Fundamentalist Day Schools Growing?" paper presented at History Department Seminar, Kansas State University, Manhattan, Kan., 20 April 1982.

20. These figures are based on information provided by Gerald Carlson of the American Association of Christian Schools, Normal, Illinois and Lee Ranson of the Association of Christian Schools International, La Habra, California. Although the Christian school movement has been more vibrant in the West and the South than in other regions of the country, it is clearly a national phenomenon. See Judith Cummings, "Non-Catholic Christian Schools Growing Fast," *New York Times*, 13 April 1983, sec. A, pp. A-1, A-22; Gleason, "A Study of the Christian School Movement," pp. 11–12; and Paul A. Kienel, "Status of American Christian Schools," paper presented at the National Institute of Christian School Administration, Winona Lake, Ind., 25–30 July 1976.

21. Bruce Cooper, Donald H. McLaughlin, and Bruno Manno, "The Latest Word on Private School Growth," *Teachers College Record* 85 (Fall 1983): 88–98.

22. George Edward Ballweg, Jr., "The Growth in the Number and Popula-

tion of Christian Schools Since 1966: A Profile of Parental Views Concerning Factors Which Led Them to Enroll Their Children in a Christian School" (Ed.D. dissertation, Boston University, 1980), pp. 85–92, 193–94; Holmes, *What Parents Expect of the Christian School,* p. 3; and Neuhaus, "Educational Diversity in Post-Secular America," pp. 316–17.

23. John F. Blanchard, Jr., "Can We Live With Public Education?" *Moody Monthly* (October 1971), pp. 33, 88–89; Timothy Cedric Evearitt, "An Analysis of Why Parents Enroll Their Children in Private Christian Schools" (Ed.D. dissertation, Illinois State University, 1979); Lanouette, "The Fourth R Is Religion," p. 1; Raney, "Public School vs. Christian School," pp. 44–45; and Nordin and Turner, "More Than Segregation Academies: The Growing Protestant Fundamentalist Schools," pp. 391–93.

24. *Engel v. Vitale,* 370 U.S. 421 (1962); *Abington School District v. Schempp,* 374 U.S. 203 (1963); and *Murray v. Curlett,* 374 U.S. 203 (1963). This belief has been strengthened by recent federal appellate court decisions sharply curtailing the right of students in Guilderland, New York and Lubbock, Texas to hold voluntary, student initiated religious meetings on school grounds.

25. Ostling, "Why Protestant Schools Are Booming," p. 45.

26. Based on a review of the literature on secular humanism, pronouncements of humanists, such as Paul Kurtz, editor of *The Humanist,* Paul Blanshard, and G. Richard Bozarth, and an analysis of the *Humanist Manifesto I* (1933), and the *Humanist Manifesto II* (1973), Whitehead and Conlan assert that secular humanism is a nontheistic religion that: "denies the relevance of Diety or supernatural agency"; affirms the "supremacy of human reason"; emphasizes the "self-sufficiency and centrality of Man"; assumes the inevitability of progress by either natural or state-aided means, particularly public education; exalts "science as the guide to human progress and the ultimate provider of an alternative to both religion and morals"; and emphasizes the "absolutism of evolution" in all realms. John W. Whitehead and John Conlan, "The Establishment of the Religion of Secular Humanism and Its First Amendment Implications," *Texas Tech Law Review* 10 (Winter 1978): 17–65 passim. For additional commentary on secular humanism and its role in public education see Wendell R. Bird, "Freedom from Establishment and Unneutrality in Public School Instruction and Religious School Regulation," *Harvard Journal of Law and Public Policy* 2 (June 1979): 125–27, 174–85; Allan Carlson, "Secular Humanism: Right-Wing Bogeyman, or Threat to Human Progress?" *Persuasion at Work* (February 1982), pp. 1–6; Harvey Cox, *The Secular City: Secularization and Urbanization in Theological Perspective* (New York: Macmillan, 1965), p. 18; Alan N. Grover, *Ohio's Trojan Horse* (Greenville, S.C.: Bob Jones University Press, 1977), pp. 28–89 passim; and Robert Russell Melnick, "Secularism in the Law: The Religion of Secular Humanism," *Ohio Northern Law Review* 8 (April 1981): 329–57.

27. Charles E. Rice, "Conscientious Objection to Public Education: The Grievance and the Remedies," *Brigham Young University Law Review* (1978): 860. See also Alan L. Lockwood, "A Critical View of Values Clarification," *Teachers College Record* 77 (September 1975): 35–50 passim; and Joel S. Moskowitz, "The Making of the Moral Child: Legal Implications of Values Education," *Pepperdine Law Review* 6 (Fall 1978): 114–26.

28. James C. Hefley, *Textbooks on Trial* (Wheaton, Ill.: Victor Books, 1976);

George Hillocks, Jr., "Books and Bombs: Ideological Conflict and the Schools—A Case Study of the Kanawha County Book Protest," *School Review* 86 (August 1978): 632–54; Donald Oppewal, "Humanism as the Religion of Public Education: Textbook Evidence," *Christian Legal Society Quarterly* 2 (Winter 1981): 7–9, 31–33; Ostling, "Why Protestant Schools Are Booming," p. 45; Gerald J. Stiles and Louis R. Rittweger, "The Dichotomy Between Pluralistic Rhetoric and Bias Practices," paper presented at the 18th annual meeting of the American Educational Studies Association, Philadelphia, 3 November 1977; Gordon Spykman et al., eds., *Society, State, and Schools: A Case for Structural and Confessional Pluralism* (Grand Rapids: Eerdmans, 1981), pp. 110–15; and Turner, "Reasons for Enrollment in Religious Schools: A Case Study of Three Recently Established Fundamentalist Schools in Kentucky and Wisconsin," pp. 48–50.

29. Legislation requiring instruction in creationism as well as evolutionism has been introduced in at least a dozen states including Illinois, Georgia, Indiana, Iowa, Arkansas, Louisiana, South Carolina, and Florida. According to Bird: "School districts in six states currently require or encourage balanced treatment of the theory of scientific creationism and the general theory of evolution, and state-approved textbook lists for five states currently include texts presenting scientific creationism along with evolution." Bird, "Freedom from Establishment and Unneutrality in Public School Instruction and Religious School Regulation," p. 165; and "Evolution, Creationism Backers Tangle over Teaching of Origins," *Christianity Today*, 18 April 1980, pp. 50–51. For an excellent analysis of the creationism/evolutionism issue and its legal and religious implications see Wendell R. Bird, "Freedom of Religion and Science Instruction in Public Schools," *Yale Law Journal* 87 (January 1978): 515–70. Various 1981/82 issues of *Acts & Facts*, a publication of the Institute for Creation Research, El Cajon, California; *American Biology Teacher; Christianity Today; Church & State; Educational Leadership; Phi Delta Kappan; Science Digest;* and *Science News* have included numerous thoughtful articles on the creationism/evolutionism issue in general, and recent litigation in California and Arkansas in particular.

30. Floyd Robertson, "The Declining Support for Public Schools," *Christian Teacher* (November–December 1976), p. 19.

31. Ballweg, "The Growth in the Number and Population of Christian Schools Since 1966: A Profile of Parental Views Concerning Factors Which Led Them to Enroll Their Children in a Christian School," p. 195.

32. John Naisbitt, *Megatrends: Ten New Directions Transforming Our Lives* (New York: Warner Books, 1982), pp. 239–40. The resurgence of conservative Protestantism since the late 1960s is described by Jackson W. Carroll, Douglas W. Johnson, and Martin E. Marty, *Religion in America: 1950 to the Present* (New York: Harper & Row, 1979); Dean M. Kelly, *Why Conservative Churches Are Growing* (New York: Harper & Row, 1972); Neuhaus, "Educational Diversity in Post-Secular America," pp. 310–11; Burton Yale Pines, *Back to Basics* (New York: William Morrow, 1982), pp. 183–208; Kevin P. Phillips, *Post-Conservative America: People, Politics and Ideology in a Time of Crisis* (New York: Random House, 1982), pp. 180–88.

33. McLoughlin, *Revivals, Awakenings, and Reform: An Essay on Religion and Social Change in America, 1607–1977*, pp. 179–216. Adjustments in institutional arrangements, including schooling, are frequently linked to religious

awakenings. The alteration of educational patterns associated with the common school movement can be understood in part as an outcome of the "Second Great Awakening."

34. Ballweg, "The Growth in the Number and Population of Christian Schools Since 1966: A Profile of Parental Views Concerning Factors Which Led Them to Enroll Their Children in a Christian School," pp. 85–96; Evearitt, "An Analysis of Why Parents Enroll Their Children in Private Christian Schools," passim; Gleason, "A Study of the Christian School Movement," pp. 97–104, 149–55; Holmes, *What Parents Expect of the Christian School;* pp. 85–87, 116–26; and Turner, "Reasons for Enrollment in Religious Schools: A Case Study of Three Recently Established Fundamentalist Schools in Kentucky and Wisconsin," pp. 236–39.

35. Proverbs 22:6.

36. William H. Willimon, "Should Churches Buy into the Education Business?" *Christianity Today,* 5 May 1978, p. 22.

37. David Nevin and Robert E. Bills, *The Schools That Fear Built: Segregationist Academies in the South* (Washington, D.C.: Acropolis Books, 1976).

38. Nordin and Turner, "More Than Segregation Academies: The Growing Protestant Fundamentalist Schools," pp. 391–92.

39. Peter Skerry, "Christian Schools versus the I.R.S.," *Public Interest* 61 (Fall 1980): 28–31. For similar assessments, see Neuhaus, "Educational Diversity in Post-Secular America," p. 319; and Lyle E. Schaller, "Public versus Private Schools: A Divisive Issue for the 1980's," *Christian Century,* 7 November 1979, p. 1087. Busing has been a factor in the establishment of some Christian schools in all regions of the country. It is unclear, however, as to whether the reaction to busing has been due to racism, resentment of federal coercion, fear of unrest, or a combination of all three. See Russell Chandler, "Popularity of Religious Schools Rising," *Los Angeles Times,* 18 June 1978, p. 14; and Towns, "Have the Public Schools Had It?" pp. 19, 50.

40. D. Bruce Lockerbie, "The Way We Should Go," *Christian Teacher* (September–October 1976), p. 7. For similar statements, see "Creed and Color in the School Crisis," *Christianity Today,* 27 March 1970, pp. 32–33; Lowrie, "Christian School Growing Pains," p. 20; and Ostling, "Why Protestant Schools Are Booming," pp. 45–46.

41. According to G. William Davidson of the Association of Christian Schools International, a majority of the 700-plus Christian schools in California are integrated. See also Denis P. Doyle, "A Din of Inequity: Private Schools Reconsidered," *Teachers College Record* 82 (Summer 1981): 661–73; Holmes, *What Parents Expect of the Christian School,* pp. 4, 73–74; and Ostling, "Why Protestant Schools Are Booming," pp. 45–66.

42. Bayly, "How Wide is the Spectrum in Christian Schools?" pp. 24–31; Ethel Herr, "Who's Salting the Schools?" *Eternity* (February 1976), pp. 16, 18, 58–59; Lockerbie, "The Way We Should Go," pp. 6–7, 29; Lowrie, "Christian School Growing Pains," pp. 19–21; and Priscilla Raue, "Don't Abandon the Public Schools," *Logos* (March–April, 1980), pp. 52–53.

43. James C. Carper, "Rendering Unto Caesar: State Regulation of Christian Day Schools," *Journal of Thought,* forthcoming.

44. Ibid. For discussions of these cases and related issues, see Bird, "Freedom from Establishment and Unneutrality in Public School Instruction and Religious School Regulation," pp. 185–95; James C. Carper, "The *Whisner*

Decision: A Case Study in State Regulation of Christian Day Schools," *Journal of Church and State* 24 (Spring 1982): 299–301; Neal Devins, "State Regulation of Christian Schools," *Journal of Legislation* 10 (Summer 1983): 351–81; and Patricia M. Lines, "State Regulation of Private Education," *Phi Delta Kappan* 64 (October 1982): 119–23. Allen Lobozzo, "Judge Rules Maine May Not Shut Unapproved Christian Schools," *Education Week*, 11 January 1984, p. 6.

45. Carper, "The *Whisner* Decision: A Case Study in State Regulation of Christian Day Schools," pp. 301–02. For discussions of deregulation and the effectiveness of state standards, see Stephen Arons, *Compelling Belief: The Culture of American Schooling* (New York: McGraw Hill Book Company, 1983); Carper, "Rendering Unto Caesar: State Regulation of Christian Day Schools"; J. Eric Evenson II, "State Regulation of Private Religious Schools in North Carolina—A Model Approach," *Wake Forest Law Review* 16 (June 1980): 405–37; and Cynthia Wittmer West, "The State and Sectarian Education: Regulation to Deregulation," *Duke Law Journal* (1980): 801–46.

46. Research is needed not only on the enrollees and graduates of these schools, but also on the climate of the schools. Alan Peshkin of the University of Illinois is currently working on an in-depth study of the environment of a Christian school. His initial findings were presented in "Fundamentalist Christian Schools: Truth and Consequences," paper presented at the annual meeting of the American Educational Research Association, Montreal, Canada, 12 April 1983.

Chapter 6

The Jewish Day School in America: A Critical History and Contemporary Dilemmas

EDUARDO RAUCH

Day School (occasionally called "All-Day" school) refers to Jewish full-time nonpublic schools, communal or congregational, which teach both the Jewish and the general studies every school day, with or without Saturdays and/or Sundays. Day school is used by Jews in contradistinction to the term "parochial" school of the Catholics, or the terms "church community" school or the "parent-society" school of the Protestants. The Jewish day school is neither a "parish school" nor even necessarily a congregational school. It is generally an autonomous, communally sponsored or locally sponsored institution with no official or binding ties with any educational or philanthropic agency. Its policies are determined by members of its own lay board. Although some schools belong to loosely organized national and local networks, the affiliated schools reflect not so much the ideology of the "parent" organization as that of the lay officials of the schools.

Although the Jewish day schools are generally regarded as communal schools with a traditional program, it is not good practice to consider them as *one* group of schools or *one form* of education. The majority are the type that is called the Orthodox-oriented day school. Over 90 percent of the day schools are in this group. Their enrollment is about 88 percent of the total. The rest of the day schools belong mostly to the Conservative movement and a small number to other much smaller splinter groups. The Reform movement, despite its central role in American Judaism, has no more than six of these institutions.

In the United States most Jewish education has been traditionally carried out through part-time programs, either in one-day-a-week

"Hebrew Schools" or in the two-to-five day a week afternoon programs. These two programs are still dominant, but much less than before. In 1958 the day school accounted for one of twelve students enrolled; in 1966 the full-time schools accounted for one of eight students enrolled in Jewish schools. In 1974 they accounted for one in five. By 1978 one out of every four Jewish students was enrolled in a full-time Jewish school.[1]

Subdivisions within the American Jewish Community can be partially explained in terms of the religious intensity of commitment of each distinct group: "The American Jewish Community is mainly composed of three distinct religious persuasions: (1) the Orthodox, who follow the traditions of Jewish life and adhere faithfully to the *Shulhan Arukh,* the basic code Jewish Law, which was formulated in the fifteenth century; (2) the Reform, or the liberal wing of the Jewish community, who stress the ethical concepts of Judaism, but do not follow the traditional practices of Orthodox Jewry; and (3) the Conservatives, who endeavor to maintain the basic rituals of Judaism while adapting them to modern conditions."[2]

What we call Jewish Orthodoxy is mainly rooted in Eastern Europe; the Reform movement had its origins in Germany. The Conservative movement on the other hand—although rooted in Europe—is truly an American product, in a way a compromise, a synthesis between the extremes of the spectrum represented by Orthodox and Reform. According to J. Milton Yinger: "Sociologically speaking, [Conservatism] was an attempt to do for the large number of Eastern European migrants, particularly in the second and third generations in the United States, what the Reform movement sought to do for the earlier migrants from Western Europe: it formed a link between the total Jewish culture of the past and the requirements and possibilities of the American present."[3] From a theological-ideological point of view, writes a Conservative spokesperson:

> We differ from our colleagues to the left of us in our unequivocal acceptance of the authority of the *Halacha,* that is, of the moral and ritual injunctions of the Torah as interpreted in the Rabbinic tradition. We differ from our colleagues to the far right of us in our understanding of the extent to which there is room for *Halachic* maneuverability within the framework of the *Halacha.* I need not stress here the well-known fact that the Talmud consists of the record not only of the areas of agreement among the Rabbis, but also their disagreements.[4]

The classification of American Jews into the three groups above described does anything but exhaust the variety of Jewish identifications in America. Although membership in a synagogue continues to be perceived both within the community and outside of it as revealing of the nature and scope of Jewish commitments, reality does much to weaken the validity of this approach. As more and more Jews no longer necessarily joined synagogues during the teens, twenties, and thirties of this century, other forms of being Jewish or retaining a Jewish identity came to the fore. Zionism as an ideology, and the Zionist movement as its concrete expression, became many times the only vehicle of Jewish identification for a considerable and ever-growing number of Jews. Nonetheless, many Zionists have also maintained synagogue affiliation. For the unaffiliated, Zionism provided—and continues to provide—"a means consistent with the American voluntary tradition whereby a Jewish consciousness can be expressed without acceptance of Judaism. There is a change from affiliation with Judaism to identification with Jewishness."[5]

There are other patterns of identification that move even farther away from the classical form of being Jewish in America, i.e., synagogue affiliation. In some cases one does not even need be affiliated or work with Jewish philanthropic or fraternal organizations or contribute to Jewish causes. "For many American Jews, serving the general community leads to the feeling that they are expressing their Judaism in their lives, whether or not they have any specifically Jewish affiliation. This secular and moralistic version of Jewish identification is American, very American."[6] Whether these secular forms of identification have any power to survive and be transmitted on to the next generation by its practitioners remains an open question and an important one for the survival of American Judaism.

While it is true that the majority of the day schools are affiliated with the Orthodox movement, not all their pupils are children of Orthodox parents. We find children from all kinds of Jewish religious and other backgrounds in these schools. It is doubtful, nonetheless, that Orthodox children will be found in Conservative schools. They might be found in the public school system, but not in Jewish schools with a religious orientation less intensive than their own.

The day schools are divided into two major groupings: (1) elementary schools with approximately 75 percent of the school units, and (2) the high schools with approximately 25 percent of the school units and growing. Of all children receiving some kind of Jewish education, 26.3 percent of them are in day schools. The rest are distributed between the one-day-a-week schools and mid-week school with the Reform congregation, and the weekday afternoon school with Conservative and Orthodox synagogues. About 50 percent of all Jewish children receive some kind of Jewish education at some time. By 1962 enrollment in forms other than the day school had begun to decline. Between 1966 and 1978 schools other than full-time suffered a drop of enrollment of about a third, according to a report by the American Association for Jewish Education. This dramatic overall decline is beginning to slow down. Between 1971 and 1975 this decline was only 11 percent. The decrease in the Jewish birth rate, it is believed, was largely responsible for the drop in school enrollments. The latest data available seems to indicate that the Jewish school population might begin to rise again.[7]

The schools of all three religious orientations would probably agree to the following paraphrase of their educational objectives:

> (1) To provide knowledge of the classical Jewish texts and the traditions embodied therein; (2) to foster a life-long commitment to the study of Torah (Bible); (3) to develop some form of personal observance; (4) to develop a facility in the Hebrew language and a familiarity with its literature; (5) to nurture an identification with the Jewish people through a knowledge of its past, and to encourage a concern for its survival and welfare the world over; (6) to stimulate a recognition of the unique place of Israel in the Jewish imagination, both past and present, and to foster the acceptance of some sort of personal obligation to participate in its development; (7) to encourage participation in American society, based on a conscious awareness of the relationship between Jewish tradition and democracy; and (8) to inculcate faith in God and trust in his beneficience.[8]

Despite this concurrence, the deep and abiding division separating the Reform from the Orthodox view of the religious life is clearly manifest in the style and manner of the schools, but the broad purpose of the Jewish school is to contribute to the continued existence of the Jews as an identifiable group.

While it is true that this set of educational objectives is backed partially at least by certain studies conducted on parents of day school children it still seems suspiciously neat and excessively optimistic. In a school system so heavily influenced by lay leadership, there are many other school and psychological parameters that must necessarily impinge on the definition of objectives. The Jewish day school is not only an attempt at creating an ideal environment for the education of Jewish children, but it is also a deliberate instrument of separation from the rest of the community of schools, for reasons that can have either positive or negative connotations, or both. These elements are not dealt with in this set of objectives.

BRIEF HISTORY

Prior to the American Revolution, Jewish children invariably studied under private tutors or attended small Jewish schools, since most non-Jewish schools were denominational. Between the end of the Revolutionary War and 1879, many day schools existed under various congregational and private auspices. This was due to the attitude of Jews toward public education. Some of the newly arrived immigrants as well as some of the native American Jews refused to send their children to secular schools permeated with Christian influences. Most Jewish schools of that period, however, failed to survive. People were not of learned stock and were increasingly satisfied with less than the minimum for their children. The Jewish community placed an increasing importance upon secular education; conditions were such that Jewish education had to become secondary to secular training. Moreover, as Oscar Handlin has pointed out:

> The dominant conditions of American education were already set before the appearance of large groups of immigrants, and the newcomers were never in a position to revise the earlier decisions. By the 1840s it had been determined that the education of youth in the United States would be public, that is, governed by the state. Such training, it was clear, would also be almost entirely free and universal. From these premises, it followed as a matter of course that there would be no religious instruction in the public schools and that no public funds would go to religious schools.[9]

Although a succession of day schools could be found during the 1840s and 1850s in cities such as Cincinnati, Chicago, Boston, Baltimore, and Philadelphia, besides those already established in New York City, it soon became clear that parochial institutions would not be able to resist the development of the public school system. Day schools were too expensive and teachers sought better careers elsewhere. And "above all, these schools were not as likely to lead to social and economic advancement which depended on contacts outside the Jewish group. In this respect, attendance at a sectarian school was actually a liability rather than an asset."[10] Many Jews considered these Jewish schools not only unnecessary, but even dangerous, and the conflicts between Catholics and Protestants destroyed any intention they might have had at advocating an arrangement for "parochial" schools for Jews.[11] Many American-born Jews went as far as to send their children to Christian "Institutes" or "Academies," whose clear purpose was the inculcation of Christianity. Generally these Christian institutions were superior to the municipal schools in their general curriculum.

The day school movement received a temporary boost when during the 1860s the Jews of New York reacted to Christian missionary attempts by establishing Hebrew schools in the Lower East Side. While their attempts at thwarting the missionary efforts were successful, the schools created as a reaction to that phenomenon were themselves to fold a decade later. By 1880, because of intermarriage and conversion to Christianity, very few descendants of the early eighteenth-century Jews were left. Many Jews of German origin—who immigrated to America in the mid-nineteenth century—were in favor of the day school and expressed regret at its decline and disappearance. Other German Jews were violently opposed to this type of education, just as the native Jew had been in an earlier period. They feared that by creating and maintaining these schools, a wall was being erected between themselves and the Gentiles.[12]

The birth and growth of the modern American day school has its origins in developments in Jewish life and in Jewish education in the United States during the late nineteenth century and the first half of the twentieth century. Between 1881 and 1920 nearly two million Jews emigrated to America from Eastern Europe.[13] These immigrants, while willing to adapt themselves to the rapid and efficient character of American life, were not ready to give up their religious and cultural inheritance as had been done by many of the Jews who had preceded them.[14] The pressures on these new immigrants were multiple and came both from the established American Jewish community and the general Gentile community. Most of this pressure was directed to bring about a change in the image, customs, and even the beliefs that these immigrants had brought from the old world. Established American Jewry felt a special and profound ambiguity about these newly arrived coreligionists. A famous American Jewish rabbi explained, for example, that the Reform movement represented "the sentiment of American Judaism minus the idiosyncrasies of . . . late immigrants." Jewish cultural societies talked about Americanizing and "humanizing" the immigrant Jews, eliminating the "Oriental" elements in the life and culture of Eastern European Jewry, "not so much a matter of religion, but of race and of habits." Handlin writes:

"The outraged 'German' Jew saw, shuffling down the gang-plank, himself or his father, stripped of the accessories of respectability. This was what he had escaped from, been Americanized away from."[15]

It was also at this time that many Americans started questioning the entire value of immigration. Others felt that acculturation was not proceeding fast enough. The melting pot concept was being questioned and some argued that American culture was already well established and the new immigrants had the task of assimilating those forms. Milton Gordon quotes an educator writing in 1909:

> These southern and eastern Europeans are of a very different type from the north Europeans who preceeded them. Illiterate, docile, lacking in self-reliance and initiative, and not possessing the Anglo-Teutonic conceptions of law, order, and government, their coming has served to dilute tremendously our national stock, and to corrupt our civic life. . . . Everywhere these people tend to settle in groups or settlements, and to set up here their national manners, customs, and observances. Our task is to break up these groups or settlements, to assimilate and amalgamate these people as a part of our American race, and to implant in their children, as far as can be done, the Anglo-Saxon conception of righteousness, law and order, and popular government, and to awaken in them a reverence for our democratic institutions and for those things in our national life which we as a people hold to be of abiding worth.[16]

Anti-Semitism was also flowering at this time and added to the pressures to which the new Jews were being submitted during those years.

Among those Jews who came to America at the end of the nineteenth century there were also those who were intensely trained in the Talmud. These Jews were especially dissatisfied with the Jewish education they found in America. Thus they opened their own schools. For them knowledge and study were not only means to religious and ethical behavior, but were in themselves a mode of worship. Neither poverty nor the pursuit of a livelihood nor the pressure they encountered in America nor the raising of a family could free a Jew from the obligation of study of Torah. But in the new world it was not easy for young people to study Torah for its own sake. For young and old the possibility that a secular education might help them out of the life of "labor in shop or store was both exciting and disturbing."[17]

Jews with these deep ambiguities and profound commitments to education were by no means the majority among the new immigrants. Poverty played an important role in the kind of educational institutions that dominated the life of these new immigrants. It was almost impossible for them, if even they would have desired it, to finance a day school system. The majority of these immigrants faced serious problems of adjustment to America, and because of their compact Jewish environment, reinforced by traditional home life and synagogue, they did not consider Jewish education a serious problem. While prior to the 1880s it was the American environment which established educational trends among American Jewry, among the new immigrants it was the institutions of their old homes which carried the greater weight. Moreover, as long as Jews lived in crowded settlements with little contact with either native Americans or other immigrant groups, they were able for a time, whether intentionally or unintentionally, to ignore the new American environment.[18] Despite the fact that most of them had a strong religious orientation, they preferred public schooling for their children. Having been excluded in Eastern Europe from educational instruction, they seized the opportunity of sending their children to public schools.[19] As Milton Himmelfarb has pointed out: "Jews have been particularly grateful for free, universal education in the United States because where most of their parents or grandparents came from, the government tried to keep them out of whatever schools there were."[20]

Marshall Sklare interprets the embrace of public education by the new immigrants in a more radical way:

> The favor that the public school system found in the eyes of the immigrant is a highly significant index of his secularization and desire to accommodate to America. And the public school in turn served to speed the process of integrating both parent as well as child into American culture. Given the attitudes of those who came to America during the period of mass migration, together with the challenges and opportunities of American life (and particularly the way such challenges and opportunities were interpreted by the immigrant), the traditional orientation to Jewish learning was abandoned and a new orientation to secular education came into being. It is possible to contend that the shift was so extreme that values actually became transposed: secular education assumed the place that Jewish education had occupied, while Jewish education was shifted to the position formerly assigned to secular education.[21]

An important element in the maintenance of a strong Jewishness among the new immigrants was the Yiddish language. It helped make public education less of a threatening experience, especially for those whose religious roots were not as deep, and who had more problems in identifying symbols of uniqueness in the new and complex environment.[22]

Jewish evaluations of the period around the turn of the century would appear to place an excessive emphasis on the Jewish will to embrace the American public education system, and apparently tend to underestimate the effect that outside pressure might have had on the decisions that the new Jewish community adopted regarding its educational priorities. While it is true that poverty must have had much to do with the way things developed and that these Jews were deeply enthralled by and thankful for the opportunities—almost magical in their eyes—that America offered them, we cannot forget how profoundly hostile an environment these new immigrants had to confront. The golden age of immigration had truly ended, if not in numbers at least ideologically, by the beginning of the century.[23] There were many pressures to stop immigration altogether or at the very least make the new immigrants into "Americans" as fast as possible. This must have had a profound effect on the attitudes of the immigrants and might have well molded their decisions for many years following their arrival to this country. Moreover, the educational patterns established by the old American Jewish community and the pressures that these Jews applied on the new immigrants must also have had a profound effect.

For American Reform Judaism, for example, this was a time when the struggle for the affirmation of the public school acquired dramatic characteristics. Statements in favor of public education, and against any type of parochial education were strong and unequivocal.[24] The roots of these attitudes might well have been a response to the rising threat of missionary schools toward the end of the nineteenth century, and the presence of the recently arrived Jews with their strong attachments to a past that Reform Jews often perceived as discomforting and threatening. The public school was perceived as a fortress against these threats and thus was not only enthusiastically but truly fanatically supported.

Samson Benderly—the most important Jewish educator in America in the first few decades of this century—symbolized in many ways the acceptance of a more-or-less established status quo in the American educational scene: Jewish education would be fine as long as it did not interfere with the public education process. In 1908 he examined the options open to American Jews:

Shall we withdraw our children from the public schools and establish schools of our own as the Catholics are doing? In such schools the Jewish spirit would predominate. The purely Jewish studies would find their proper place in the curriculum and our children's health would not be endangered. This plan, even if practical otherwise, should be banished from our minds. In spite of the fact that isolation in the midst of a Christian environment greatly contributed to our preservation in the past, we have paid dearly for this isolation. What we want in this country is not Jews who can successfully keep up their Jewishness in a few large ghettos, but men and women who have grown up in freedom and can assert themselves wherever they are. A parochial system of education among the Jews would be fatal to such hopes.[25]

Benderly clearly sided with supplementary Jewish education as the only realistic option for the American Jewish community. On the other hand, he strongly opposed religious instruction within the public schools and made it clear that he did not accept the Sabbath and/or Sunday Jewish schools as an adequate alternative. For Benderly, only a double school system would do; one in which children would attend Jewish schools only after their daily participation in the public schools.

A new atmosphere and alternative ideological developments would be necessary before the day school could become a legitimate alternative to supplementary education. While the Jewish playwright Israel Zangwill sang the glories of assimilation in his famous play *The Melting Pot* (1908),[26] it was a spokesman for cultural Zionism, the young American-born rabbi, Judah L. Magnes, who ardently responded during a sermon: "The symphony of America must be written by the various nationalities which keep their individual and characteristic note, and which sound this note in harmony with their sister nationalities. Then it will be a symphony of color, of picturesquesness, of character, of distinction—not the harmony of the Melting Pot, but rather the harmony of sturdiness and loyalty and joyous struggle."[27]

The Zionist movement played no minor role during these years of confusion, attempting to rally Jewish group consciousness. By calling for the reestablishment of a Jewish State in Palestine, Zionism could appeal to all Jews regardless of their social, political, and religious differences. It was a powerful antidote against assimilation by appealing to a common denominator called ethnic heritage.

It was in such an intellectual environment that a theory of cultural pluralism could arise. Even so, it would not be until well into the thirties that such theory would become a significant political force. The most prominent representative of such a theory was to be Horace Kallen, a deeply committed Zionist stirred by the hope of a Jewish national revival. John Higham calls cultural pluralism "a revolt against the monistic systems that prevailed in the late nineteenth century. It rejected their rationalistic spirit and their inclination toward a stratified view of society. The antiformalists denied a privileged status to any fixed point of view or any social category. They accepted the multiformity of experience and the relativity of values. Their refusal of any single, all-embracing scheme of things acquired a pluralistic bent when it became a positive celebration of irreducible diversity."[28] It is interesting to note that Higham believed that cultural pluralism received its philosophical credentials from William James, especially through his book *A Pluralistic Universe* (1909). Kallen was a student of James' at Harvard. Writing in 1915 in the journal *The Nation*, Kallen laid out the basic premises of his theory while not as yet calling it cultural pluralism. After making an historical analysis of the struggles of many minorities against assimilation throughout history and the failure of many political systems in obliterating differences among people, Kallen proceeded to describe in lyrical terms the beauty of a society in which pluralism would be a palpable reality.[29] Higham indicates with great insight that cultural pluralism could only appeal to those minority spokesmen who saw advantage in a permanent minority status, and who no longer perceived themselves as in the periphery but rather at the center of the American experience. Thus, cultural pluralism would prove most attractive to those who were already largely assimilated. In this light, cultural pluralism was in itself a product of the American melting pot. Kallen in a way prophesied this development when analyzing the process by which human groups assimilate to larger societies:

> In the first phase [the immigrants] exhibit economic eagerness, the greed of the unfed. Since external economic differences are a handicap in the economic struggle, they "assimilate," seeking thus to facilitate the attainment of economic independence. Once the proletarian level of such independence is reached, the process of assimilation slows down and tends to come to a stop. The immigrant group is still a national group, modified, sometimes improved, by environmental influences, but otherwise a solitary spiritual unit, which is seeking to find its way out on its own social level. . . . Americanization has not repressed nationality. Americanization has liberated nationality.[30]

But this social situation, adequate to the flourishing of cultural pluralism, would not develop until the late thirties. Ethnic hatred reached its zenith in the years prior to, during, and immediately after the First World War. This morbid "Americanism" expressed itself by a rejection of all deviant groups.

Whether ethnicity came to be accepted in the thirties or not, or whether cultural pluralism really achieved any status in American life until much later remains a question to be explored. Perhaps Jews became more acceptable as "different" when instead of insisting on a total differentiation from other groups in society, they limited that appeal to difference in the realm of religion. Such a shift in the Jews' self-perception is described by Judah Pilch:

> Judaism in America has been taking a new turn from the thirties on, when the chapter of adjustment to conditions of life and culture in America ended. With the passing of the Yiddish language as a folk possession; with the break-up of typical Jewish neighborhoods; with the replacement of the leaders of European origin by American born; with the development of suburbanism, the process of acculturation became an accomplished fact. Ideas were expressed that *religion, now as ever, was the beginning and the end*, our very life and the length of our days. The nationalist-secularist approach was being questioned, together with its emphasis on the study of the Hebrew language. The institutionalized religion of suburbia began to hold sway in the new neighborhoods.[31]

Will Herberg in the fifties converted this social observation into a theory by noting that the American ethnic group does eventually lose its separate identity which is replaced by a religious community. Herberg visualized religion as the only lasting dimension of culture and the foundation of American pluralism.[32] Was this religious interpretation of the Jewish condition in America an adaptive response to an inflexible reality or a true evolution of self-understandings? The fact that Jews apparently became more acceptable as different, that they could start thinking of establishing separate schools only when they reduced their claims to difference from all encompassing ethnic-cultural to more limited religious dimensions, is an historical fact that deserves more exploration. But these developments only describe one dimension of the changes that accompanied the growth of the day school in America.

Well into the second decade of this century the public school remained as practically the only full-time educational alternative for the Jewish community. Landesman, writing about a borough of New York City, stated that "Jewish children of school age, with few exceptions, attended the public schools. There was no all-day Jewish school in Brownsville until 1912 when Yeshiva R'Chaim Berlin opened one for boys. Only a small group attended in the early years, no more than 200 as late as 1918."[33] In Baltimore, according to Isaac M. Fein:

In spite of all the efforts of both individual schools and the Board of Jewish education, many children did not recieve any Jewish education. Although rabbis and school officials tried hard to enroll all Jewish children, over two thousand did not attend any Hebrew school in 1917. . . . Day schools, which had been the basis of Jewish education until the middle of the 1870s, came back to life in the second decade of the twentieth century.[34]

Between 1917 and 1939, twenty-eight day schools were founded. Many parents desiring a Jewish all day education, often not available to their offspring in their immediate communities, moved into various day school neighborhoods. In their early development, the day schools initially reflected the ideological orientation of the founders. Gradually, however, they mirrored the needs of their respective communities and the influence of their lay boards and parent groups. Many of the newly organized schools met with the indifference of both parents and communal leaders. With immigrant culture on the decline, emphasis shifted to that of the children. Here education was critical. By 1935, in New York, the percentage of children between the ages of six and sixteen who received any Jewish education had dropped to 25 percent and seven years later was still falling. Bureaus of Jewish Education in various cities and a national association attempted to put life into the parochial and part-time school system. But the inescapable question remained: What were these institutions to teach and why?

The year 1940 marks the beginning of the period of phenomenal growth for the Jewish day school movement. More than 360 schools, 95 percent of all existing day schools were established after this date. In 1940, at the beginning of this era, there were 35 schools with about 7,700 pupils. By 1958 there were 214 schools with 43,000 students, and by 1964 the number of schools had risen to 306 and the enrollment to 65,000. In 1976 there were 80,000 students enrolled, and by 1980 the number surpassed 100,000.

Of all the children who were in church communal schools in 1958 only one percent were in Jewish day schools, while the percentage of Jews in the American population was around three percent. Between 1941 and 1950 enrollment increased at an average yearly growth of 1,500 pupils. Between 1951 and 1960 the annual rate was of 3,200 students. During the sixties, however, the average increase declined to less than 1,800 pupils per year. Between 1970 and 1972 there was almost no increase at all. Between 1941 and 1972 the number of communities served by the schools increased from 7 to over 125. The enrollment growth of the day school in the United States between

1940 and 1964 was four times as great as the enrollment increase of the supplementary Jewish schools (Sunday and weekday schools) during the same period. Fifteen years ago day school students constituted about 12.5 percent of all pupils in Jewish schools of any kind. This percentage had risen to 14 percent by 1971, to 20 percent by 1976 and to 26 percent by 1978. While there has been a dramatic overall decline in the number of students enrolled in all Jewish schools due largely to a decline in the Jewish birthrate—18 percent between 1967 and 1971 and 11 percent between 1971 and 1975—the full-time day school has experienced a steady growth. The latest enrollment data seem to indicate that the Jewish birthrate might be rising again.

The growth of the Jewish day school enrollment is also particularly impressive when compared to the growth of public and Catholic parochial schools. Between 1940 and 1963 the number of pupils in Jewish day schools rose 745 percent as compared with rises of 129 percent and 53 percent in the parochial schools and public schools respectively.[35]

Despite the rapid growth of the day school one must not forget that even in 1958, during a period of phenomenal growth, 75 percent of the Jewish community was still opposed to the day schools in principle. Even so, 25 percent support is a considerable minority, and it was felt among many leaders that such a number warranted financial community support for the day school "for those who want them," but only given on the basis of the cost of Jewish studies and for schools that met objective educational standards of "modern schooling and give adequate attention to the general education of their pupils."[36]

Jewish schools reflect the mobility of the Jewish population. As Jews began to move out into the suburbs from metropolitan areas, the educational enterprises followed suit. Between 1951 and 1964 city schools doubled their enrollment, while suburban schools multiplied sevenfold. In 1958 Jewish school enrollment was proportionately higher in smaller communities than in the larger ones and higher in towns than in big cities.[37] This gap has continued to grow steadily.

Finally, it is interesting to point out that the growth pattern of the Jewish all-day school is a sound indication that increasingly larger percentages of elementary day school graduates are continuing their Jewish education in Jewish high schools.

ABOUT THE CURRICULUM OF THE DAY SCHOOL

The autonomy of the Jewish day school is reflected in the variety of the educational programs and patterns of program scheduling. While there are many obvious differences, there are also many similarities in these important phases of the day school operation. Although there are no curricular guidelines for each group of kindred day schools, the curricula of these schools are similar for three reasons: (1) their common purpose and similar educational philosophies; (2) the frequent educational exchanges between school principals; and (3) the emulation by many day schools of certain programs and practices of the more established schools. Most schools include subjects such as prayer, the first five books of the Bible (Chumash), learned comments to these five books by the medieval scholar Rashi, prophets, Hebrew language, arts, laws and customs, history, sections of the Talmud (Mishna, Gemara), ethics, and Israel.[38]

But there are obvious and serious ideological and theological problems with this simplistic summary of the character of the curriculum in the day school movement. We have already touched on some of these problems when discussing the differences between the Orthodox and Conservative factions of American Jewry. For the Orthodox "the philosophy of Jewish education may be said to be built upon the belief in a personal God, a revealed truth, and the teaching of this truth. By exercising his free will toward the fulfillment of the divine precepts, each individual, no matter of what group, may attain immortality. The will to do presupposes a knowledge of what to do, obtainable only through proper instruction."[39] On the other hand a Conservative spokesperson writes:

> The conventional [Orthodox] day school philosophy tends toward fundamentalism in outlook. It presents our religious tradition as a divine incursion into history with little allowance for a creative human dimension, and it tends to see the tradition as a finished and closed system toward which it urges unswerving loyalty. Our movement long described itself a "historical Judaism," which focuses on historical factors in the development of tradition. This does not negate a divine initiative in the precipitation of the visions in which Jewish beliefs arose. But it acknowledges a creative human dimension working in symbiosis with the divine.[40]

If curriculum building is confronted with honesty following a careful reading of such disparate philosophies, one cannot but conclude that the end products for each one of these streams of thought will be very different. For reasons of unity within the community, scarcity of resources, and often perhaps because of indifference to philosophical niceties, these gaps have been glossed over. The consequences have been both confusion and a weakening of purpose, and the almost total elimination of the discussions of basic life premises. When the compromise is around something, anything "Jewish" within the curriculum, the risk is that soon there will be nothing left.

One of the basic features of the day school program is pupil participation in religious activities. The "doing" phase of the day school curriculum provides important incidental educational experiences. Experiences around the religious holidays are regularly planned. Hebrew is generally the language of instruction in the Hebrew classes of the coed schools. Yiddish and English are used in most of the all-boy schools. Over 90 percent of the schools outside New York employ Hebrew or a combination of Hebrew and English in their classes.

As to the General Studies curriculum, the course of study of the local state board of education is generally followed in the Jewish day schools. The same texts and materials used in the public schools are employed. Teachers and principals of the General Studies departments are engaged on the basis of their competence in general education. Many of them are not Jews. In most schools, the Hebrew program is scheduled for the morning while the rest of the classes carry on their general studies work; in the afternoon, the program of each class is reversed. In some of these parallel program schools, the Hebrew and General Studies are alternated between morning and afternoon on a weekly basis. A variety of other combinations have been tried. As Sklare has argued:

> Despite the wide differences among day schools, sophisticated observers claim that all of them suffer from a similar defect: the two-track approach. The result of such compartmentalization is that the secular curriculum never receives the benefit of cross-fertilization by Jewish culture and vice versa. To its detriment Jewish culture is doomed to exist in splendid isolation from the general culture. Furthermore, the student may be taught one thing in the secular curriculum and its precise opposite in the Jewish curriculum. Sensitive educators concede the danger of curricular separatism and the consequent desirability of integrating secular and Jewish studies, but little progress has been made.[41]

In a recent book an Orthodox teacher and spokesperson makes the point most forcefully:

> There is at least one serious shortcoming in our educational philosophy. In our day schools and Yeshiva high schools, the curriculum is divided into *Limudei Kodesh* and *Limudei Hol,* sacred studies, the

teaching of Jewish subjects on the one hand, and secular studies of a general nature on the other. . . . The two areas of knowledge cannot be kept apart in the mind and soul of the student. If one may paraphrase the words of Maimonides from the Introduction to his *Guide for the Perplexed,* by this kind of educational process one either does violence to one's intellect by one's faith, or one violates one's faith by one's intellect.[42]

While this spokesperson expressed anguish over the problem, another scholar has observed: "The Conservative Movement in Judaism, and certainly the Reform Movement, is not at all preoccupied with the challenge of secular studies. This question is not dealt with on a philosophical basis in the publications of these movements, as neither of them recognizes a threat in the general studies, philosophy and sciences towards its conception of Judaism."[43] Both sides express desire to "build a bridge" and/or "integrate" the curricula, but little is said about how this would be done. It is not at all sure, moreover, whether all educators within the Orthodox movement see such "integration" as a good thing. As Bennett Solomon has pointed out, integration refers to much more than an articulation of curriculum materials. Issues such as the integration of secular and religious worlds and the integration of Judaism and Americanism within the life of the child are equally challenging goals. The aim is to achieve an "integrating individual" rather than an "integrated personality," a static form which leaves little space for what must remain as an ever unfinished task.[44]

What does integration mean? Is integration possible or desirable? Is the gap to be easily dismissed as nonthreatening as some Conservative spokespersons seem to think or is it to be raised as one of the basic paradoxes of the human condition, and confronted as such? While this area holds one of the most important challenges in education, it is also an area where we seem to have the least degree of understanding.

In a fine paper, Joseph Lukinsky "complicates" matters even further by pointing out the delicate nuances, trappings, and possibilities implied in integration. He calls for an open, fluid, undoctrinaire approach, always seeking for new insights, connections, and even the lack of them. The truth is ultimately one perhaps, but it is at the very least evasive. This is a verity we must learn to live with.[45]

FINANCING THE DAY SCHOOLS

While the day school movement continues to grow, with both schools and pupil enrollment increasing annually, the cost of maintaining such institutions has increased disproportionately. Tuition payments defray about 50 percent of the overall school budgets. The difference between tuition and school costs is made up through fund raising projects, individual endowments, federal assistance, and communal funding from congregations and Federations (the central fund-raising bodies of each constituted Jewish community throughout the United States).

Day school supporters have been turning increasingly to Federations as a major source for the additional funding needs.[46] The increasing readiness in the recent past on the part of Federations to help finance the day school movement represented a radical change in the attitude of the community towards what continues to be a minority phenomenon within Jewish life. Generally, Federation funding tends to subsidize a variety of activities that on the whole represent a much higher community consensus than is the case with the day school. A glowing example of this attitude or policy is the overwhelming portion of the total amount raised that goes to the State of Israel. The fact that the community as a whole had been ready to help the survival and growth of the day school showed that attitudes regarding the importance of full-time Jewish education had undergone basic qualitative changes. What was opposition, sometimes vicious, only a few years ago had become at the very least warm acceptance toward the day school. The practical consequence had been that a majority of parents who still would not have dreamed of sending their own children to a day school had been ready to help other Jewish parents to do so. In the last few years, however, the trend seems to be turning again, as Federation contributions to Jewish education have decreased on all fronts. This is a grave development and teacher salaries seem to have been the most serious victim of this disturbing trend.[47]

REASONS FOR THE GROWTH OF THE DAY SCHOOL

It is not easy to explain the fantastic growth of the day school movement. When studying reasons for this growth, given by a variety of authors, we soon have the feeling that often the reasons are mixed and perhaps confused with justifications. The American Jewish community feels that in some way or other it is going against the grain of contemporary American life by setting up and supporting the Jewish day schools. The growth of the day school has resulted more from a phenomenon of decrease in resistance, a giving in to growing evidence of inescapable need, than any real growth in enthusiasm. Even now, after all this impressive growth, only 13 percent of the total Jewish child population is going to Jewish day schools. Many leaders—such as prominent members of the Reform Movement—who until recently were dramatically against the day school and who championed the public school, today have changed their minds and stated their belief in the need for such an alternative within Jewish education. With evident reluctance but no less courage, an important leader of the Reform movement said as early as 1961: "We will likewise have at least to discuss the question of the Jewish day school. There is increasing dissatisfaction with the few hours instruction presently afforded in our congregational schools and, while the majority within our own movement may resist, for still a long time, any temptation to yield to the growing clamor for the day school, the trend to the parochial school is already making great inroads in the Conservative movement."[48] Similar statements, growing rapidly in confidence and boldness, have continued to emanate from a variety of sectors within the Reform movement. Local congregations have established a small number of Reform day schools.

Many others do not know which side to take in the Jewish day school/public school controversy and end by confusing the outside observer by adopting both sides of the issue and declaring deep enthusiasm for both systems of schooling. Rabbi Robert Gordis, a highly respected scholar within the Jewish community and a Conservative movement leader, makes the two following statements within the context of the same article: "I cannot conceive of meaningful survival of Judaism in America . . . without day schools as an integral element in the system of Jewish education." A few paragraphs later we read: "The day school, laudable as its objectives are, represents an act of separation from the general community. . . . If we stratify American life completely and permanently . . . the results are bound to be deleterious."[49]

The American Jewish Congress, one of the central American Jewish organizations, in a statement adopted in October 1966, declares in the same paper on the one hand that: "The A.J.C. believes that the Jewish community possesses the resources—intellectual, spiritual, financial—to support and sustain effective institutions of Jewish education. We urge . . . that local Jewish Federations and Welfare funds around the country—the traditional sources of support for meeting communal needs—include as beneficiaries in their allocations all forms of Jewish education, including Jewish day schools." Then later in the same statement we find the following: "We remain, as always, devoted to the American public school and its central role in the democratic process, and we shall continue our efforts to strengthen public education as an instrument for all American people."[50]

Whatever the possible rationalizations and explanations for the apparent discrepancies, these statements and others not quoted here express confusion both about the objectives and needs for day school education and the ideological value of the public school as part of the American system. They are probably a reflection of an age of change, when we are moving from an ideology favoring homogeneity to a greater tolerance of diversity, from an ideal of melting pot to an exploration of cultural pluralism, from an age deeply enthralled by reason to an exploration of myriad religious experiences. But these statements also reflect some of the dilemmas that torment the contemporary Jew and that have no easy resolution. As Michael Rosenak has observed: "Jewishly speaking, the less 'particularistic' a Jew is, the less 'parochial,' the more assimilated he tends to become. Conversely, the more 'Jewish' the less he tends to be concerned with society at large. We may say, today as well as in the nineteenth century, that 'good Jews' tend to be sectarian, whereas anti-sectarian Jews (i.e., those who take the world seriously) are often tempted to become non-Jews. . . . The dichotomy between our 'human' ideals and our 'Jewish' ones, which is almost unavoidable when the Jews constitute a congregational community rather than a society, poses a classical *Galut* [Exile] dilemma."[51]

For many Jews America was simply a place to escape persecution, discrimination, hunger, and the premature death that haunted their lives in the great centers of Eastern European Jewish life. For these Jews there was no justification powerful enough for a continued Jewish existence which could equal the sufferings they had had to bear because of their Jewishness. Thus many Jews "were led to think that the solution to human conflicts must lie beyond all particularisms and the last great task of the Jewish people would be to abdicate its own separate existence, thus supplying an example and model for Christianity."[52]

The profound ambiguities about the day school which we have explored above, represent a dramatic change in the attitudes of Jewish leadership as compared with statements and polls of only a few years before. Ambiguity in this case means a certain openness to change, an exploration, sometimes courageous, of old cliches and accepted forms of thought and action.

How did these changes come about? Why did the day school slowly but surely become an issue which could legitimately be discussed in most forums of Jewish communal life? How did the taboo against

private and separate education become challenged? A brief analysis
of the most important factors is outlined below.

1. Many authors feel it is safe to assume that the wartime and
postwar upsurge in religious sentiment in the United States helped
stimulate greater Jewish communal interest in Jewish education. As
we have already seen, this upsurge in religious sentiment apparently
was preceded in the thirties by a qualitative change in the self-perception of the American Jew. The Jew no longer sees himself necessarily
as an ethnic group, but rather as a religious group, or even more
sophisticatedly as a "religious civilization" as described by Mordecai
Kaplan.[53] This might have been a safer category to be included in,
one more acceptable to many sectors of the American public, rather
wary of "foreigners" during the period before and following the First
World War. Being a safer category in terms of external threats, it
might have made the Jew more comfortable in his/her niche and
therefore readier to act on his/her own behalf. Louis Katzoff writing
in 1949 stated that: "It then follows that the theory of cultural pluralism need not come into the generally accepted Conservative thought
process. Since Judaism *is* a religion, and fits into the pattern of American Democracy despite its civilizational characteristics, it need not
have a recourse to the thesis of cultural pluralism—which is secular in
essence—in order to justify its perpetuation. So long as the synagogue
is *central,* Judaism theoretically stands on a firm foundation in con-
firming its existence and in furthering Jewish life in America."[54]
Katzoff speaks of justification, a clear indication of the importance
the Jewish community has given to their image in the outside world,
whatever their internal condition. This would seem to indicate that in
the years that followed the Second World War and even some years
before it, Kallen's theory of cultural pluralism in itself was no longer
adequate justification for nonassimilationist streams within American
Jewish life. It would gain new life in the late fifties and sixties, fueled
by the Civil Rights movement and the black awakening. Dushkin,
however, argues that the upsurge in religious sentiment that followed
the war cannot explain it all because while the day school increased
over 135 percent in the period between 1945 and 1946, in the same
period nonpublic Catholic and Protestant schools only increased 60
percent.[55]

But religious revival there was, fed by the spread of Hitlerism, the
desolation of war, and the collapse of many socialist dreams. It was
increasingly difficult to remain unaffiliated, and with the death of so
many secular gods it seemed to be time to probe more traditional
routes. Handlin expressed this in lyrical terms: "Sinking back into the

pillowed round of ritual, the disillusioned puffed up new illusions, created a romantic vision of the old ghetto, a secure and self-contained place of piety and good deeds, and longed to be taken back."[56]

The Orthodox section of the community suspected the depth of this so-called religious revival and saw it more as a threat than good news. Curiously enough they found reasons in this perceived threat to give greater emphasis to the day school. Emmanuel Rackman argued that: "To prevent the institutionalized synagogue from turning Judaism into a Temple cult and the rabbi into a public relations man, Orthodoxy today is transferring its prime emphasis from the synagogue to the school—preferably to a yeshiva [Orthodox day school]. This shift of emphasis is in part a kind of holding operation, aimed at recreating an elite of scholars who will preserve Judaism through a period of agnosticism and nonobservance."[57]

For one group within American Jewish life it was the return to religion that opened the way for more day schools. For another group it was what they perceived as the ritualization of religion that moved them to give extra impetus to the day school movement.

2. The prosperity of the postwar era made possible the establishment of many schools and increased the probability of their support and maintenance. This is partially a good explanation, but, again, it was not only the lack of money that was stopping prewar Jewry from setting up their own schools. Moreover, postwar Jewry could perfectly well have sent their children to private schools instead of getting involved in the complex process of setting up a school system of their own.

3. Certainly the example set by the early pioneers by creating schools almost singlehandedly during the first part of the twentieth century had a deep effect. The success of these schools paired with the increasing disillusionment with the poor accomplishments of supplementary Jewish education led many parents, not fully committed to the day school idea, to send their children to this type of school. Irving Greenberg expressed the problem in ironic terms: "We must reckon [with] student and teacher lateness and absences; the ballet lesson and dentist appointments that receive first priority; the host of distractions and interruptions. . . ; the fact that [such schools] are generally of marginal concern to rabbis upon whom congregations place . . . a host of other rabbinical obligations. . . ; the frequent lack of commitment of teachers and administrators. . . ; the frequent absence of standardized and/or properly evaluated curricula."[58] In 1959 the Dushkin-Engelman study could report: "Evidently, Jewish educators are right in insisting that *our problem is no longer that of getting*

our children to Jewish school, but rather of having them stay in the schools long enough to make that education valuable."[59]

4. Two momentous occurrences in Jewish history probably had a profound effect on the growth of the day school movement. One was the creation of the State of Israel in 1948 which brought about both the resurgence of an intense pride in identification with Jewish life and a burning interest in having closer ties with the newborn state. This implied the acquisition of a more thorough knowledge of Hebrew and the traditions as tools for that new joyful relationship. The day school seemed to be the institution would be able to supply these tools. Although writing only a couple of years ago and referring to the specific effects of the Six Day War (1967), Michael Rosenak characterized well the quality of the relationship between Israel and American Jewry as it had developed over the years, culminating in the aftermath of the war:

> Paradoxically, the Six-Day War and the Jewish response likewise testified to the sense of security and "belongingness" enjoyed by Jews in America. They felt free to express their fears, their relief, and their triumph without worrying overmuch how much "non-religious" (in the Protestant sense) emotions would be received by their fellow Americans. Their unabashed reactions to what was transpiring in Israel, their open admission of what that meant for *them,* indicated that, perhaps for the first time, American Jews *as Jews* were willing to acknowledge and to articulate the concrete "space dimension" of Jewish existence and commitment and its quasi-political dimensions."[60]

Perhaps such feelings were more subdued before 1967, but they were there, growing quietly and changing the relationship of American Jews with America.

The second occurrence was the Nazi Holocaust which destroyed the great majority of European Jewry. Schiff expresses the rather detached view that "American Jewry came to the realization that the American Jewish community could no longer depend upon Eastern Europe as a source of Jewish creativity, scholarship, and religious leadership."[61] In this new situation the day school would become the training ground for future Jewish leadership. Although valid, this explanation seems to avoid the rather haunting question as to the deeper impact which the Holocaust might have had on the Jewish psyche, and its possible effects in stimulating more intensive Jewish education. Emil Fackenheim, the Jewish theologian expresses, it seems to me, in dramatic terms these deeper effects:

The Jew is singled out for special contradictions. In America he enjoys a freedom and security unparalleled in history; yet he is but twenty years separated from the greatest and as yet uncomprehended Jewish catastrophe. His trust and joy in the modern secular world cannot but coexist with radical distrust and profound sorrow. Authentic Jewish religious witness in this age must both face up to Auschwitz and yet refuse a despair of this world which, wholly contrary to Judaism, would hand still another victory to the forces of radical evil. Insofar as he is committed to Jewish survival, the Jew has already taken a stand against these forces. But survival—for survival's sake—is an inadequate stand. The Jew can go beyond it only if he can reopen the quest of Jeremiah and Job, who for all their agony refused to despair either of God or the world.[62]

The Jew cannot any longer trust the world and yet he/she knows they must learn to trust again. Where can this trust be found, rebuilt, nurtured? For some, for many, understanding and the rebirth of the self cannot be anywhere else but at the source itself: the Jewish tradition, pulled out of the closet of memories and nostalgia and confronted again with profound dedication and unwavering loyalty.

5. The post-World War II immigration undoubtedly also had notable effects. Many of these immigrants were intensely religious and as Marshall Sklare writes:

> They came out of necessity rather than choice. They were firmly committed to giving primacy to Jewish culture. Unlike their Orthodox predecessors in the United States they disdained conformity to American culture and even took pride in their refusal to conform to the prevailing culture in such externals as dress and hairstyle. In fact, their version of the American dream was that they should have the freedom to reestablish the way of life they had enjoyed before the holocaust. Thus without hesitation they proceeded to organize their own schools—schools that would give primacy to Jewish culture and shield their children and others from the influence of the secularism of the public schools.[63]

Their example and success no doubt spilled over, and convinced many of the value of Jewish education. The Holocaust survivors were and are a special breed. Silent, achievement-oriented, they have had the feeling that they owe the world nothing, that they have paid their price so as to be permitted to do almost anything in their own specific way. They are not trying to convince anybody of their goodness or of their right to certain behaviors or actions. To exorcise their perennial nightmares they have worked hard, incessantly and compulsively, and have excelled and accrued great achievements in almost any field with which they have become involved. It has been their silent efforts, sometimes guided by mysterious aims, coupled with the pained impact the Holocaust has had on American Jewry that has brought about a dramatic and growing commitment to full-time Jewish education.[64]

6. The failure of the public school plus the urban patterns of migration, with many blacks coming into the innercity and Jews moving out into the suburbs, also had a great impact. For most of these Jews the logical eduational choice would have seemed to be a nonsectarian private school. But these were difficult to find, so many parents chose to send their children to day schools instead, where they often found superior physical facilities and an ecumenical approach to all segments of the Jewish community.[65] For Jews the failure of the public school was not only characterized by the deterioration of discipline, quality of teachers, or juvenile delinquency. Rather, in the past the public school was supposed to be the place that would meld ethnic and cultural differences. This does not occur any longer as it did when the Jews lived in crowded heterogeneous urban centers. Today Jewish children attend public schools with children of similar racial, economic, and social backgrounds. The only thing that differentiates these children is their religion. That is a difference that carries no importance in the context of public education. As Philip Arian has suggested: "Since the public school-Hebrew school (part-time Jewish school) framework is a product of a past relationship it behooves us to question whether this framework is appropriate for our day. We need to evolve a rationale for the relationship of today between our being American and our being Jewish even as the concepts of melting pot and cultural pluralism projected for former days."[66]

Some Jews were going beyond all this and questioning the very basic goals and ideals of the public school. Marvin Fox wrote in 1953: "Hebrew day school must be candidly explicit in announcing that it is committed to a particular set of values which are embodied in Jewish religion and rooted in the whole of established Jewish tradition."[67] He was arguing against the current philosophy and practice of "value-free" education and making it clear that he was against the Jewish day school becoming something like an expanded copy of the public school, adding to an identical secular curriculum for both schools some hours of Bible and Hebrew language. He wanted a genuinely distinctive Jewish school opposing the strong trend in public schools in line with scientific naturalism. Fox claimed that this philosophy was taking over the school system as some new gospel, threatening with a new kind of intellectual totalitarianism. He saw the day school as one place where the struggle against the disregard for intellectual values would take place and where intellectual achievements would occupy a more honored position. He called for a revival of the classical Jewish values of learning for its own sake and felt that the Jewish day school could demonstrate how Judaism reconciled human equality with reverence for authority. He also saw the day school as an important bulwark against the terrible moral confusion of our time, and felt that the development of moral sensitivity was something the public school could not do.

It took courage to make this affirmation, but maybe the time had come. Sklare explains: "Until the nineteen-forties parochial education constituted a heretical idea. Obedience to the American system of public education was a religious commandment. By the post-World War II era there had emerged a group of first, second, and third generation Jews who felt safe enough as Americans to reject public education. Unlike their predecessors they did not require the common school in order to validate their American identity."[68]

7. An additional and very important reason for the growth of the day school is no doubt the great concern that exists among American Jewry over the declining Jewish birthrate and the great increase in intermarriage. To this we can add the evident alienation among younger Jews and the widespread "Jewry identity crisis." This can all be packaged under one label: concern with Jewish survival. Most Jewish parents are painfully conscious that they do not have the tools or sometimes the will to play a role in stemming these developments and have turned over this task either to the synagogue or to the school.[69]

8. On a more philosophical level, Zevi Scharfstein attributes the greater openness to Jewish education to the classical conflict between generations. Comparing the immigrant generation with those that followed, Scharfstein felt that it was much easier now to establish a Jewish school than during the peak immigration period. He thought that the immigrants were perplexed and frightened, and with the old and new wrestling in their hearts they did not know how to combine their past and present. Some chose the old ways, others severed all links with their own past. Further, Scharfstein remarked:

They and their children became separated by a great rift—not of ideology, which sometimes is fruitful, but of distrust and disrespect. The second generation which had lost the culture of the fathers was cut off without having acquired the new culture except in its out-

ward features, and these mostly distorted. They had no need for
Jewish education. And the third generation is getting lost in search
of itself and its way in life. They resent their emptiness and carry a
grudge against their parents who denied them the understanding
of their cultural roots. They look for leaders.[70]

Scharfstein concluded therefore that many of the impediments
against Jewish schooling were gone. The situation, he believed, was
ripe for a dramatic growth in the number of educational institutions.

OPPOSITION AND CRITICISM OF THE DAY SCHOOL

Although open opposition to the day school within the context of
the organized Jewish community is rapidly dwindling, there are still
many circles that express legitimate fears as to the possible consequences of a very developed system of Jewish day schools. Most of
these fears are centered around the fact that Jews might face the
danger of isolating themselves again, thus doing a serious disservice
to American democracy but also, on a more pragmatic ground, offering Protestants and Catholics too good an example to follow. Behind
this looms the spectre of the revival of anti-Semitism as a consequence
of that isolation. Paradoxically, anti-Semitism has been a factor in
both stimulating the growth of the day school and an argument
against it. Many parents see a good Jewish education as a tool to
struggle against anti-Semitism, should it ever reassert itself in some
vicious form, while the opponents of the day school see its isola-
tionism as a stimulant of anti-Semitic prejudice. Himmelfarb wrote in
1964: "For Jews, America is the open and hospitable country that it is
because the public school expresses its true spirit. They see the public
school as simultaneously an instrument for individual progress and
the symbol of a benign inclusive national ideal. They take *e pluribus
unum* seriously and they take pluralism seriously, and for them the
public school is a kind of quintessential America which has succeeded
remarkably well in reconciling the two."[71]

There are also what we could call political-survivalist arguments as
the one made by David Singer: "Public education brings Jews into the
mainstream of American life and thus closer to those levels of power
which determine both individual and group status; obviously, a
strong case for the public school can be made precisely on the
grounds of Jewish group interest."[72] Jack Cohen feels that "the act of
isolation can just as easily distort [the pupils'] view of America, ren-

dering them unfit to participate in a pluralistic society, destroying their capacity to be objective about cultural differences between themselves and their neighbors, and depriving them of the ability of self-criticism."[73] As we have seen earlier, this argument has been partially refuted by demographic changes. On more positive ground Cohen believes that the public school will suffer great damage if the more talented Jewish clientele leaves its fold. Himmelfarb did not agree that there would be damage to the public school as a consequence of the Jewish day school movement.[74] Cohen, on the other hand, maintained that "the removal of superior students from the public school in a local area can often have profound consequences on the curriculum of public school in that area. Good students who remain are frequently unable to have the special programs which the presence of just a few more students on their level would be able to secure them. Moreover the local parent groups are deprived of the participation of highly competent men whose help is needed to secure improvements in the public school."[75] This argument, raised in 1964, seems all the more interesting in our time when we are witness to the serious decay of the public school.

SOME ADDITIONAL AND FINAL THOUGHTS

The paradox created by the Jewish day school, the ambiguous feelings of the Jewish community, its desire for change and permanence, its wish to become part of America and still be faithful to its own past, its pride in a newly discovered world, and its fear for its own waning identities are all marvelously expressed as early as 1920 in Isaac Berkson's *Theories of Americanization*. In his book Berkson attempted to find rationales for the survival of Judaism in a world open to alternatives, but wary of difference.[76]

Berkson visualized democracy almost as a new religion and accepted Darwinism as proof that the conception of absolute values and purposes could not be held as true. Relativism, claims Berkson, is the only tenable position. The point of departure cannot but be the individual in his own situation.

Berkson might have exaggerated. Judaism could not survive theologically within the framework that he had created for himself. Was this Berkson's "sacrifice" in order to make Judaism an acceptable alternative in America? After all, serious Darwinism made Genesis obsolete and thus the Jewish religion could not possibly overlap with democracy as a form of religion. Moreover, a truly religious system could not possibly accept relativism as a premise nor the individual as point of departure in any philosophical analysis.

Paradoxically, after what appears as almost an act of suicide as a Jew, Berkson proceeds to surprise his readers by making an unyielding defense for the right of survival of Jews as a group preserving both their religious and cultural heritage. After rejecting theories such as Americanization (which emphasized the Anglo-Saxon contribution as model for the ideal American), the Melting Pot theory (which called for the integration of all groups into a new American identity, while giving up their own), the Federation of Communities theory (a federative system of ethnic groups, all living side by side), Berkson proposed a Community theory which, while leaving aside all racial connotations, made the basis for the life of every ethnic group its own culture, freely transmitted from generation to generation through the school which was to become the center of community life.[77]

The same man who had called democracy the new religion and enthusiastically embraced Darwin's view of evolution also wrote: "The central idea in Jewish life is Torah. In legend and in literature, it is for the sake of the Torah that Israel was called into being; it is for the sake of Torah that Israel has been spared annihilation. . . . It was the Torah that was revealed from Sinai. It was for the sake of the Torah that Israel entered the Promised Land. It was because Israel sinned against the Torah that he was exiled."[78] No Orthodox Jew could have put it more emphatically. It is very difficult to reconcile—and is indicative of the times—the first and second series of Berkson's ideological statements.

While Berkson seemed to have understood that it would take a very complex and sophisticated school system to bring about his Community theory, he could not reconcile in his mind the existence of both Catholic parochial schools and Jewish day schools. While defending the right of existence of day schools on rather feeble arguments such as that they were under "lay control" and that only a "fraction of one percent of Jewish children attend parochial school," he strongly attacked the Catholics for wanting to establish a system of parochial schools which he saw as educationally constricting. He did feel that the Jewish day school would also disappear once the public schools better accomplished their role and saw the ideal solution in the setting up of complementary schools to function side by side with the public school.[79]

Although Jews seemed to have explored all the possibilities of adaptation to America, they never were ready to *assert* any position until some other group preceded them down that road. There has been a fear of selfishness, an almost morbid altruism. As a group the Jews seem to have been always too ready to sacrifice their own identities for "some higher ideal" that rarely comes to be. Perhaps it is fear, simple, instinctive, primeval, ingrained through centuries of persecution and death, which has not given the Jew enough freedom to assert him/herself.

A second important element that has limited the growth and development of an original Judaism in America has been the lack of faith that American Jewry has had in being able to make a contribution to American culture without first alientating its own values. Jewish creativity in America has been limited to the creation of Jewish institutions and a literature of limited outreach. All other creativity by Jews as individuals has been expression of painful alientations, often deeply significant, but no longer Jewishly rooted. There have been no attempts to create Jewishly from within, by absorbing in organic fashion from the American environment and experiences and sublimating them into new expressions legitimately rooted and continuous with the historical tradition. Schools have a special opportunity for experimenting in this area, and democracy offers the most legitimate opportunity to do so in more than two millenia. For some reason Jews have not had the confidence to prove democracy right in one of its utmost qualities.

A third important factor is that until recently Jews have not had the courage to confront the threatening possibility that their existence as a group with certain beliefs, might be incongruous within the accepted conceptual frameworks of the contemporary Western world. A modern Jewish writer claims: "Modernity is not only a condition, but an ideology. As an ideology, it stands in opposition to Jewish understandings, and therefore in tension with them." "This tension," writes Leonard Fein, "along with the way Jewish Americans respond to it, provides the central ideological context within which Jewish education takes place, and the failure to acknowledge it is a continuing source of educational confusion."[80] For Fein, modernity seeks to be rational, while Judaism remains partially mysterious; modernity is committed to Universalism while Judaism sees as a priority a commitment to other Jews, and, while modernity invokes achievement, "Judaic tribalism" retains a significant measure of ascription.

As Berkson before him, Fein makes the point that in America "one of the most startling psychological consequences of modernity [read democracy in Berkson] has been the transformation of personal identity into an area of option, where people are not only permitted but actually encouraged to choose who it is they want to be. . . . The American alternative has been all the more attractive to Jews because of America's persistent flirtation with the doctrine of election, with the notion that America is the new Promised Land, and, by implication, Americans the new Chosen People."[81]

Both Fein and Berkson seem to be discussing the same problem, but both arrive at different conclusions. Berkson's was a valiant attempt to close the gap between Judaism and modernity; Fein rejects such a possibility. He writes, "Many Jews, despite their enthusiastic embrace of ideological modernity, find themselves still inexplicably encumbered by a residual core of Jewish instinct." We cannot imagine Berkson talking in such terms. When he was writing in the twenties such thoughts would have probably been qualified as racial heresy. Fein recognizes the advantages of writing from his position when he says: "American secularism is no longer so compelling an alternative to Judaism. . . . The demythologization of America . . . has forced people to begin to examine other alternatives." The consequences for education arising from this analysis follow easily: "A primary deprivation of the present generation of Jewish children is in the area of instinct . . . substantially greater attention needs to be paid the development of a Judaic id (Juidism?) and less, relatively, to the development of a Judaic superego . . . conscious attention to the development of instinct will help to bring about something else . . . the education system must become the site for a set of Jewish experiences of the sort that might be available in 'real' life were the family and the community not so weak as they have become."[82]

Fein does not analyze what the consequences of such a bold scheme could be for American Jewry and how such a focus could assure the active participation in Jewry in American democratic life. What Fein's article does indicate, nonetheless, is possibly a new attitude among some of the more liberal leaders of the Jewish community in giving controversial Jewish concerns a high place in the list of priorities, without questioning to an exaggerated degree what the consequences will be in relation to the outside world. This attitude, if exaggerated, could be dangerous; but if never employed in the analytical process, it becomes a serious weakness both in the philosophizing and planning stages of any attempt at imaginative community development.

NOTES

1. Alvin Irwin Schiff, *The Jewish Day School in America* (New York: Jewish Education Committee, 1966); "Decline in Rolls at Jewish Schools Found Slow-

ing," *New York Times,* 27 December 1976; Alexander Dushkin and Uriah Engelman, *Jewish Education in the United States,* Report of the Commission for the Study of Jewish Education in the United States, 1959, vol. 1 (New York: American Association for Jewish Education, 1959), p. 60; and American Association for Jewish Education, *Jewish School Census 1978/1979* (New York: American Association for Jewish Education, 1979).

2. *Encyclopedia of Education,* 5th ed., s.v. "Jewish Education."

3. J. Milton Yinger, "Social Forces Involved in Group Identification or Withdrawal," *Daedalus* 90 (Spring 1961): 255.

4. Simon Greenberg, "The Religious Policy of the Solomon Schechter Day School," *Synagogue School* 24 (Spring 1966): 12.

5. Joseph L. Blau, *Judaism in America—From Curiosity to Third Faith* (Chicago: The University of Chicago Press, 1976), p. 101.

6. Ibid., p. 102.

7. "Decline in Rolls at Jewish Schools Found Slowing," *New York Times,* 27 December 1976; American Association for Jewish Education, *Jewish School Census 1978/1979* (New York: American Association for Jewish Education, 1979).

8. Walter I. Ackerman, "Jewish Education—For What?" *American Jewish Year Book* 70 (1969): 17–18.

9. Oscar Handlin, *Adventure in Freedom—Three Hundred Years of Jewish Life in America* (New York: McGraw-Hill Book Company, Inc., 1954), p. 70.

10. Ibid., p. 71.

11. Hyman B. Grinstein, "In the Course of the Nineteenth Century," in *A History of Jewish Education in America,* ed. Judah Pilch (New York: American Association for Jewish Education, 1969), p. 30.

12. Ibid., p. 34.

13. Howard Morley Sachar, *The Course of Modern Jewish History* (New York: Dell Publishing Co., 1958), p. 311.

14. Ibid., p. 315.

15. Handlin, *Adventure in Freedom—Three Hundred Years of Jewish Life in America,* pp. 144, 157ff.

16. Milton M. Gordon, "Assimilation in America: Theory and Reality," *Daedalus* 90 (Spring 1961): 269.

17. Handlin, *Adventure in Freedom—Three Hundred Years of Jewish Life in America,* p. 116.

18. Oscar Janowsky, ed., *The American Jew—A Reappraisal* (Philadelphia: The Jewish Publication Society, 1967), p. 128.

19. A recent authoritative study questions whether many of the traditionally inclined immigrants can be described as anything more than nominally Orthodox. See Charles S. Liebman, "Orthodoxy in American Jewish Life," *American Jewish Year Book* 66 (1965): 27–28.

20. Milton Himmelfarb, "Those Catholic Schools," in *The Jews of Modernity,* ed. Milton Himmelfarb (New York: Basic Books, Inc., 1973), p. 161.

21. Marshall Sklare, *America's Jews* (New York: Random House, 1971), p. 157.

22. Blau, *Judaism in America—From Curiosity to Third Faith,* p. 46.

23. John Higham, *Send Those to Me—Jews and Other Immigrants in Urban America* (New York: Atheneum, 1975), chap. 4 passim. In this masterly chap-

ter Higham makes the point that our stereotyped image of immigration—
shared by Emma Lazarus in her immortal poem "The New Colossus" written
in 1881—as almost a welcome phenomenon in the America of the dying
nineteenth century is rather distant from the truth. Discussions about the
meaning of the Statue of Liberty at its inauguration (1881) never referred to
the fact that America had been built on immigration and an open border
policy. Instead speeches tended to refer abstractly to the concept of liberty
and other philosophical niceties. Lazarus' poem in fact, so poignantly pointing to the dramatic and compassionate meaning of immigration was totally
ignored until the 1930s, and it was only then that a small plaque with the
poem was laid at the statue.

24. David Sanford Cohen, "American Reform Judaism and the Jewish Day
School" (Master's thesis, Hebrew University, Jerusalem, Israel, 1974).

25. Nathan H. Winter, *Jewish Education in a Pluralist Society: Samson Benderly
and Jewish Education in the United States* (New York: New York University
Press, 1966), p. 48.

26. Israel Zangwill, *The Melting Pot* (New York: Macmillan, 1909), p. 37.
"America is God's crucible, the great Melting Pot where all races of Europe
are melting and reforming! Here you stand, good folk, think I, when I see
them at Ellis Island, here you stand in your fifty groups, with your fifty
languages and histories, and your fifty blood hatreds and rivalries. But you
won't be long like that, brothers, for these are the fires of God you've come
to—these are the fires of God. A fig for your feuds and vendettas! Germans
and Frenchmen, Irishmen and Englishmen, Jews and Russians—into the
Crucible with you all! God is making the American."

27. Arthur A. Goren, *New York Jews and the Quest for Community—The Keh-
illah Experiment, 1908–1922* (New York: Columbia University Press, 1970),
p. 4.

28. Higham, *Send These to Me—Jews and Other Immigrants in Urban America,*
pp. 199–200.

29. Horace M. Kallen, "Democracy Versus The Melting Pot," *The Nation,*
25 February 1915, pp. 217–20, as it appears in John J. Appel, ed., *The New
Immigration* (New York: Jerome S. Ozer Publishing Corporation, 1971), p.
111.

30. Ibid.

31. Judah Pilch, "Jewish Educational Philosophy," in *Judaism and the Jewish
School,* ed. Judah Pilch and Meir Ben-Horin (New York: Bloch Publishing Co.
and American Association for Jewish Education, 1966), p. 107.

32. Will Herberg, *Protestant-Catholic-Jew, An Essay in American Religious So-
ciology,* rev. ed. (New York: Doubleday & Co., 1960).

33. Alter R. Landesman, *Brownsville—The Birth, Development, and Passing of
a Jewish Community in New York* (New York: Bloch Publishing Co., 1969),
p. 155.

34. Isaac M. Fein, *The Making of an American Jewish Community—The History
of Baltimore Jewry from 1773 to 1920* (Philadelphia: The Jewish Publication
Society of America, 1971), pp. 191–92.

35. Schiff, *The Jewish Day School in America,* chaps. 5 and 6 passim; Amy
Malzberg, *Jewish Day Schools in the United States* (New York: Jewish Communal
Affairs Department, The American Jewish Committee, 1971), pp. 5–9; Hillel

Hockberg, "Trends and developments in Jewish Education," *American Jewish Year Book* 73 (1972): 194–235; Jewish Telegraphic Agency Report, n.p. 1973, supplying statistical data on the state of the day school in America; Dushkin and Engelman, *Jewish Education in the United States,* p. 60; Daniel J. Elazar, *Community and Polity—The Organizational Dynamics of American Jewry* (Philadelphia: The Jewish Publication Society of America, 1976), pp. 290–333; "Decline in Rolls at Jewish Schools Found Slowing," *New York Times,* 27 December 1976.

36. Dushkin and Engelman, *Jewish Education in the United States,* pp. 155–56.

37. Ibid., p. 55.

38. Schiff, *The Jewish Day School in America,* chap. 8 passim.

39. William W. Brickman, "Education for Eternal Existence: The Philosophy of Jewish Education" in *Judaism and the Jewish School,* ed. Judah Pilch and Meir Ben-Horin (New York: Block Publishing Co. and American Association for Jewish Education, 1966), p. 207.

40. Ben Zion Bokser, *Solomon Schechter Day School Education and the Conservative Movement* (New York: Solomon Schechter Day School Association Resource Library pamphlet 105, n.d.).

41. Marshall Sklare, *America's Jews* (New York: Random House, 1971), p. 168.

42. Eliezer Berkovits, *Crisis and Faith* (New York: Sanhedrin Press, 1976), p. 169.

43. Aaron Nussbaum, "The Integrated Curriculum in the Conservative School," *Igeret* 3 (May 1968): 1.

44. Bennett I. Solomon, "A Critical Review of the Term 'Integration' in the Literature on the Jewish Day School in America," *Jewish Education* 46 (Winter 1978): 4.

45. Joseph Lukinsky, "Integrating Jewish and General Studies in the Day School: Philosophy and Scope," in *Integrative Learning: The Search for Unity in Jewish Day School Programs—Proceedings of an Invitational Working Conference,* ed. Max Nadel (New York: American Association for Jewish Education, 1978), p. 1.

46. Elazar, *Community and Polity—The Organizational Dynamics of American Jewry,* p. 333.

47. American Association for Jewish Education, *Budgeting and Financing in Jewish Day Schools 1979–80–81* (New York: American Association for Jewish Education, 1981).

48. Cohen, "American Reform Judaism and the Jewish Day School," p. 52.

49. Rabbi Robert Gordis, "The Day School and the Public School: A Strategy for Jewish Survival Today," reprinted from *Congress Bi-Weekly,* (New York: American Jewish Congress, n.d.).

50. "Where We Stand on Jewish Education," A Statement of the American Jewish Congress adopted in New York, October 1966 (mimeographed).

51. Michael Rosenak, "On the Teaching of Israel in Jewish Schools," *Jewish Education* 42 (Winter 1972–73): 9.

52. Michael E. Meyer, "Beyond Particularism: On Ethical Culture and the Reconstructionists," *Commentary* 51 (March 1971): 72. See also Handlin, *Adventure in Freedom—Three Hundred Years of Jewish Life in America,* p. 246.

53. Mordecai M. Kaplan, *Unity in Diversity in the Conservative Movement* (New York: United Synagogue of America 1947), pp. 14–15.

54. Louis Katzoff, *Issues in Jewish Education—A Study of the Philosophy of the Conservative Congregational School* (New York: Bloch Publishing Co., 1949), p. 102.

55. Dushkin and Engelman, *Jewish Education in the United States*, p. 50.

56. Handlin, *Adventure in Freedom—Three Hundred Years of Jewish Life in America*, p. 248.

57. Emmanuel Rackman, "Institutionalized Cult or Congregations of the Learned?" in *Judaism and the Jewish School*, ed. Judah Pilch and Meir Ben-Horin (New York: Bloch Publishing Co. and American Association for Jewish Education, 1966), p. 224.

58. Irving Greenberg, "Jews or Zombies," *Boston Jewish Advocate*, 20 September 1966.

59. Dushkin and Engelman, *Jewish Education in the United States*, p. 226.

60. Rosenak, "On the Teaching of Israel in Jewish Schools," p. 11.

61. Schiff, *The Jewish Day School in America*, p. 76.

62. Emil L. Fackenheim, "On the Self-Exposure of Faith to the Modern-Secular World," *Daedalus* 96 (Winter 1967): 193.

63. Sklare, *America's Jews*, p. 170.

64. Dorothy Rabinowitz, *New Lives—Survivors of the Holocaust Living in America* (New York: Alfred A. Knopf, 1976).

65. David Singer, "The Growth of the Day-School Movement," *Commentary* 56 (August 1973): 53–57.

66. Philip Arian, "Realities and Challenges Facing Jewish Education in the 70s," in *Jewish Education in the 70s: Challenge and Promise* (New York: Yearbook Educators Assembly of the United Synagogue of America, 1970), p. 6.

67. Marvin Fox, "Day Schools and the American Educational Pattern," *The Jewish Parent*, September 1953, p. 12.

68. Sklare, *America's Jews*, pp. 169–70.

69. Singer, "The Growth of the Day-School Movement," pp. 53–57.

70. Zevi Scharfstein, "Preparing the Hearts for Jewish Education," in *Judaism and the Jewish School*, ed. Judah Pilch and Meir Ben-Horin (New York: Block Publishing Co. and American Association for Jewish Education, 1966), p. 141.

71. Himmelfarb, *The Jews of Modernity*, p. 162.

72. Singer, "The Growth of the Day-School Movement," p. 57.

73. Jack J. Cohen, *Jewish Education in Democratic Society* (New York: The Reconstructionist Press, 1964), p. 310.

74. Milton Himmelfarb, "Reflections on the Jewish Day School," *Commentary* 30 (July 1960): 29.

75. Cohen, *Jewish Education in Democratic Society*, p. 301.

76. Berkson, *Theories of Americanization—A Critical Study with Special Reference to the Jewish Group*.

77. Berkson himself makes the point: all four theories were proposed by Jews.

78. Berkson, *Theories of Americanization—A Critical Study with Special Reference to the Jewish Group*, p. 100.

79. Ibid., pp. 153–59.

80. Leonard J. Fein, "Suggestions Toward the Reform of Jewish Education in America," *Midstream* 18 (February 1972): 41.

81. Ibid., p. 44. No attempt is being made at equating modernity with democracy. Nevertheless there are some valid overlapping elements in Berkson's and Fein's utilization of these two terms.

82. Ibid., p. 46.

Part Two

Contemporary Concerns

Chapter 7

Reflections on the Continuing Crusade for Common Schools: Glorious Failures, Shameful Harvests, or . . . ?

CHARLES R. KNIKER

In a society in which one out of four persons typically spends Monday through Friday, September through May, in school, it is difficult to imagine that there was a time in American history when there was extensive debate about the importance of formal education. But debate there was. As late as the 1870s there were sporadic efforts to resist the formation of the common or free public schools.[1]

By the 1830s, however, a number of Americans in the youthful republic believed that some type of state-sponsored educational institution was needed to supplement the few excellent private academies and to replace the many inadequate schools and female seminaries. In 1837 a brilliant forty-year-old attorney, Horace Mann, gave up a promising political career to become Massachusetts' first Secretary of the Board of Education. He correctly foresaw that he would encounter jealousy, misrepresentation, and prejudice as he introduced a new common school system, but he could write: "If I do not succeed in it, I will lay claim at least to the benefit of the saying, that in great attempts it is glorious even to fail."[2]

From our perspective, Mann and others who came to be identified as "friends of education" achieved a number of glorious successes. In their time they were more aware of the opposition of the powerful, the lethargy of the timid, and the bickerings of those who already had or who dreamed of having alternative schooling systems. Those whose preferred curriculum had been shunted aside were particularly critical. Ten years after Mann had made his initial proposals for

169

the common school, Mathew Hale Smith, a Boston clergyman, attacked him in print. Criticizing the public schools for divorcing Bible studies from instruction, prohibiting sectarian religious texts, and substituting reason for the rod, Smith was certain the fledgling institution had already produced a "shameful harvest" of rebellion and crime.[3]

Who was right? Were the relationships of defenders of public education and advocates of religious schooling typically this strained? Did (and do) the public schools have a unique mission which religious schools cannot and should not imitate? In sum, a major educational question facing America today is what reasons justify a common school system? This essay attempts to answer those questions. To do so it reviews the five major "expectations" given historically for the development of the common school system (a term replaced gradually by "public schools").[4] Promoters of common schools believed that the new form of education would provide:

- training in common citizenship skills
- a common creed (i.e., transmission of widely held values)
- common experiences (mixing peoples of diverse backgrounds so that unity could be promoted)
- common opportunities for unequal persons (especially members of different social and economic classes)
- commonly agreed to reforms to improve society through the solution of social problems.

Each of these five expectations or goals will be treated in terms of how it was initially perceived and introduced (origins), how it evolved in terms of curriculum and student behaviors (objectives), and how public and religious schools and their leaders reacted to the implicit or explicit criticisms against religious schools embedded in the expectations, especially when it was tied to research studies (outcomes). The debates on these five issues and the degrees of cooperation or competition between public and private schools over the years is a story which is disturbingly contemporary. A final section considers some of the latest developments in the relationship between public and religious schools and suggests that a new expectation may have to be formulated.

Five general comments should be made at the outset to explain the title of this essay. First, for whatever consolation it may bring American education—public and private—has always been the victim of extensive and often unwarranted criticism. It cannot be otherwise in a country which has liberty as its cornerstone. Our institutional "bricks" are mortared by uneasy alliances not conformity. The staunchest defenders of public and private education in *every period* of American history perceived they were being attacked and prepared elaborate rationales for their systems.

Second, buttressed by recollections of Thomas Nast's anti-Catholic cartoons it is easy to conclude that common school admirers and parochial school supporters were constantly at war. While there is no doubt that genuine conflicts have existed, a careful reading of primary documents indicates that, especially at the local level, individuals and groups were more inclined to reasonable accommodation than unbending encounter. State legislators, more often than not, have been concerned that students receive a basic education and have cared less whether it was in a publicly or privately sponsored school.

Third, the adjective "common" is worthy of reappropriation. Both historically and currently it embodies the most critical dimensions of the rationale for government-sponsored schooling. As Justice H. S. Orton wrote in the Edgerton, Wisconsin, case in 1890:

> The common schools are free to all alike, to all nationalities, to all sects or religions, to all ranks of society, and to all complexions. For these equal privileges and rights of instruction in them all are taxed equally and proportionately. The constitutional name, "common schools," expressed their equality and universal patronage and support. *Common* schools are not common, as being low in character or grade, but *common* to all alike, to everybody and to all sects or denominations of religion, but without bringing religion into them. . . . As the state can have nothing to do with religion, except to protect everyone in the enjoyment of his own, so the common schools can have nothing to do with religion in any respect whatever. They are completely *secular* as any of the other institutions of the State, in which all the people, alike, have equal rights and privileges.[5]

A related reason why common school is a preferable term to public school is that the adjectives public and private have become inadequate. To separate public and private schools along the traditional lines of financing, control, curriculum, or access is becoming more and more difficult, because of exceptions found in local practices, state laws, and federal court decisions.[6]

Fourth, the reader may wonder if it is somewhat artificial to examine the five expectations separately. Quite correctly, he/she could note that most speakers and writers on the subject usually incorporate three or four of the goals. They are intimately interrelated. My response is that the concept of the common school is like a prism which casts intense light and generates tremendous heat. That light, in terms of input and output, can vary immensely. Our reflection upon its various color components, helps us better understand how brilliant it will be in the future.

Fifth, to study public education is to examine a crusade, complete with flaming rhetoric attacking and defending the emerging school system. Joseph Gusfield, in *Symbolic Crusade,* reminds us that a crusade has several layers of meaning. Just as his study showed that the temperance movement was as much an attempt by the WASP culture to control the political destiny of immigrant groups as it was an effort to modify drinking habits, so we must be sensitive to the motivations behind the messages of the public school's defenders and critics.[7]

COMMON CITIZENSHIP SKILLS

The soil in which the common school grew was the years from the War of Independence through the Civil War. A new nation was born, and political leaders referred to the country as "the great experiment." As a result of the Louisiana Purchase, the size of the country was doubled. Population rose from 4 million to 40 million. In 1820 the country had twelve cities of 10,000 or more; by 1860, over one hundred. Eight of the cities had over 100,000, and New York City had become the third largest city in the world. The cities reflected the growth in commerce and industry as well as technological advances.

Progress in urbanization and industrialization required responsibilities and would exact a price. Revisions in the political order were called for, and Andrew Jackson and the Democratic Party—the party of the common man—symbolized the belief that individuals could rectify social ills. The importance of participation in the electoral process was reflected in numerous scenes on artists' canvases of political debates and crowds awaiting election results. The abuses of technological advances required other forms of action as well. The exploitation of the immigrants and slaves, family separations, and pollution in the cities brought forth new institutions—mental asylums, orphanages, prisons, hospitals, and—the common school.[8]

Origins

Thomas Jefferson and his contemporaries recognized the coming problems of democracy. They realized that corruption would occur and excesses were inevitable. According to Jefferson: "Every government degenerates when trusted to the rulers of the people alone. The people themselves therefore are its only safe depositories. And to rend even them safe, their minds must be improved to a certain degree. . . . An amendment of our constitution must here come to the aid of the public education."[9]

His sentiments were echoed in the halls of state legislatures and in the offices of school officials prior to Horace Mann's formulation of his annual reports. In Illinois, for example, an Education Act passed in 1825 reflected the sentiments of Governor Coles, who had been secretary to Madison and a personal friend of Jefferson. Its preamble began: "To enjoy our rights and liberties we must understand them;—their security and protection ought to be the first object of a free people;—and it is a well-established fact no nation has ever continued long in the enjoyment of civil and political freedom, which was not both virtuous and enlightened." Thaddeus Stevens, a Pennsylvania legislator, commented in 1837: "If an elective republic is to endure for any great length of time, *every* elector must have sufficient information. . . . It is the duty of government to see that means of information be diffused to every citizen. This is a sufficient answer to those who deem education a private and not a public duty—who argue that they are willing to educate their *own* children, but not their *neighbor's* children." In that same year, John Pierce, Michigan's superintendent of schools, noted: "Without education, no people can secure themselves against the encroachments of power. . . . Children of every name and age must be taught the qualifications and duties of American Citizens, and learn in early life the art of self-control. . . . And to accomplish this object, our chief dependence must necessarily be the free school system."[10]

Horace Mann could and did argue this same point many times. In his *Tenth Annual Report* to the Massachusetts Board of Education, however, he mentions a "postulatum" to counter his growing concern that individuals who resist taxation for public schools may cause the downfall of the country. He wrote:

> In later times, and since the achievement of American Independence, the universal and ever-repeated argument in favor of Free Schools has been, that the general intelligence which they are capable of diffusing, and which can be imparted by no other human instrumentality, is indispensable to the continuance of a republican government. This argument, it is obvious, assumes, as a postulatum, the superiority of a republican over all other forms of government.[11]

Others, especially professional educators and politicians, joined Mann in insisting that the welfare of democracy itself was dependent upon the training of future citizens, and they concurred that democracy, increasingly identified as the best example of Christianized civilization, was the most appropriate form of human government. Although isolated attacks upon that position have occurred historically, it is only recently that a significant number of Amercian writers have challenged democracy's favored role.[12]

Objectives

Sooner or later, rhetoric must be translated into the reality of a curriculum. What surfaced in terms of national commission recommendations and state and local district curriculum guides? What were common student objectives in textbooks? How did these change over the years? Generally speaking the answers to these questions center on five citizenship objectives which surfaced in essays, reports, speeches, and textbooks—patriotism, knowledge of American history, awareness of the political process and voter responsibilities (civics), ability to communicate and ability to discern (critical thinking). The five remain remarkably unaltered over the years, although different periods have resulted in various objectives receiving higher priority than others.

The five are summarized in remarks given by W. E. Anderson, superintendent of Milwaukee schools, in 1888. The graduate, Anderson stated,

> should read English intelligently and intelligibly upon all common subjects of knowledge—history, geography, and general literature. He should be able to read a newspaper editorial, a magazine article, a poem, a popular lecture, and to give it such expression as will evince his understanding of the thought presented by the author. He should have a fairly accurate knowledge of the Constitution of the United States, the general plan or the practical workings of the Government as shown in the organization of Congress, and the manner of electing the President. . . ; and further, he should understand the necessity and importance of legal tribunals. . . . He should know something of his prerogatives as a citizen, his duties and rights as regards the exercise of franchise.[13]

In summary, Anderson's remarks reflect the popular belief that patriotism is the primary objective to be supported by the other four.

Patriotism is alluded to in most state documents inaugurating their systems of common schools. During the Revolutionary War period, Jefferson, Madison, and Webster—who offered a "federal catechism"—had spoken often of the need for loyal citizens. Textbooks in history and geography were the tools employed to teach young Americans. Although the first United States history textbooks for lower schools had appeared in the 1780s and 1790s, graded texts did not appear until the 1830s. These comprehensive texts, according to Cremin, transmitted much information and moralizing, "teaching the superiority of Americans and American institutions, the inferiority of colored peoples, the truth of the Protestant Christian religion, and . . . the evils of slavery."[14]

History books would make relatively few changes over the years. Yes, the Committee of Ten and several commissions over the years have requested that publishers make less of American superiority and do more with the promotion of world citizenship. Yes, social and intellectual histories have been expanded at the expense of the celebration of war victories. But not to a major extent. Civics, on the other hand, was a minor school subject in the 1800s. It gained visibility as a separate course only in the twentieth century. The climate during and following World War I promoted interest in civics in schools. The late 1930s and the late 1970s have also witnessed efforts to emphasize civics in public schools.[15]

Over the years there have been few disputes that general communication skills and exercises in critical thinking should be part of the curriculum. Even now we are still in the throes of the back-to-the-basics movement. Yet, what has been downplayed over the years is the application of the latter, in particular teaching students how to discriminate between "good" and "bad" political views. During the war in Vietnam, when the antischool movement was flourishing, Robert M. Hutchins reminded readers of the necessity for having such skills in a democracy. He concluded:

> The purpose of the public schools is not accomplished by having them free, universal, and compulsory. They may do many things for the young: they may amuse them, comfort them, look after their health, and keep them off the streets. But they are not public schools unless they start their pupils toward an understanding of what it means to be a self-governing citizen of a self-governing political community.[16]

Outcomes

To what extent has the public school been successful in meeting these five citizenship objectives? The focus of the essay dictates that the answer to the question is more likely to reflect widely held perceptions rather than summaries of empirical studies.

Public Schools. From the beginning advocates of common schooling argued that their proposal would bring improved civic conditions. A typical speech in the 1870s was given by F. A. Sawyer, a United States senator from South Carolina, who was convinced that people in non-schooled countries or nations with private systems, were likely to be "rude, ill-educated, thriftless, inert, almost savage, intent on no purpose of elevating, purifying, civilizing, christianizing themselves, but obedient to every impulse of passion, blind to every inducement to virtuous advancement." He maintained that a "constant flow of information" was needed to maintain free government, something which the public schools provided best. Finally, he was convinced that common schools had resulted in fewer law-breakers, better family relations, more security of property, and more contented laborers.[17] Such assertions are easier to proclaim than prove.

Since then, defenders of public schooling have contended that the "constant flow of information" has produced remarkable citizenship results. Today, they maintain that "evidence" of the success of the public school includes America's high literacy rate, the numbers of students who pursue postsecondary educational opportunities, the positive correlations of schooling with voter participation, involvement with civic projects, and income. Moreover, polls point out that a majority of Americans are generally satisfied with schools and that those who are most critical of public education are those who have the least amount of contact with it.[18]

Within this panoply of skills, media criticism has been directed more at the lack of communication skills than the lack of citizenship knowledge. At the turn of the century, there was a concern about poor student performance in general and spelling in particular; in the 1950s there were accounts of "educational wastelands" and more recently there have been stories about "literacy hoaxes." The public seems fascinated with the declining tests scores, which, of course, refer to the SAT, a test designed to predict success in college.[19]

Weaknesses in citizenship education have been pointed out, from time to time. The years just prior to and following World War I were filled with stories and fears about lack of patriotism. Within the last twenty years there has been some evidence that students do not recall much information about American history or retain knowledge about voting procedures.[20]

Religious Schools. Those who promoted common schools, as some of the previous quotations attest, criticized the sectarian schools for being divisive (a point to be examined on several grounds throughout the essay). One of the criticisms has been that such schools did not foster patriotism in students. That particular charge did not reach its full fury until the 1880s. It was a topic debated at the National Education Association in 1889 and 1890. Catholic leaders, such as John Ireland, tried to walk the fine line between defending the need for public schools and yet claiming a distinctive need for Catholic schools which was not antipatriotic. The Catholic schools exhibit at the World's Columbian Exposition in 1893 stressed how patriotic the schools were. But some Catholic leaders, such as John J. Keane, presented double messages. In 1888 he acknowledged the criticism that parochial school parents and school officials were un-American. He disagreed: "To suppose that they . . . [begin schools] . . . through any want of public spirit, through any want of interest in the public weal, through any want of devotedness to our country . . . would be unreasonable and unjust. Quite the contrary is true." The following year he would argue that "the real welfare of our country depends on denominational schools rather than a national system of public schools."[21]

Past and present, there is no body of evidence that this author knows of which seriously challenges the ability of religious schools to "produce" graduates who are as knowledgeable about American history, or are as loyal to the country, as are public school graduates. If anything, it seems that there is more evidence to support the fact that parochial schools of the past—Roman Catholic and German Lutheran in particular—were fiercely patriotic. Today, the Christian day school movement has a penchant to provide what liberals view as overzealous patriotism.[22]

Ironically, one area of dispute, as witnessed in recent court disputes across the country, is in the areas of ability of students in basic skills and critical thinking skills. Studies of parochial school pupils suggest they perform as well, if not better, than do public school students. In part, due to the shorter history of Christian day schools, the evidence on them is not as complete, or viewed as accurate, as that compiled on Catholic students.[23]

COMMON VALUES

The soil which was so hospitable for the seed of republicanism was similarly receptive to the kernel of common values. The Protestant-dominated culture assumed that there would be a supporting body of common virtues which would be a witness to the new democratic Zion. How that list, rarely delineated, changes over time is a fascinating topic of investigation. Two thorny questions arise: Can morality be taught without religion? If religion (or Bible-reading) can be retained in public schools, can it be nonsectarian and effective? (Such long-standing questions are still with us, particularly today in the guise of the issue of secular humanism.)

Origins

"Learning," wrote Benjamin Rush, Philadelphia surgeon and Revolutionary War leader, "is friendly to religion, in as much as it assists in removing prejudice, superstition, and enthusiasm, in promoting just notions of the Deity, and in enlarging our knowledge of his works." Mann's *Twelfth Annual Report* contains his extensive defense of moral education in public schools and his defense of having the Bible read in the schools without interpretation. Advocates of religious schools did not subscribe to the idea that religion could be separated from moral training. It surfaced in the New York disputes in the early 1840s and was to be a recurring theme in both Protestant and Catholic school publications thereafter.[24]

A slightly different rationale for moral instruction in public schools emerged in the 1850s. Horace Mann and others argued that parochial schools, due to the nature of their support, were committed to sectarian doctrines which prevented them from providing an environment where students could really discover ultimate truths. At the 1858 session of the National Teachers Federation, Mann insisted that "any institution which stifled discussion or relied upon authority without investigation, was wrong and hostile to progress." Mann's remarks were made in a heated debate entitled, "Parochial Schools, Are They in Harmony with the Spirit of American Institutions?" The debate became so fierce that a "song" recess had to be called. Later Mann made one concession. He acknowledged that some denominational schools did encourage "open" discussions on moral issues, but he believed most did not. He and several other public school advocates refused, however, to recognize the argument that the parochial schools were providing a necessary function in some communities where public schools were neglecting instruction in morals.[25]

By the end of the 1880s "secular" moral instruction was entrenched in public schools, although subject to increasing attacks. The religious diversity of the country promoted growing dissatisfaction with devotional Bible reading. By the turn of the century a number of midwestern states had experienced cases which usually resulted in the justices establishing a middle ground. Bible reading for devotional purposes was prohibited, but schools were permitted to carry on moral instruction. Most Catholic leaders and a number of Protestant clergy were convinced, from the 1850s on, that secular moral instruction was wrong. Religion had to be the basis of morality. They concluded, therefore, that since "it does not lie within the province of the State to teach religion . . . the church must do so in its own schools." On the one hand, the absence of former critics of this sensitive school policy issue made it easier for public schools to carry on a Protestant-flavored morality; on the other hand, the new schools were a visible scar, marring the face of the body politic.[26]

Objectives

What were *typical values that common schools* could teach? A typical list is found in the 1870 verdict of the *Minor v. Board of Education of Cincinnati* case. Justice Hagans, speaking for the Ohio Supreme Court, ruled that the Bible could be retained in common schools and used to teach children "the principles and duties of morality and justice, and a sacred regard to truth, love of country, humanity, universal benevolence, sobriety, industry, chastity, moderation, temperance and all other virtues which are the ornaments of human society."[27]

The *Report of the Commissioner of Education for the Year 1888–1889* contained an extensive collection of comments about religious and moral instruction in public schools, among them a debate between D. L. Kiehle of Minnesota, then state superintendent of schools, and Bishop James McGolrick of the diocese of Duluth. After McGolrick had argued that the public schools could not teach religion or morality, Kiehle responded that there was no "practical difficulty" in inculcating such recognized Christian principles as "temperance, purity, and charity." Another public educator, Austin Bierbower of Chicago, agreed: "All men, no matter what their religion, or whether they have any religion, recognize the same virtues—truth, honesty, purity, love, politeness, etc." *Our Country*, in 1893, summarized Protestant sentiments of the times by stating that public schools could and should teach three religious principles: the existence of God, the immortality of man, and man's accountability. An essay contest sponsored by an anonymous Californian in 1906 on the topic "Moral Training in the Public Schools" brought over 300 entries. Five of the best responses were published in 1907 and included, in addition to

philosophical statements justifying such training in state schools, curricular suggestions based on the author's values. The winning essay
called for inculcation of such "school virtues" as regularity, punctuality, silence, industry, neatness, accuracy, and obedience, in addition to certain religious principles.[28]

The twentieth century has witnessed three intense periods of activity concerning values instruction in public education. Each era has
lasted fifteen to twenty-five years following a major war. In each
period—following World War I, World War II, and the Vietnam
conflict—there have been major Supreme Court decisions involving
religion and education and national pronouncements on specific values to be transmitted to students.[29]

More specifically, what values were called for? From approximately
1920 to 1945 Americans witnessed the character education movement. Slightly earlier (in 1918), the National Education Association
(NEA) issued what has come to be known as "the seven cardinal
principles" of secondary education. They include: good health, command of fundamental processes, worthy home membership, vocational direction, citizenship, worthy use of leisure time, and ethical
character. Temperance and sexual purity, dominant concerns of the
previous century's statements had faded in favor of family and health
matters, understandable in light of the waves of immigrants and perceptions of problems in urban America in the first decades of the
twentieth century. Following World War II and Korea, there was a
second movement, focused on moral and spiritual values. There was
much stronger emphasis on world citizenship and social justice, although the foremost value was "the uniqueness of the human personality." There has been no comparable national statement about values
education in the post-Vietnam years, but the pervasiveness of the
values clarification movement, together with the work of Lawrence
Kohlberg on moral reasoning, suggest that it has duplicated the popularity of the two previous trends. Values clarification, rightly or
wrongly, has been perceived as emphasizing personal freedom of
choice above societal norms or conventions—a moral narcissism.
Rather than precise lists of moral virtues, the process of valuing is
most significant.[30]

What has happened to Bible reading and direct instruction about
religion in public schools in the twentieth century? George Albert Coe
observed in 1917: "The argument shifts back and forth between the
value of the Bible as literature, and its value for religious guidance."
He saw even the former effort as a thinly disguised Protestant ruse to
maintain its sway over the curriculum. The strategy of released time

(religious leaders came in to schools to offer Bible instruction for short periods of time) was crippled by the *McCollum* decision (1948). In disarray, religious leaders opted for four plans: Some continued to press for sectarian instruction; others urged no sectarian doctrines be taught, but asked for a curriculum which would "impel" students toward the acceptance of some religious faith; still others favored teaching *about* religion; and some wanted no sectarian instruction whatsoever. Mainline Protestants, together with many Jewish leaders, worked for the third or fourth options. For fundamentalist leaders, the *Schempp/Murray* decision of 1963 confirmed the fears of the *McCollum* case—"secular humanism" had triumphed in the public schools. So they began to develop their alternative schools.[31]

Outcomes

In his last report to the Massachusetts Board of Education, Horace Mann stated that public schools were not meant to be theological seminaries, but he believed they would prove to be places which provided adequate moral instruction for the nation's future citizens. U.S. Senator F. A. Sawyer agreed some years later (1870), and he challenged sectarian schools to prove that their graduates were any better, morally, than common school products. Another speaker before the National Teachers Federation in 1880, the president of the University of Minnesota, thought public school and college graduates were better because they had been secularized, which for him meant they had been taught how to reason.[32]

Public Schools. Evidence on morality, especially paper-and-pencil tests, is usually regarded with suspicion. There was not much testing of the affective domain in pupils until the early twentieth century, and today that research is usually regarded as biased. Even early intelligence tests asked "moral dilemma" questions! Probably the first systematic study of national significance was Hartshorne and May's research project, Character Education Inquiry, conducted at Teachers College, Columbia University, from 1924 to 1929. As might be expected, they found children who attended progressive private schools markedly more "honest in their school work than are children who attend conventional public schools." They did point out high correlations with social class and found certain ethnic groups more honest than others.[33]

Some advocates of public schooling, meanwhile, continued to try to discredit those supporting private schools. In the post-World War II years, when parochial schools were beginning their boom, some liberal educators charged that countries with sectarian school systems were "centers of social insanity and human cruelty." They offered no proof for their assertions. Today, the arguments about the effectiveness of values clarification and moral development programs have still not been settled. Most studies seem to suggest that the impact of these programs has been marginal.[34]

And yet, more programs in morals education are being introduced into the public schools. The school is still perceived to be a force for morality. Regarding the specific issue of teaching about religion, the majority of mainline Protestant denominations favor the teaching about religion option previously described. Little research has been done on the effectiveness of this approach.[35]

Religious Schools. Historically, Catholic schools have found some famous Protestants whose comments have coincided with this perspective on morals instruction. Professor Louis Agassiz was quoted as saying that his study of prostitutes in New York City had indicated that the "soiled doves" traced their fall to *"influences that met them in the public schools."* Washington Gladden was supposed to have said that the divorce of religion from education was the cause of the rise of pauperism and crime. Within the past few decades there has been more criticism of the public schools by advocates of religious schooling for the government schools' permissiveness, especially in the area of sexuality. Mel Gabler, a Texan noted for his attempts to have school curricula reviewed, is convinced that humanistic textbooks are belittling the concept of sexual virginity and sexual abstinence, and are teaching the legitimacy of abortion, premarital sex, homosexuality, and incest.[36]

The evidence of the recent Coleman report and related studies indicates that parochial schools claim that their students are more disciplined and that instruction is imparted in more orderly fashion. Such reports do not claim, however, that students in religious schools are better morally. Supporters of the Christian day schools would claim that their graduates are better morally.[37]

COMMON EXPERIENCES

By the 1880s Bible reading and moral instruction in public schools began to experience more and more opposition. Some former advocates believed it was producing too much divisiveness, contrary to the third expectation of common schools—that they were to bring unity from the diversity of the nation of immigrants. At first glance what we are about to discuss—the importance of having the various children of the community in the same school, sharing in common experiences—may appear to be only a slightly different shade of the previous color in the prism of the rationale for common schools which we examine. But upon closer investigation it becomes more distinct. Public schools were and are needed for more than *talking* about a common creed. They will help the new immigrant understand the old settler, one ethnic group relate to a second, and the rich and poor better see that they have more similarities than differences. To foster a climate in which diverse religious groups, ethnic groups, or special interest groups are encouraged to build separate schools contributes to the demise of the common school and diminishes the greatness of the nation.[38]

Origins

A major need for having the common school was the growing heterogeneity of the population. Between 1830 and 1860 every country in Europe had sent new citizens to America—a total of 4.5 million— with the largest number of immigrants from Scandinavian countries, Germany, and Ireland. The American common school, through the promotion of patriotic songs and national holidays, was to give the new children an understanding of American ways. Calvin Stowe, in 1836, viewed the common school's mixing of children from diverse backgrounds as the "surest palladium" for building a strong nation.[39]

To promote such a task for the public schools was to raise a serious question about the function of the private schools, which had existed in most parts of the country for almost two hundred years. The debate in 1858 at the National Teachers Association meeting did not prevent that group from finally resolving

> that in endeavoring to promote the great cause of general education, this Association will not recognize any distinction on account of locality, position or particular departments of labor, but that all teachers, whether in colleges, academies, public, private, or parochial schools . . . shall be regarded by us as brethren and fellow laborers in one common cause.[40]

The resolution concluded that private schools were necessary, in the present condition of things, and saw them as "indispensable aids in public education," but urged states to provide the means of education for all youth.

Such a sentiment has continued in the nation's history. The Supreme Court verdict in *McCollum* noted:

> The public school is at once the symbol of our democracy and the most pervasive means for promoting our common destiny. In no activity of the State is it more vital to keep out divisive forces than in its schools. . . . "The great American principle of eternal separation"—Elihu Root's phrase bears repetition—is one of the vital reliances of our Constitution system for assuring unities among our people stronger than our diversities.[41]

Objectives

How are the curriculum and extracurricular activities of the school to promote unity? The texts of the nineteenth century had of course been used as "guardians of traditions," promoting a host of common values, including punctuality, respect for property, honesty, capitalism, courage, and patriotism. Its twin towers were that virtue would be rewarded and vice punished. Books were to be supplemented by experiences, however. According to accounts of immigrant children, former slaves, and American Indians, teachers and peers introduced the newcomers to strange new types of music, food, clothes, sports, and vocational possibilities. The price could be terribly high, from embarrassment in the classroom to literal loss of family.[42]

In the first decade of the twentieth century high schools were encouraged to become social centers. Such centers were to offer courses for both secondary students and adults, but also were to provide informal programs and meeting sites so that community members could become better acquainted. As one song put it: "It's at the center, the social center/ The place where everybody feels at home/ Forgets the external/ Becomes fraternal/ And knows the time for friendliness has come." Such friendliness evaporated during World War I. By 1919 legislatures in eight states had virtually mandated instruction in English and prohibited the use of foreign language in elementary schools. Yet, the U.S. Commissioner of Education John J. Tigert in 1924 told the NEA that faith in education was so strong that "citizens of all races, nationalities, and creeds support it morally and materially, without prejudice and without protest." It was so, he added, because it was there that "the Christian and the Jew, the Protestant and the Catholic, and Theist and the Atheist, the native born and the foreign born, all sit down together to learn the most fundamental things of life."[43]

Perhaps the most articulate argument in support of common experiences in the recent past has been given by Robert Maynard Hutchins. He began his 1973 article by noting that the Constitution of the United States contemplates government by discussion, with all citizens participating in it. Such an assumption does not assume agreement; in fact, it assumes disagreement. He continues:

> The doctrine of every man for himself, or every nation for itself, loses its charm in an interdependent world. This doctrine has to give way before the idea of a world community. . . . To consider most of the topics of current education discussion is irrelevant to the real issue we face. So is the great antischool campaign, except that if it succeeds we shall be deprived of the institution that could most effectively assist in drawing out our common humanity.[44]

Outcomes

In the 1800s the WASP culture was clearly dominant, and it was easy enough for educational leaders such as William T. Harris to call for students in public schools and their parents to learn how to compromise. Reading between the lines, it was obvious who was expected to compromise if a difficulty arose. After World War I especially, WASP leaders felt more threatened by those out of the mainstream. Private schools became more of a challenge. In 1924 Payson Smith, the State Commissioner of Education for Massachusetts, informed the NEA that there were challenges to the widely held belief (and goal) of the melting pot. He was convinced that there was a minority "who think that they can serve their country by trying to array class against class, section against section, and racial group against racial group." He argued that to promote unity was not the same as promoting uniformity. The future of the Republic was at stake.[45] You will note that there is little which follows that is empirical data. What can be noted are the perceptions, and these perceptions suggest that we are still a divided nation.

Public Schools. By the end of the 1940s it seemed to leaders of the public schools that the evidence was mounting that there was an increasingly divisive fragmentation within American society. The *Mc-Collum* case, following the *Everson* case, which permitted public funds to be used for the transportation of pupils to private schools, signaled a wider battle for tax dollars. B. O. Smith reiterated in 1949 what members of the John Dewey Society had claimed in 1944—that the private schools were promoting "cleavages and tensions." James Con-

ant was widely quoted in 1952 when he remarked, on several occa-
sions: "The greater the proportion of our youth who attend independent schools, the greater the threat to our democratic unity."[46]

The same year the *Schempp/Murray* cases were decided, the NEA
adopted a resolution beginning: "American public education is
founded on the conviction that the public school is indispensable to
national unity." It closes with the words: "Free public schools are the
cornerstone of our social, economic, and political structure and are of
utmost significance in development of our moral and spiritual values. . . . The public school is not expendable."[47]

About that time a new curriculum innovation was beginning, a
reform calling for a multicultural perspective in textbooks. The call
reflected the growing political power and pride of racial and ethnic
groups. Almost thirty states have passed legislation requiring human
relations training or multicultural education, which includes recognition of the religious differences in the country. As with most reforms,
this one has led to a backlash as the public schools wrestle with unity
and diversity.[48]

Religious Schools. In 1889 a non-Catholic educator, speaking to the
NEA, charged that spokespersons for the parochial schools had "no
sense of obligation to the whole, no civic breath, no thought of any
children but their own." Such an accusation, indirectly, branded the
Catholics as antipatriotic and arrogant. The Catholics, as have other
sponsors of religious schools, have tried to dispel the idea they were
against the concept of unity.[49]

Of the five reasons for having public schools (and the criticisms
they imply of religious schools), this is the most difficult to dispute. As
has been shown there is evidence to show that religious schools have
graduates who are loyal citizens who are not significantly better or
worse than public school graduates. It is harder to counter the argument for unity through interaction when private schools deliberately
place students in separate facilities.

A counter-argument which applies here and in the next expectation is that religious schools have served a variety of students over the
years. Many denominational leaders can point out that their schools
have blended students from "both sides of the economic tracks," and
that they have served a disproportionately high number of minority
students.

COMMON OPPORTUNITIES

One of the hallmarks of democracy is its contention that all citizens
have an equal opportunity to achieve happiness and success. Convert-

ing theory to practice is always difficult, however, as witnessed in the deliberations of the Continental Congress. Numerous individuals and groups since that time, including a raft of revisionist historians and lawyers today, have reminded us that America has fallen short of reaching the ideal, in the public school as well as other governmental arenas.

As will be noted, the thrust of this expectation has been altered over the years. In the 1830s the focus was on correcting the evils of pauperism and narrowing the gap between rich and poor. Providing equal educational opportunity for racial and ethnic minorities did not emerge as a major thrust until the twentieth century.

Origins

The supporters of the common schools reflected a wide range of political, social, and economic perspectives. The *Working Man's Advocate* of 31 October 1829 reported the formation of an association to promote national education because "industry is at present un-protected, oppressed, despised, and indirectly deprived of its just reward . . . because there is . . . no system of education . . . which se-cures the equal maintenance, protection, and instruction of youth—of the children of the poor man as of the rich . . . free from aristocratical distinctions." A few years after Horace Mann had stated in his final report that education could serve as the balance wheel of society, Governor James Grimes of Iowa noted that education was "the great equalizer of human conditions. It places the poor on an equality with the rich. It subjects the appetites and passions of the rich to the restraints of reason and conscience, and thus prepares each for a career of usefulness and honor."[50]

By the end of the nineteenth century there were three arguments that were used to buttress the expectation that the public schools gave students of diverse backgrounds common (i.e., equal) opportunities. Observing the demographic patterns in urban and rural settings as well as the increasing school enrollments, public school advocates pro-posed that the school parallel an athletic contest, where the rules would be fair for all participants. They assumed that different out-comes (grades, honors, and eventually jobs) would be the result of intelligence differences and the individual efforts made by students, and not related to economic caste or ethnic background. Second, it was widely believed that the providing of educational opportunities would diminish domestic unrest. If poor people were convinced that they had a chance to break out of their economic plight, they would be less inclined to strike or riot. Third, the feeling was widely held that a well-educated population would result in a changing work force, which meant a general improvement of the living standard for the nation. This essay will look at the first argument most closely: Did and does the common school provide equal opportunity for students?[51]

Objectives

In contrast to the expectations previously discussed, common opportunities relate more to general policy matters than to specific curriculum topics and student objectives. A particular manifestation of this expectation is seen in funding decisions by local districts and state legislatures.

Even the staunchest defenders of public schooling today admit that historically American schools have mirrored the racial biases of our society. Yet, in this century, in our speeches and our legislation, we can find numerous calls for equal opportunities. John J. Tigert, U.S. Commissioner of Education in 1925, told the NEA: "The public high school is the bridge that the American system of education has erected to make practical its faith that equal opportunitites should be provided for the education of all regardless of wealth, birth, or occupation." He posited that the democratic atmosphere of America would not long support a dual education system, but would eventually provide "a free road to knowledge for every child from the kindergarten to the university."[52]

Even during that time, there was systematic discrimination against the poor and racial minorities. It is easier to document the ways in which blacks were denied funding for dual systems or racially isolated schools in northern urban centers than it is to detail economic discrimination. The keystone case outlawing dual school systems was *Brown v. Board of Education of Topeka, Kansas* (1954). Since that time, a number of other court cases have supported that verdict which called for equal educational opportunities. A variety of desegregation remedies, including site selection, pairing, busing, magnet plans, and metropolitan educational parks have been tried. Affirmative action programs related to admissions standards have also been put in place.[53]

Within the instructional environment, efforts have been made to eliminate stereotypes in textbooks and to make the curriculum multicultural. Several agencies have developed which aid local districts in evaluating curriculum and instructional practices which may foster racial bias (and work toward its elimination).[54]

How has the public school responded to the economic disparities found among its student population? The answer to that question is one of the most debated issues facing American education today because it is grounded on the philosophical question of whether the school's mission is complete when it provides an equal *chance* for everyone or if it has an obligation to secure more equal *income* for all.

While the poor have never been invisible, they have not always received special consideration in the curriculum. By the 1880s, however, it was generally agreed that most poor students would be receiving only a rudimentary education. Since they were not going on to college, they should therefore receive more of a job-related education. Industrial education (manual arts) and vocational education were introduced and greatly expanded in the early twentieth century schools. By the 1950s and 1960s there was a backlash to these curricula. Some argued that the academic curriculum was watered down too much. Others were convinced that vocational education needed to be expanded even more. Some thought it was sufficient, but needed to be updated. James Conant, writing in the 1960s, was convinced that comprehensive high schools were needed which offered better college-preparation *and* vocational education.[55]

Since the mid-1960s there have been several specific federal actions directed toward improving educational opportunities for low-income students. The Elementary and Secondary Education Act of 1965 marked a breakthrough in legislation because it permitted federal funding to be distributed to schools, private or public, that had specified percentages of poverty-level students. The formation of the Department of Education in 1980, in part, was justified on the basis that a large share of its budget would be just for equal educational opportunity. Not all efforts at the federal level can be called successes, however. The *Rodriguez* case (Texas), which attempted to clarify whether there was unequal funding for low-income districts that needed to be rectified, was returned to the State of Texas for further action.[56]

Outcomes

Have these various programs and legislation improved equal educational opportunity for the poor and minorities? At first it seems this question should be easy to answer because we have enormous amounts of data about the socioeconomic, racial, and ethnic backgrounds of students. The answer, however, is not so simple because statistics, as always, have to be interpreted. It is interesting to note how the political persuasions of today's commentators color their reading of the data. Supporters of public schools read the evidence and say that schools have done what reasonably could be expected in a pluralistic society, considering the difficulties of funding. They are convinced, moreover, that if educational funds are diverted to alternative schools, educational equality will decline. Public schools will become the "dumping ground" for those with the most severe emotional and instructional problems. Looking at the same data, critics counter that the public school never has achieved the dream of equality that Horace Mann and others promoted. They argue that America is a pluralistic nation which requires distribution of the educational resources to various "publics." When that occurs, greater educational equality and opportunities will come.

Public Schools. Defenders of "the system" can marshal both historical and current evidence on their behalf. (1) Prior to the advent of the common schools, private academies, more often than not, served the wealthy and slighted the poor. Voluntary systems will curtail, not enhance, opportunities for equal treatment. (2) Biographies of famous Americans from any period reveal many came from humble backgrounds. They were served well by public schools. (3) If public schools have been as unjust as their critics claim, what explains the overall decline in the percentage of students attending nonpublic schools? Is it cost alone that can explain the relatively recent decline in Catholic school enrollment? (4) In the 1870s the dropout rate in public schools was approximately 98 percent; it is currently 23 percent. Considering the huge expansion of the system, it is evident that greater percentages of the poor and racial groups are graduating as well as attending post-secondary schools. (5) Contrary to popular opinion, desegregation remedies have worked more effectively than usually reported in the media. Programs for disadvantaged learners, such as Project Headstart, have improved students' performance levels. Senator Ernest F. Hollings summarizes the unique role and problems of the public school in this way:

> The public school, in contrast, must take all comers—regardless of background, regardless of special problems. Additionally, the public institution must abide by congressional laws and court decisions that the private school can ignore. Those who argue that public and private schools are directly competitive and that pupil performances can be directly compared ignore this basic dif-

ference. The public school is bound by both law and conscience to reach out to every child as a matter of his or her birthright. . . . In contrast, many private schools have been built for the specific purpose of closing the doors of economic and social opportunity.[57]

Those who claim that the public schools have never fulfilled their obligation to provide equal chances for the poor and minorities offer four counter-arguments: (1) Historically, reports of visitors (Matthew Arnold in 1894–95, for example), biographies, and court decisions reveal discrimination has been rampant. (2) Sociologists, such as Patricia Sexton, have demonstrated class bias in large city systems. (3) While retention rates have gone up, so have unemployment rates for racial minorities. Schooling has not helped minorities with employment, a typical promise of the early proponents of the common schools. (4) The number of illiterates and functional illiterates in the nation is an embarrassment. What is done in schools, even if it is true that more poor and minority students are in attendance, cannot be considered successful. As the Coleman and Jencks reports reveal, one's social class, not school variables, is the best predictor of achievement in the classroom. Virgil Blum summarizes the stance of critics of the public schools today:

> The greatest degradation of poverty is the unavailability of choice. Most poor parents in America are suffering that degradation. In the education of their children they have no choice of religious and moral values, no choice of educational environment, no choice of dedicated and committed teachers, no choice of personal involvement in the education of their children. The state through its truancy laws forcibly compels parents to send their children to schools, but monopolizes the resources so that only the government schools get significant public assistance. The net result is that parental rights remain only theoretical for most poor people.[58]

Religious Schools. Understandably, backers of religious schools and other private schools are quick to respond to the criticisms implied in the expectation of common opportunities. Before turning to specific current research studies, it is important to note that studies in the field are few in number. Denis Doyle reports, however, descriptive data are now available on a fairly consistent basis and its quality is improving. He cautions that estimates on student enrollment trends have become volatile. *The Condition of Education* for 1979 predicted a leveling off of private school enrollments through 1984. The 1980 *Condition of Education* shows a more rapid decline in the public sector and what can only be described as a dramatic increase in private school enrollments through 1989 (possibly a 12 percent increase).[59]

From the recent studies which have been done, five points can be made. First, it is difficult to expect religious schools to be fully desegregated when their membership has few minority members. (The two largest parochial systems, Catholic and Lutheran, are from denominations which have only a 2 percent black membership.) Yet, despite the historic membership patterns, these denominations and others have made strides in opening their schools to minority groups. As several studies indicate, in innercities in particular, minority and poor families enroll their children in private schools in disproportionate percentages. (Over 25 percent of the students in New York City, 40 percent in Boston, and 50 percent in Albany, New York, are in private schools.) Third, it is argued that certain federal policies discourage racial and economic integration of private schools.[60]

Fourth, the most extensive study, *Public and Private Schools* (1981), does point out that religious schools (which account for between 85 and 90 percent of the private school enrollments) do have disproportionate numbers of high- and low-income students. Also, the study confirmed that while religious schools are disproportionately low in terms of black enrollments, they are not low in terms of Hispanics. The authors of the text make the point that individual private schools, in various parts of the country, may be less segregated (or more desegregated) and better representative of their community's racial composition than the public school. Finally, the authors of the study conclude, about Catholic schools in particular:

> [They] more nearly approximate the "common school" ideal of American education than do public schools . . . [and] the achievement levels of students from different parental educational backgrounds, of black and white students, and of Hispanic and non-Hispanic white students are more nearly alike in Catholic schools than in public schools or other private schools.[61]

In summary, the religious school proponents could argue that they believe that they have made an extensive contribution to the fabric of the commonwealth. Based on their motivation of service, they have taken their share of "difficult" students. If, in fact, religious schools were to go out of existence, the public would be saddled with immense fiscal burdens and problems of social integration that would cause a wave of new schools to emerge.

COMMON REFORMS

The final expectation is the logical conclusion of the other four. They focus on transmitting knowledge and attitudes about the past glories and accomplishments of the nation, and urge citizens, by uniting them through common values and experiences, to maintain social cohesion. The American ethos, however, also accepts the perspective that the future can and should be made better. Society expects schools to prepare students to bring about constructive changes in the social order. Such changes are to be made through persuasion rather than revolution, cooperation rather than conflict.

To make significant changes in society implies a mobilization of will and immense effort. Who decides what changes are good and necessary? How and at what pace are reforms instituted? What penalties are paid by those who refuse to comply? Such questions underscore the issue of control of the educational process which shadows the expectation of common reforms.

Origins

In the post-Revolutionary War years, many of the comments about schools mentioned societal benefits such as reduced crime rates. According to Benjamin Rush, bachelors would benefit from paying public school taxes by being able to sleep better at night and needing to spend less for bolts and locks. Horace Mann concurred. In addition he envisioned the schools being used to upgrade the general health and economy of the nation. Political leaders agreed.[62]

By the late 1880s many educational leaders were convinced that state systems of education were the only viable approach to bring about meaningful societal changes. Rhode Island State Commissioner of Education Thomas Stockwell noted:

> Only State action is able to cope with the problem, and only State interest can be relied upon to cover the entire field. Nor does the action of the State in this matter necessarily paralyze local effort.
>
> It is only as the State takes the control in these matters that we can be sure, first, that schools will be provided within reasonable distance of every home; and second, that the schools thus established will be practically equal in the character and quality of the education which they furnish. Local power is not infrequently unable to provide the proper accomodations; again, for one cause or another, it is unwilling to do so. . . . What shall be taught and how it shall be

taught are fundamental questions, and should not be left to the arbitrament of local feelings, or judgments even, which are often too narrow both in their premises and in their conclusions.[63]

Not all educators leaped to the same conclusion. Voices were raised in protest about too much control being gathered in one place. John Dewey reflected a position which acknowledged the role of the state school in bringing about changes, but cautioned about excessive use of force.
He maintained that:

—education is the fundamental method of social progress and reform.
—all reforms which rest simply upon the enactment of law, or the threatening of certain penalties, or upon changes in mechanical or outward arrangements, are transitory and futile.
—education is a regulation of the process of coming to share in the social consciousness; and that the adjustment of individual activity on the basis of this social consciousness is the only sure method of social reconstruction.[64]

Objectives

To prepare students to be "change agents," in today's parlance, may be admirable, but how is that (and was that) to be accomplished? Educators in the late nineteenth and early twentieth centuries believed that the emerging areas of knowledge had to be incorporated into the curriculum. Music, drawing, physiology, nature study, and physical exercise became common in elementary schools. Secondary schools offered more sciences, modern languages, home economics, physical education, as well as music and art.[65]

Under American legal parameters states rather than the federal government determine curriculum requirements. A survey in 1979 of states found an amazing array of mandated subjects, including the dangers of drug and alcohol abuse, driver education, sex education, ecology, career education, and recently, computer literacy and peace education.[66]

A current trend in some parts of the country is "futuring." The educators promoting this curricular innovation assume that the world is changing rapidly (e.g., Alvin Toffler's *Future Shock*) and propose that students be taught skills in questioning conventional wisdom and in anticipating future developments.[67]

Outcomes

Before turning to the discussion of the effectiveness of schools in preparing students to reform society, it is appropriate to note how slowly schools tend to change. First, public or private schools, by their very nature, tend to be conservative institutions, transmitting what patrons of that system deem valuable. Studies of curriculum change indicate that more curriculum innovations fail than succeed in being adopted. Second, because a number of changes that American society proposes have moral and religious implications, there are legal restraints. Justice Jackson, in *Everson* (1947), noted that the "state may pay out tax-raised funds to relieve pauperism, but it may not under our Constitution do so to induce or reward piety. It may spend funds to secure old age against want, but it may not spend funds to secure religion against skepticism."[68]

Public Schools. There is little research on students' ability to do "futuring." If anything, there does seem to be a consensus among writers that today's students are likely to have more cognitive knowledge than some previous generations of students, but are less able to integrate such knowledge, or have the ability to reflect upon new situations.[69]

Critics have charged that public schools are a monopoly that will change only under extreme pressure. They contend that efforts to improve student performance, through community control efforts or minimum competency examination requirements, for example, are typically opposed by teacher organizations. Champions of public education counter that the status quo is more likely to be preserved under family choice or voucher options. Robert Hutchins posited: "What would happen if the schools or compulsory attendance at them were abolished and 'the making of citizens' were left to parents? The status quo would be maintained—or would deteriorate."[70]

Religious Schools. Historically, there has been some evidence that private schools were "the experimental stations for public schools." The 1981 Coleman study could not find support for that role today. Moreover, as even the critics of public education admit, approximately 70 percent of the money spent on educational research comes from governmental funds.[71]

The differences in public school student and religious school student performance which exist today, according to *Public and Private Schools*, are most likely to be that the religious school student will have higher cognitive achievements and be more disciplined in the classroom. In summary, the evidence suggests that students in private schools are somewhat more conformist (to cultural norms) than public school students. Such a conclusion implies they would be less oriented toward alternative futures.[72]

A NEW EXPECTATION

From the business world and theological circles comes the message that we are in an era of shifting worldviews.[73] One of the major premises of the emerging worldview is that there has been too much centralization of power—in government, in medicine, in business, in agriculture, and in religion. What is called for is more power for intermediate groups, e.g., voluntary associations and smaller business groups. The high-tech age we are in, advocates of the new order would argue, make international corporations less necessary. Individuals, who have been stripped of too much meaning already, could regain control of their lives.

Signs of the new worldview include: increased political instability (the growth of many new small nations and rapidly changing political alignments); a more positive view of pluralism; the emergence, within America and other nations, of many new religious and social groups; the formation of specialized companies and voluntary associations (for business, social, and medical purposes); the emergence of new professions; and the call by numerous individuals and many special-interest groups for "right." It is understandable that this new worldview will be met with various degrees of support and resistance. No worldview is ever completely dominant. Remnants of the other views will endure.

To describe the educational expectation which results from this emerging worldview, I am using a term which I heard Bruno Bettelheim use to describe preschool children at play—*collective individualism*. Children in such an environment are first and foremost concerned about themselves and are often oblivious of others. Yet, at times they are aware of others in the group and, in fact, want to engage in activities with them. But relationships are fragile, easily made, easily broken. Structure is needed, to be sure, but it is at a minimum.

According to interpreters of this movement, those still wedded to the former worldview (which supports the necessity of state control), will want to have some standards set by the state. The "collectives" are likely not to be as reactionary as the representatives of the old order, state government officials and legislators who favor tightening educational standards.[74] They may support the lessening of rigid state regulations; they may applaud a multicultural curriculum, but they are likely to call for some minimal standards (including the maintenance of the five expectations described in this essay). Interestingly, many mainline Protestant denominations fit this category. In the early 1980s several denominations saw fit to publish study guides for their members urging them to reconsider the needs of public education. One can speculate, using Gusfield's terms, whether denominations are waging a symbolic crusade to regain their lost prestige and power or are correct, theologically, that the self-love of individuals has become excessive (and hence sinful)?[75] Other "collectives," more conservative religiously, are selective about which values they would want the public schools to teach. If they become convinced that there is no hope to rescue the public schools from the "pit" of secular humanism into which it has fallen, they will desert it.[76]

We are already seeing examples of "individualist" behavior. The rise in the number of parents who are going to jail rather than submit to school regulations, the increase in nonpublic schools, the proliferation of at-home instruction packages are just several examples. Far from a unified group, the "individualist" camp includes political socialists who ask the schools to stick to the basics and give up political indoctrination (Jonathan Kozol), as well as religious fundamentalists who refuse to cooperate with the state in any way.[77]

CONCLUSION

Historically, the interactions between the "friends of common school education" and advocates of religious schooling have ranged from embarrassing ignorance to admiration and imitation. Strategically, public schools and private schools have avoided each other or tried to abolish each other. More often, there has been accommodation or assimilation.

Quoting a public school supporter, David Tyack entitled his history of American education text, *The One Best System*. This essay has recalled that five expectations were used to justify the common school's development as "the one best system"—a replacement for the private schools. It is the opinion of this writer, as a "collective," that while all five reasons still have merit, only two (common experiences and common opportunities), have relevance today. Readers must decide whether they can join the writer in supporting public schools and religious schools for the following reasons:

1. That public schools and religious schools both retain a responsi-

bility to prepare students for participation as citizens and there is no meaningful difference in how well they do that task now.

2. That the common values taught in public schools, with the exception of religion studies, are not substantially different than those taught in religious schools; that public schools can and do have an obligation to include some treatment of the role of religion. (Failure to do so is likely to exacerbate the movement to nonpublic schools.)

3. That public schools *can* offer, to an extent not always possible in religious schools, more experiences to build unity from diversity. There is no substitute for personal experiences with members of diverse racial and ethnic backgrounds. More interactions are sorely needed in our society.

4. That public schools still have the mandate to provide common opportunities, which religious schools *may* also provide, but are not compelled to meet. Although there is much evidence that public schools have failed far too often at this task—it stands as an indictment of our culture—critics have not convinced me that religious schools and other private schools would achieve more equality of educational opportunity.

5. That public schools and religious schools are similar in their preparation of students to be social reformers.

In closing, I would reiterate a point I made in the introduction. The words, government schools and state schools, are now replacing the term "public" schools. Frequently, those words are used in a pejorative sense. As this essay has pointed out, the term "common" school has a proud history and has an intent which is still valid. Therefore, supporters of public education need to reappropriate the term "common school." We are more than individuals. Each of us is a member of many publics. Sooner or later, we must learn how to communicate with those publics as we face intimate personal problems and urgent social concerns. Self-contained educational systems, whether they are religious, economic, racial, geographical, forfeit that necessary function of the "common" school.

A special word needs to be said to readers who are professional educators in the public sector. The key to your survival will be your responsiveness to your clients. For the openness of the public schools is one test of whether it is truly a "common" school. If your needs must be met at the expense of the students, if you ignore valid criticisms from patrons, if you blame others for all your problems, then society can legitimately ask others to become our next common school.

The common school is a human institution. It has had its share of glorious failures. It has had its share of shameful harvests. It deserves the chance to continue striving for its ideal—glorious harvests.

NOTES

1. A general sourcebook for the period 1830–1870 is Sol Cohen, comp., *Education in the United States: A Documentary History*, 5 vols. (New York: Random House, 1974). Robert B. Everhart, ed., *The Public School Monopoly: A Critical Analysis of Education and the State in American Society* (Cambridge, Mass.: Ballinger Publishing Co., 1982), pp. 23–188, contains several selections which offer detailed descriptions of the individuals who opposed the emerging public system. Daniel F. Reilly, *The School Controversy, 1891–1893* (Washington, D.C.: The Catholic University of America Press, 1944; reprint ed. Arno Press and The New York Times, 1969), p. 33, describes the efforts of Zach Montgomery, a San Francisco editor who traveled California in the late 1870s protesting the public school movement.

2. Horace Mann to Mary Peabody Mann, 2 July 1837, cited by Cohen, *Education in the United States: A Documentary History*, 2: 1075.

3. Mathew Hale Smith, *The Ark of God on a New Cart* (Boston, 1847), pp. 11–12, cited by Cohen, *Education in the United States: A Documentary History*, 2: 1154.

4. Lawrence A. Cremin, *American Education: The National Experience, 1783–1876* (New York: Harper & Row, 1980), p. iii.

5. The words of Justice Orton, from *Wisconsin v. Weiss* (Edgerton, Wisconsin, 1890), are found in U.S., Bureau of Education, *Report of the Commissioner of Education for the Year 1888–1889*, 1: 630–31.

6. Cohen, *Education in the United States: A Documentary History*, 2: vii, provides yet another description of the meaning of "common school" in the early 1800s. For further discussion of the interpretations of "public" and "private" schools, see Richard Pratte, *The Public School Movement: A Critical Study* (New York: David McKay Co., 1973), pp. 27–37. The terms "state school" and "government school" are terms often used by critics of public education today and scarcely hide the antagonism against centralized control they imply.

7. Joseph R. Gusfield, *Symbolic Crusade* (Urbana, Ill.: University of Illinois Press, 1966).

8. In addition to Cremin, *American Education: The National Experience, 1783–1876;* and Cohen, *Education in the United States: A Documentary History*, 2, see Frederick M. Binder, *The Age of the Common School, 1830–1865* (New York: John Wiley, 1974).

9. Paul L. Ford, ed., *The Works of Thomas Jefferson*, 10 vols. (New York: G. P. Putnam, 1904), 4: 60–65.

10. *Illinois Sessions Laws* (1825), p. 121, cited by W. G. Walker, "The Development of the Free Public High School in Illinois During the Nineteenth Century," *History of Education Quarterly* 4 (December 1964): 264–79; "General Education—Remarks of Mr. Stevens," *Hazard's Register of Pennsylvania*, 15 (1835): 283–86, cited by Cohen, *Education in the United States: A Documentary History*, 2: 1064; Michigan Senate, "Report of the Superintendent of Public

Instruction of the State of Michigan," *Senate Journal*, 1837, Doc. no. 7, cited by Cohen, *Education in the United Staetes: A Documentary History*, 2: 1025.

11.   Horace Mann, *Tenth Annual Report of the Secretary of the Board of Education* (Boston: Dutton and Wentworth, State Printers, 1847), cited by Cohen, *Education in the United States: A Documentary History*, 2: 1096.

12.   Iowa, "Report of the Superintendent of Public Instruction," *Journal of The Senate of the State of Iowa*, 5th General Assembly (1854), Appendix, pp. 129–30; J. N. McJilton, "Preparation of Pupils for Citizenship," *Proceedings of the National Teachers Association* (Syracuse: C. W. Bardeen, 1860), pp. 269–90. For current critics, see Samuel Bowles and Herbert Gintis, *Schooling in Capitalist America: Educational Reform and the Contradiction of Economic Life* (New York: Basic Books, 1979).

13.   U.S., Bureau of Education, *Report of the Commissioner of Education for the Year 1888–1889*, 1: 617.

14.   Cremin, *American Education: The National Experience, 1783–1876*, p. 394.

15.   A general source on the history of curriculum development is Robert S. Zais, *Curriculum: Principles and Foundations* (New York: Thomas Y. Crowell, 1976). For a more detailed discussion on civics, see Edward A. Krug, *The Shaping of the American High School, 1880–1920* (Madison: University of Wisconsin Press, 1969), pp. 353–61; and R. Freeman Butts, *The Revival of Civic Learning* (Bloomington, Ind.: Phi Delta Kappa, 1980). An example of the most recent efforts is Richard C. Remy, *Handbook of Basic Citizenship Competencies* (Alexandria, Va.: Association for Supervision and Curriculum Development, 1980).

16.   Robert M. Hutchins, "The Role of Public Education," *Today's Education* (November–December 1973), p. 82.

17.   F. A. Sawyer, "The Common Schools—What They Can Do for a State," *Proceedings of the National Teachers Association* (Syracuse: C. W. Bardeen, 1870), p. 913. A similar statement was made by John J. Tigert, then U.S. Commissioner of Education, to the National Education Association in 1925 (the year of the *Pierce* decision). See John J. Tigert, "The Faith of the American People in Public Education," *Addresses and Proceedings* (Washington, D.C.: National Education Association, 1925), pp. 5–10.

18.   Arthur J. Newman, ed., *In Defense of the American Public School* (Berkeley, Calif.: McCutchan, 1978) contains thirty-five selections, past and present, which provide examples of the positive results of public education. Harold L. Hodgkinson, "What's Still Right with Education," *Phi Delta Kappan* 64 (December 1982): 231–35, is an update of an earlier article by the same author. For annual data on various educational benefits such as citizen participation in government, see such sources as National Center for Education Statistics (hereafter cited as NCES), *The Condition of Education, 1978* (Washington, D.C.: U.S. Government Printing Office, 1978), p. 260; NCES, *The Condition of Education, 1979* (U.S. Government Printing Office, 1979), p. 36.

19.   For an analysis of the criticisms which emerged during the 1950s see Lawrence A. Cremin, *The Transformation of the School* (New York: Knopf, 1961), pp. 338–43, 347. For more recent criticisms, see Paul Cooperman, *The Literacy Hoax: The Decline of Reading, Writing, and Learning in the Public School and What We Can Do About It* (New York: Morrow Quill, 1978); and Allan

Nairn and Associates, *The Reign of ETS: The Corporation That Makes Up Minds* (Washington, D.C.: Learning Center, 1980).

20. John Dewey was highly disturbed when three New York City teachers were fired in 1917 for their *lack* of patriotism. See John Dewey, "Public Education on Trial," *New Republic*, 29 December 1917, p. 245. During the 1970s the National Assessment of Education Progress (NAEP) began periodic surveys of student performance in ten areas, including social studies and citizenship. One summary of their findings is located in B. Frank Brown, *Education for Responsible Citizenship* (New York: McGraw-Hill, 1977), pp. 1–3.

21. Two references for this general area are Reilly, *The School Controversy, 1891–1893*, pp. 1–38; and Tom Jones, "Public v. Nonpublic Education in Historical Perspective," Stanford University, Institute on Research on Finance of Government Report TTT-6, February 1982. For Keane's remarks, see U.S., Bureau of Education, *Report of the Commissioner of Education for the Year 1888–1889*, 1: 625–26. For a story of the World's Columbian Exposition exhibit, see U.S., Bureau of Education, *Report of the Commissioner of Education for the Year 1892–1893;* 1: 510–520.

22. George M. Marsden, *Fundamentalism and American Culture, The Shaping of Twentieth-Century Evangelism: 1870–1925* (Oxford: Oxford University Press, 1980) provides a historical overview. Jerry Falwell, ed., *The Fundamentalist Phenomenon: The Resurgence of Conservative Christianity* (Garden City, N.Y.: Doubleday and Co., 1981) illustrates the general point of view among the "moral majority" about patriotism. In Christian day schools it is common to see patriotic cermonies.

23. Edward M. Gaffney, Jr., ed., *Private Schools and the Public Good: Policy Alternatives for the Eighties* (Notre Dame, Ind.: University of Notre Dame Press, 1981); and James Coleman et al., *Public and Private Schools* (Washington, D.C.: National Center for Educational Statistics, November 1981).

24. Rush's 1786 words are cited by Newman, *In Defense of the American Public School,* p. 12; Horace Mann, *Twelfth Annual Report of the Secretary of the Board of Education* (Boston: Dutton and Wentworth, State Printers, 1849), cited by Cohen, *Education in the United States: A Documentary History,* 2: 1104–09; Neil G. McCluskey, ed., *Catholic Education in America: A Documentary History* (New York: Bureau of Publication, Teachers College, Columbia University, 1964), pp. 65–77; and for an extensive treatment of religion (and especially Bible-reading) in public schools, see David L. Barr and Nicholas Piediscalzi, eds., *The Bible in American Education: From Source Book to Textbook* (Philadelphia: Fortress Press, 1982).

25. The topic of "Religious Instruction in Public Schools" was featured in *The American Journal of Education* 2 (August 1856): 153–72. For Mann's comments on parochial education, see National Teachers Association, *Proceedings of the National Teachers' Association* (Syracuse: C. W. Bardeen, 1858), pp. 36–38.

26. For court case summaries and analyses, see Donald E. Boles, *The Bible, Religion, and the Public Schools* (Ames, Ia.: Iowa State University Press, 1975); and Charles R. Kniker, "Changing Perceptions: Religion in the Public Schools, 1848–1981," *Religious Education* 77 (May–June 1982): 251–68. To gain some idea of the shifting positions of professional educators, look at the annual meeting reports of the National Teachers Association and its successor, the National Education Association. The 1869 *Proceedings* contained

statements on this topic from a number of administrators. For Catholic reactions, see McCluskey, *Catholic Education in America: A Documentary History*, pp. 90–94.

27. Justice Hagans, in *Minor v. Board of Education of Cincinnati* (1870) as printed in *The Bible in the Public Schools* (New York: Da Capo Press, 1967), p. 371.

28. U.S., Bureau of Education, *Report of the Commissioner of Education for the Year 1888–1889*, 1: 614–15, 628; Robert Michaelsen, *Piety in the Public School* (New York: Macmillan Co., 1970), pp. 120–21 describes the background of *Our Country;* and *Moral Training in the Public Schools* (Boston: Ginn and Co., 1907), pp. 3–52.

29. Charles R. Kniker, *You and Values Education* (Columbus, Ohio: Charles E. Merrill Co., 1981), pp. 12–27.

30. National Education Association, Commission on the Reorganization of Secondary Education, *Cardinal Principles of Secondary Education* (Washington, D.C.: U.S. Bureau of Education, Bulletin No. 35, 1918); and National Education Association, Educational Policies Commission, *Moral and Spiritual Values in the Public Schools* (Washington, D.C.: National Education Association, 1951). See also Ellis Ford Hartford, *Moral Values in Public Education* (New York: Harper and Brothers, 1958); Louis Raths, Merrill Harmin, and Sidney Simon, *Values and Teaching* (Columbus, Ohio: Charles E. Merrill Co., 1966); David Purpel and Kevin Ryan, *Moral Education—It Comes with the Territory* (Berkeley, Calif.: McCutchen, 1976); and Reo M. Christenson, "Clarifying 'Values Clarification' for the Innocent," *Christianity Today*, 10 April 1981, pp. 36–39.

31. George Albert Coe, *The Social Theory of Religious Education* (New York: Charles Scribner, 1917), pp. 26-–61; see also R. Freeman Butts, *The American Tradition in Religion and Education* (Boston: Beacon Press, 1950) and B. Othanel Smith, "What Do the Sectarians Want?" *Progressive Education* 26 (February 1949): 121–24, 128. For the parochial school and fundamentalist reactions see Otto F. Kraushaar, *American Nonpublic Schools: Patterns of Diversity* (Baltimore: The John Hopkins University Press, 1972); and Timothy D. Crater, "The Unproclaimed Priests of Public Education," *Christianity Today*, 10 April 1981, pp. 44–47.

32. Mann, *Twelfth Annual Report of the Secretary of the Board of Education* (1849), cited in Cohen, *Education in the United States: A Documentary History*, 2: 1108; Sawyer, "The Common Schools—What They Can Do for a State," p. 922; William W. Folwell, "Secularization of Education," in National Education Association, *Addresses and Proceedings* (Boston: Alfred Mudge and Sons, 1882), pp. 42–45.

33. Clarence J. Karier, "Business Values and the Educational State," in *Roots of Crisis: American Education in the Twentieth Century*, eds. Clarence J. Karier, Paul Violas, and Joel Spring (Chicago: Rand McNally, 1973), pp. 6–29; Vernon Jones, *Character and Citizenship Training in the Public School* (Chicago: University of Chicago Press, 1936); and Hugh Hartshorne, *Character in Human Relations* (New York: Charles Scribner's Sons, 1933), pp. 224–25.

34. Smith, "What Do the Sectarians Want?" p. 122; and Alan L. Lockwood, "The Effects of Values Clarification and Moral Development Curricula on School-Age Subjects: A Critical Review of Recent Research," *Review of Educational Research* 48 (Summer 1978): 325–64.

35. R. Freeman Butts et al., *The School's Role as Moral Authority* (Washington, D.C.: Association for Supervision and Curriculum Development, 1977). In 1971 the National Council on Religion and Public Education (NCRPE) was formed as a consortium of organizations to support the U.S. Supreme Court's 1963 *Schempp/Murray* decision which prohibited devotional Bible reading but allowed teaching about religion in public schools. More recently, five Protestant denominations prepared a study guide entitled *The Church and Public Education* for use by their members. The denominations included the American Baptists, Church of the Brethren, Presbyterian Church in the U.S., United Church of Christ, and United Presbyterians. The document is reprinted as the total issue of *Church and Society* 70 (November 1979): 1–66. The American Lutheran Church in June 1981 also developed a major statement on the topic of the church and public education.

36. The quotations of Agassiz and Gladden are cited by Reilly, *The School Controversy, 1891–1893*, pp. 35–36; and Mel Gabler, interview in *Moral Majority Report*, 30 July 1980, p. 5. A similar evaluation of the problems of values education and sex education in public schools is found in a pamphlet issued by the Catholic Bishops of Pennsylvania in 1977. Some fundamentalists are now urging that the godless public schools be viewed as missionary fields. See Barbara J. Hampton, "Why Some Parents Go to School with the Kids," *Christianity Today*, 3 September 1982, pp. 23–25.

37. Coleman, *Public and Private Schools*, chap. 5; Andrew M. Greeley and Peter H. Rossi, *The Education of Catholic Americans* (Chicago: Aldine Publishing Co., 1966); Ronald L. Johnstone, *The Effectiveness of Lutheran Elementary and Secondary Schools as Agencies of Christian Education* (St. Louis: Concordia Seminary, 1966); and Jonathan Roos, "Education in Baptist School is Better, say Trial Witnesses," *Des Moines Register*, 28 October 1982, p. 1.

38. Austin Bierbower, quoted in U.S., Bureau of Education, *Report of the Commissioner of Education for the Year 1888–1889*, 1: 627; Sawyer, "The Common Schools—What They Can Do for a State," p. 924.

39. See Cohen, *Education in the United States: A Documentary History*, 2: 825, 994, and 1063 for representative statements on unity. A modern-day advocate for unity is R. Freeman Butts, *Public Education in the United States: From Revolution to Reform* (New York: Holt, Rinehart and Winston, 1978). A contemporary challenge is found in Stephen Arons, *Compelling Belief: The Culture of American Schooling* (New York: McGraw-Hill, 1983).

40. National Teachers Association, *Proceedings of the National Teachers' Association* (1858), p. 38.

41. *McCollum v. Board of Education*, 330 U.S. 203, 231–32 (1948).

42. Leonard Covello, *The Teacher in the Urban Community* (Totowa, N.J.: Littlefield, Adams, 1970): Booker T. Washington, *Up from Slavery* (New York: Doubleday, Page and Co., 1901); Mary Antin, *The Promised Land* (New York: Houghton Mifflin, 1912); and Margaret Connell Szasz, *Education and the American Indian: The Road To Self-Determination Since 1928* (Albuquerque: University of New Mexico Press, 1977).

43. Krug, *The Shaping of the High School, 1880–1920*, pp. 256–57; and Tigert, "The Faith of the American People in Public Education," p. 8.

44. Hutchins, "The Role of Public Education," p. 80.

45. Harris is quoted in U.S., Bureau of Education, *Report of the Commissioner of Education for the Year 1888–1889*, 1: 633–34. Payson Smith, "The

Challenge to American Education," *Addresses and Proceedings* (Washington, D.C.: National Education Association, 1924), p. 139.

46. John S. Brubacher, ed., *The Public Schools and Spiritual Values* (New York: Harper and Brothers, 1944), pp. 6, 84; Smith, "What Do the Sectarians Want?" p. 122; and James Conant, *My Several Lives: Memoirs of a Social Inventor* (New York: Harper & Row, 1970), chap. 34.

47. National Education Association, *Addresses and Proceedings of the One-Hundred-And-First Annual Meeting* (Washington, D.C.: National Education Association, 1963), pp. 190–91.

48. For some perspective on this movement see William A. Hunter, *Multicultural Education through Competency-Based Teacher Education* (Washington, D.C.: American Association of Colleges for Teacher Education, 1974). Butts, *The Revival of Civic Learning*, pp. 1–23, provides arguments against multicultural education centered around the point that diversity is stressed at the expense of unity.

49. Reilly, *The School Controversy, 1891–1893*, p. 37; and James Michael Lee, "Religion and Public Schools: A Pluralistic View," *California Journal of Teacher Education* 9 (Spring 1982): 17–18.

50. Newman, *In Defense of the American Public School*, p. 5; Cohen, *Education in the United States: A Documentary History*, 2: 1025; George Smith, "Nineteenth-Century Opponents of State Education: Prophets of Modern Revisionism," in Everhart, *The Public School Monopoly: A Critical Analysis of Education and the State in American Society*, pp. 139–44; and Iowa, *Journal of The Senate of The State of Iowa* (1854), p. 15.

51. Typical statements can be found in Walker, "Development of the Free Public High Schools in Illinois," p. 272; Sawyer, "The Common Schools—What They Can Do For a State," pp. 917–18; and Judge Orton's remarks in the Edgerton, Wisconsin case, in U.S., Bureau of Education, *Report of the Commissioner of Education For the Year 1888–1889*, 1: 631.

52. Tigert, "The Faith of the American People in Public Education," p. 9.

53. Charles R. Kniker and Natalie A. Naylor, *Teaching Today and Tomorrow* (Columbus, Ohio: Charles E. Merrill Co., 1981), pp. 323–29; and Terry Eastland and William J. Bennett, *Counting by Race: Equality from the Founding Fathers to Bakke and Weber* (New York: Basic Books, 1979).

54. The Council on Interracial Books for Children, *Guidelines for Selecting Bias-Free Textbooks and Storybooks* (New York: Council on Interracial Books for Children, n.d.). A typical text used in college courses for future teachers is James A. Banks, *Teaching Strategies for Multiethnic Studies*, 2nd ed. (Boston: Allyn and Bacon, 1979).

55. C. H. Edson, "Schooling for Work and Working at School: Perspectives on Immigrant and Working-Class Education in Urban America, 1880–1920," in Everhart, *The Public School Monopoly: A Critical Analysis of Education and the State in American Society*, pp. 145–88; and James B. Conant, *Slums and Suburbs* (New York: The New American Library, 1961).

56. Everhart, *The Public School Monopoly: A Critical Analysis of Education and the State in American Society*, pp. 75, 212–13, 316.

57. Franklin Parker, "What's Right with American Education," *Illinois Schools Journal* 47 (Spring 1967): 26–32; Hodgkinson, "What's Still Right With Education," pp. 231–35; James William Noll, ed., *Taking Sides: Clashing Views on Controversial Educational Issues*, 2nd ed. (Guilford, Conn.: Dushkin

Publishing Group, 1983), pp. 136–71; and Ernest F. Hollings, "The Case Against Tuition Tax Credits," *Phi Delta Kappan* 60 (December 1978): 277–80.

58. Everhart, *The Public School Monopoly: A Critical Analysis of Education and the State in American Society,* pp. 205–06, 221, 244–57; Patricia Sexton, *Education and Income* (New York: Viking Press, 1961); James S. Coleman et al., *Equality of Educational Opportunity* (Washington, D.C.: U.S. Government Printing Office, 1966); Christopher Jencks, *Inequality* (New York: Harper & Row, 1972); and Virgil C. Blum, "Why Inner-City Families Send Their Children to Private Schools: An Empirical Study," in Gaffney, *Private Schools and the Public Good: Policy Alternatives for the Eighties,* p. 19.

59. Denis P. Doyle, "Public Funding and Private Schooling: The State of Descriptive and Analytic Research," in Gaffney, *Private Schools and the Public Good: Policy Alternatives for the Eighties,* pp. 73–74.

60. See Thomas Vitullo-Martin, "How Federal Policies Discourage the Racial and Economic Integration of Private Schools," in Gaffney, *Private Schools and the Public Good: Policy Alternatives for the Eighties,* pp. 25–43. See also Andrew Greeley, *Minority Students in Catholic Schools* (New York: Transaction, 1982).

61. Coleman, *Public and Private Schools,* p. xxxi.

62. Bush quoted in Newman, *In Defense of the American Public School,* p. 64; Mann cited in Cohen, *Education in the United States: A Documentary History,* 2: 1102; and Iowa, *Journal of The Senate of the State of Iowa* (1854), p. 130.

63. Thomas B. Stockwell, quoted in U.S., Bureau of Education, *Report of the Commissioner of Education for the Year 1888–1889,* 1: 621.

64. Reginald D. Archambault, ed., *John Dewey on Education: Selected Writings* (New York: Modern Library, 1964), pp. 437–39. For a strong position on too much state control, see Charles Burgess, "Growing Up Blighted: Reflections on the 'Secret Power' in the American Experience," in Everhart, *The Public School Monopoly: A Critical Analysis of Education and the State in American Society,* pp. 60–61.

65. Kniker and Naylor, *Teaching Today and Tomorrow,* pp. 266–67.

66. Earl J. Ogletree, "The Status of State-Legislated Curricula in the United States," *Phi Delta Kappan* 61 (October 1979): 133–35.

67. Harold G. Shane, with M. Bernadine Tabler, *Educating for a New Millennium* (Bloomington, Ind.: Phi Delta Kappan, 1981).

68. Donald E. Orlosky and B. O. Smith, "Educational Change: Its Origins and Characteristics," *Phi Delta Kappan* 53 (March 1972): 412–14; and Justice Jackson, *Everson v. Board of Education,* 330 U.S. 1, 24–28 (1947).

69. Charles E. Silberman, *Crisis in the Classroom* (New York: Random House, 1970).

70. Everhart, *The Public School Monopoly: A Critical Analysis of Education and the State in American Society,* pp. 77–108, 325–28.

71. U.S., Bureau of Education, *Report of the Commissioner of Education for the Year 1894–1895,* 1: 1318.

72. Coleman, *Public and Private Schools,* chap. 5.

73. "The Restructuring of America in the Decade Ahead," *Public Affairs Forum* (Malvern, Pa.: The Society of Chartered Property and Casualty Underwriters, 1981), pp. 1–15; and Rockne McCarthy, *Society, State, and Schools* (Grand Rapids, Mich: William B. Eerdmans Publishing Co., 1981), pp. 9–10, 13–50.

74. Patricia M. Lines, "State Regulation of Private Education," *Phi Delta Kappan* 64 (October 1982): 119–23.

75. Parker J. Palmer, *The Company of Strangers: Christians and The Renewal of America's Public Life* (New York: Crossword Publishing Co., 1981). See denominational statements mentioned in note 35 supra.

76. Bill Freeman, "How I Slid into Education's Permissive Pit and Climbed Out Again," *Christianity Today*, 10 April 1981, pp. 40–42.

77. Jonathan Kozol and John Holt would be representative of the political left, while the pastor and members of the church in Louisville, Nebraska, would represent the religious right.

Chapter 8

Tuition Tax Credits and Educational Vouchers

JAMES F. HERNDON

The Donaldsons, a family of five, have an income of a little over $20,000 a year. At a cost of $200 a year each, two children attend Catholic elementary schools. The third goes to a Catholic high school, which costs her parents $400 a year. The Donaldson children could attend public schools, but no one on either side of the family has ever done so. Catholic schools were not just the obvious but the only choice. The elder Donaldsons must sacrifice to make that choice, but because they take their religion seriously they do what they feel they must. They wonder, though, why they should be required to pay tuition to Catholic schools and be taxed to support public schools which they do not use.

Consider another family, the Millers, who live across town and whose income is too low to afford tuition at church schools. By necessity, the three Miller children attend public schools to parts of whose curriculum their parents have serious religious objections. The children seem nevertheless to do all right, especially since—in their parents' view—their formal schooling is supplemented by religious teaching at home and in church. The parents do wish, though, that they could somehow send their children to their church school full-time.

The Donaldsons have the choice the Millers do not, even though they pay—doubly as they see it—to have and exercise that choice. This absence of choice across all incomes and the perceived double payments for those who have the choice have led in the last several decades to calls for legislation to right what many see as an imbalance between public and private education.[1] Other arguments, leading to much the same conclusions, center on the threat to diversity in education that would follow from a financially induced demise of private

207

schools and on what is felt to be the failure of the public schools to educate properly, or at least as well as private schools are thought to do.[2] Some degree of public support for private schools is the suggested cure for each of these real and imagined, present or likely conditions.

However the case is put for public support—diversity, quality, income disparity, double taxes—it is eventually an argument for choice, for providing parents options they can afford for the schooling of their children. The parents' reasons for wanting a choice are secondary; they may wish to have religious education, or not; they may wish to have better, or more disciplined, or more "basic" instruction than that given in public schools; they may wish to escape racial integration; or they may simply want to send their children to a school closer to home. What is primary is that they have a choice, that the choice be independent of financial circumstance, and that they can choose without undue penalty through taxes or otherwise for making the choices they do.

The need for choice can be defended in a number of ways. Stephen Arons, for example, cites the First Amendment of the Constitution as requiring choice in its insurance of free exercise of religion, a guarantee made worthless if parents must pay what they cannot afford to secure that exercise. He also points to the Fourteenth Amendment's (and by judicial inference, the Fifth Amendment's) guarantee of equal protection of the laws and asks how that can be squared with what he believes to be double taxation.[3] A number of economists contend that a state monopoly in any enterprise reduces or destroys competition and, in the bargain, raises costs, lowers efficiency, and degrades the quality of the product being delivered.[4] A line of thought similar to that of the economists stresses the plural character of American society and the social gains to be had from preserving institutional pluralism in education, a pluralism that may be extinguished by the dead hand of state monopoly. Freedom of choice, provided if necessary by giving public money to parents or to private schools directly, would insure diversity, stimulate competition, rid parents of double taxation, and allow free exercise of religion within all income levels.[5]

An idea so appealing, and promising so much, is not likely to be ignored by politicians. Nor has it been. Many plans to provide parental choice have been devised by state legislatures and the occasional city council since World War II,[6] and in the last fifteen years or so, increasing interest has been shown at the federal level.[7] Most of the state schemes have foundered on constitutional barriers, while federal plans have been lost in budgetary, political, and constitutional disagreements between President and Congress. But despite this none too encouraging experience, politicians at all levels keep trying to fashion programs that could surmount the legal and political barriers that have been so frustrating so far.

These efforts have generally taken one or both of two forms that we shall label broadly as tuition tax credits and educational voucher systems. Simply defined, a tuition tax credit is a decrease in one's financial obligation to government. It can be equal to, or in some way proportionate to, what one pays in tuition to a private school. A full tuition tax credit for the Donaldsons, for example, would be $800, which amount they would subtract from what they owed the taxing authority. The Millers would not receive a tuition tax credit since they paid nothing in tuition to a private school.[8]

To help families like the Millers, whose income might be so low that they paid no taxes at all, some tuition tax credit plans would simply provide a grant large enough to allow these families to pay tuition at a private school. This kind of grant would be a form of negative income tax and would resemble the refunds many taxpayers receive from the Internal Revenue Service for overpayment of taxes. The educational voucher system, a somewhat more straightforward method than tuition tax credits, would also help the Millers, as well as any other family with children in private schools. Under this system, *all* parents—those using both public and private schools—would receive a certificate equal in cash value to the estimated cost of educating their children for one year in elementary or secondary schools. The parents could shop in their communities for the schools that best met their children's needs, pick the appropriate school, and send their children there. They would later deliver their certificate, or "voucher" to the school authorities who would send it on to a government office for payment.[9]

Both plans are normally hedged with provisions for administration and against fraud and racial discrimination, but they are in essence as described. Vouchers go further in promoting choice and would probably induce the competition and efficiency their supporters favor to a greater degree than would tuition tax credits. The latter would solve the problem of double taxation, if not fully, then at least in part. Vouchers would offer choices to parents regardless of family income, while tuition tax credits would do so only if some allowance for "refundability" were made. Both would likely encourage pluralism by indirect subsidies to private schools.

The most eloquent defender of aid to private schools has been

Senator Daniel Patrick Moynihan, Democrat of New York. The issue, Moynihan says, is whether "it is to be U.S. policy to foster state monopoly in the field of education or to help individuals obtain for themselves and their children the education they prefer at the schools and colleges they select."[10] Tax relief for parents who must pay the bills is only just: "To deny aid to such persons and thereby make it more difficult for them to obtain the education they seek for their families is to submit to paternalism and to statism."[11] As for constitutional issues involving church and state, Moynihan argues that earlier in our history "public support for all manner of church schools was common and unremarked"[12] and that "if there is a constitutional bar at the federal level, the only thing to do is pass a bill and let the Supreme Court decide."[13]

Senator Ernest F. Hollings, a South Carolina Democrat, has been Moynihan's most insistent opponent in the Senate. He contends that tuition tax credits "would turn our nation's educational policy on its head, benefit the few at the expense of the many, proliferate substandard segregation academies, add a sea of red ink to the federal deficit, violate the clear meaning of the First Amendment to the Constitution, and destroy the diversity and genius of our system of public education."[14] Private schools, Hollings has said, can be selective in admissions, turn away those with discipline, language, and learning problems, and enroll "those fleeing from the innercity, integrated school."[15]

The Moynihan-Hollings debate is not of just academic interest. Bills providing for tuition tax credits have been before the last two Congresses, and in the most recent Congress the Administration presented a plan for educational vouchers. The latest version of tuition tax credits offered families with adjusted gross incomes of up to $40,000 a credit of 50 percent of tuition costs, to a maximum of $300 per child. Families with incomes between $40,000 and $60,000 would have their credit reduced, and those making more than $60,000 would get no credit.[16] The Administration's voucher plan was restricted to parents of children chosen to take part in compensatory education programs. In those school districts offering the choice, parents would use vouchers to send their children where they thought educational opportunities were greatest.[17]

This legislation has been supported and opposed by numerous groups and individuals. Those opposed have been the mainline professional associations of educators and people favoring public schools, while those in support of tax credits and vouchers have been organizations of private schools and most of the organizations of the politically "far right." Crowded Congressional agendas, the concern over rising budget deficits, and effective lobbying by opponents have conspired to keep tax credit and voucher proposals from drawing the kind of legislative support that would lead to their acceptance, either in Congress or in the nation at large.[18]

But even if greater popular and Congressional support should materialize, another barrier may block the path of tuition tax credit and vouchers. Any bill containing tuition tax credits for parents of children in religious schools will certainly be challenged in the courts. And almost as certainly, one can predict that the United State Supreme Court will be called on to decide its constitutionality. What then?

CONSTITUTIONAL BARRIERS

In 1973, in *Committee for Public Education v. Nyquist*,[19] the Supreme Court struck down New York legislation that gave grants to religious schools for maintenance and repair and provided tuition grants for low income families and tax deductions for others. To the degree that tax deductions and tax credits have like effects, the ruling in *Nyquist* would seem to be precedent enough for holding federal tuition tax credits unconstitutional. Many opponents of tax credits have suggested just that and have said so with considerable certainty.[20] But if we examine how the Court arrived at the rule it applied in *Nyquist*, as well as a more recent decision of the Court, and one or two incidental comments it made in *Nyquist*, we may not be so sure.

The Supreme Court began to construct the rule used in *Nyquist* as long ago as 1899, in *Bradfield v. Roberts*.[21] Against an argument that federal assistance to a hospital run by a religious order amounted to a subsidy of religion, the Court held that the aid went to support medical and not religious activities and saw nothing constitutionally amiss in the provision of federal money to an institution that coincidentally claimed a religious affiliation. A similar result was reached thirty-one years later in *Cochran v. Louisiana*,[22] where the Court held that the state's policy of supplying secular textbooks for use in nonpublic schools was an effort to help children and not religion. In *Everson v. Board of Education*,[23] decided in 1947, the Supreme Court upheld New Jersey's practice of reimbursing parents of nonpublic school children for transportation costs on grounds that such state aid as there was went to assist children in getting to school safely and only incidentally (though not unconstitutionally) benefited the schools or their sponsoring organizations. In each of these cases, the Court confined its attention to the immediate beneficiaries of government aid, hospital patients or school children, and not to more remote or indirect recipients. Medical treatment, secular learning as might be had from textbooks, and safe transportation of school children are all legitimate, secular objectives a government may spend money to achieve. That in the process a religious institution may derive some indirect benefit is not of sufficient constitutional importance to defeat the state's pursuit of lawful ends.

Besides extending the theory first set out in *Bradfield*, *Everson* also gave the Court a statement of what the establishment clause of the First Amendment means, a statement to which the Court (and others) have referred numerous times. In Justice Black's words, it means:

> Neither a state nor the Federal Government can set up a church. Neither can pass laws which aid one religion, aid all religions, or prefer one religion over another. Neither can force nor influence a person to go or to remain away from church against his will or force him to profess a belief or disbelief in any religion. No person can be punished for entertaining or professing religious beliefs or disbeliefs, for church attendance or nonattendance. No tax in any amount, large or small, can be levied to support any religious activities or institutions, whatever they may be called, or whatever form they may adopt to preach or practice religion. Neither a state nor the Federal Government can, openly or secretly, participate in the affairs of any religious organizations or groups, and vice versa.[24]

But in applying this rule to the facts in *Everson*, Black held that in insuring against a religious establishment, the Court must not prevent a state from conferring its benefits on all its citizens regardless of their religious beliefs. It would surely do just that, Black said, were the Court to disallow the use of public funds to pay the transportation costs of parochial school children if those funds supported a general program of benefit to all school children. To deny support to the families of children attending religious schools would, Black continued, make the state an adversary of religion. "State power is no more to be used so as to handicap religions than it is to favor them."[25]

The idea that government was to avoid hostility to religion was established by the Court in *Pierce v. Society of Sisters*,[26] a 1925 case in which the Court found the denial by Oregon of accreditation to religious schools to be an act so unfriendly that it denied children enrolled in religious schools their rights to free exercise of religion. The

Court reaffirmed the principle in 1952, in *Zorach v. Clauson*,[27] a case involving released time in the public schools for religious instruction away from school premises. Here the Court found that the public schools' actions were not an unconstitutional establishment of religion but only an accommodation of schedule to religious interests. The First Amendment, Justice Douglas wrote, does not require separation of church "in every and all respects."[28] To deny accommodation of religion in the ways at issue in *Zorach* would make church and state "aliens to each other—hostile, suspicious, and even unfriendly."[29] And that the First Amendment does not permit.

These cases, then, point to several principles the Court derived from the words of the First Amendment which it could use to decide both the cases at hand and those that might arise in the future: government cannot found or aid a church, nor can it dictate religious belief. It may, however, in its pursuit of legitimate secular objectives aid those who are coincidentally associated with religious institutions in the same way and for the same reasons that it helps those without any such association. And, finally, whatever it does in avoiding the establishment of religion, government must not go so far that it becomes hostile to religion.

These several principles were made more concise in *Abington School District v. Schempp*,[30] a 1963 case in which the Supreme Court declared that required Bible reading in public schools was an establishment of religion and therefore in violation of the Constitution. Conceding that "our national life reflects a religious people," [31] the Court said that religious freedom is just "as strongly imbedded in our public and private life."[32] The joining of religion and state imperils that freedom, a circumstance the Court said had led to its earlier decisions in favor of a "wholesome neutrality."[33] To maintain that neutrality, any state policy or program touching on religious interests must have "a secular legislative purpose and a primary effect that neither advances nor inhibits religion."[34]

Armed with this test, the Supreme Court found in *Board of Education v. Allen*,[35] a 1968 case, that New York's practice of lending secular texts to children in religious schools did not violate the First Amendment because the state's purposes were secular and, because the state's actions benefited the children or their parents and not the schools, the primary effects of the state's policy neither advanced nor inhibited religion.

In a case having nothing directly to do with schools, *Walz v. Tax Commission*,[36] decided in 1970, the Court added a third element to the *Schempp* test and set in place the test to be applied in all subsequent cases, including *Nyquist*, the case most relevant to tuition tax credits. In *Walz*, the Court faced a challenge to the New York City Tax Commission's policy of allowing tax exemptions to religious institutions on property used only for religious purposes. Rather than seeing such exemptions as an establishment of religion, the Court found the Commission's policy to be part of a program extending exemptions to many nonprofit organizations. Since that program had a secular purpose and was not aimed at supporting or sponsoring religion, the Court could not find it in violation of the *Schempp* test. But the Court went further. In his opinion for the majority, Chief Justice Burger wrote that, "determining that the legislative purpose of tax exemption is not aimed at establishing, sponsoring, or supporting religion does not end the inquiry. . . . We must also be sure that the end result—the effect—is not an excessive entanglement with religion."[37] Though more precise meanings of "entanglement" were to be given in later cases, what it meant here, apparently, was any action by government to become involved in religious affairs as it carries out whatever policy is at issue. Since the Court saw no such possibility here, the exemption was upheld.

Now the Court had a three-part rule it could and did apply to a number of cases concerning public support for parochial schools. The first two parts stemmed from *Schempp*, the third from *Walz*. Any aid that government might offer to religious schools had to have: (1) a secular legislative purpose; (2) a primary effect that did not advance or inhibit religion; and (3) an absence of excessive entanglement of church and state. In 1971, in *Lemon v. Kurtzman*[38] and two companion cases,[39] the Court struck down statutes in Pennsylvania that reimbursed private schools for costs of teachers' salaries, texts, and materials in secular subjects and in Rhode Island statutes that provided up to 15 percent in salary supplements for teachers of secular subjects in nonpublic schools. The surveillance by the state which would be required to guarantee that secular teachers were not involved in sectarian instructional or other activities struck the Court as exactly the kind of "entanglement" that *Walz* forbade. The Court also thought that the annual appropriations required to support these programs would engender a degree of political divisiveness that the First Amendment sought to preclude.

Shortly after *Lemon*, in 1973, the Court turned to *Nyquist*. Under legislation adopted by New York, the state would offer direct grants to schools for maintenance and repair of physical facilities and would provide financial aid in a two-part package to parents of children in parochial schools. Part one allowed parents with annual incomes of less than $5000 to receive reimbursements of up to half of what they paid in tuition, but no more than $50 for each elementary school child and no more than $100 for each child in a secondary school. Parents whose incomes were too high to qualify for reimbursements would, under part two, receive a tax deduction which fell as income rose. Measuring these provisions of the law against the three-part test, the Court found, first, that New York had clearly secular purposes in view, and on that score the law could be upheld. The record showed that the state was seeking to insure a healthy and safe educational environment through its maintenance and repair grants, and that through these grants and through its effort to aid parents the state was trying legitimately to retain pluralism and diversity and to relieve enrollment pressures on overburdened public schools. All of these objectives were, in the Court's view, constitutionally permissible.

In applying the "effects" test, however, the Court reached quite different conclusions. Since no effort was made in the law to restrict the maintenance and repair grants to secular facilities, the section authorizing those grants had a primary effect of advancing religion and was therefore a violation of the First Amendment. If the state is not permitted to give money to build religious facilities, it cannot pay for maintenance and repair of those facilities. Tuition reimbursements and tax deductions also failed the effects test. Writing for the Court, Justice Powell said:

> By reimbursing parents for a portion of their tuition bill, the State seeks to relieve their financial burdens sufficiently to assure that they continue to have the option to send their children to religion-oriented schools. And while the other purposes for that aid—to perpetuate a pluralistic educational environment and to protect the fiscal integrity of overburdened schools—are certainly unexceptionable, the effect of the aid is unmistakably to provide desired financial support for nonpublic, sectarian institutions.[40]

The Court met the argument that the absence of state support would imperil parochial schools and therefore threaten rights to free exercise of religion with its own argument that the social importance of the state's purposes in conferring aid on religious schools cannot "justify an eroding of the limitations of the Establishment Clause now firmly implanted."[41] Justice Powell then distinguished the upholding of tax exemptions in *Walz* from the circumstances in this case by pointing out that tax exemptions for churches were meant to reduce entanglement of church and state and conferred only "indirect and incidental"[42] benefits, whereas the tax benefits at issue in *Nyquist* would "increase rather than limit the involvement between church and state."[43]

Because the New York statute could be held constitutionally invalid on the basis of the effects test alone, the Court found no need to determine whether the law would also fail the entanglement test, at least in the sense that "continuing state surveillance"[44] would be needed to enforce the law. In a concluding section of Powell's opinion, however, the Court did express itself on the matter of entanglement in the sense of political controversy over public aid to religious schools. After noting that "pressure for frequent enlargement of relief" in those sections of the law dealing with reimbursement and tax deductions "is predictable,"[45] the Court gave warning:

> We know from long experience with both Federal and State Governments that aid programs of any kind tend to become entrenched, to escalate in cost, and to generate their own aggressive constituencies. . . . The potential for seriously divisive political consequences needs no elaboration.[46]

Finally, to relate this case to our discussion of tax *credits* (*Nyquist* dealt, after all, with reimbursements and tax *deductions*), let us note that the Court saw no substantial difference between credits and deductions. Justice Powell simply quoted the lower court: "[I]n both instances the money involved represents a charge made upon the state for the purpose of religious education."[47] If one is unconstitutional, then so is the other.

Following *Nyquist*, the Court held invalid a Pennsylvania law similar to New York's in *Sloan v. Lemon*.[48] Two years later, in *Meek v. Pittenger*,[49] the Supreme Court allowed Pennsylvania to loan secular textbooks to parochial schools but disallowed the loan of materials and equipment and the state's provision of certain auxiliary services. To insure that these services, as well as materials and equipment supplied by the state, were not being put to sectarian uses, the state would have to indulge in a program of audit and review that would necessarily amount to a constitutionally forbidden degree of entanglement in the affairs of religious schools. In 1977 the Court decided *Wolman v. Walter*[50] in which it upheld textbook loans, state-supplied standardized testing and scoring, as well as diagnostic and therapeutic services. The Court refused, however, to approve transportation for field trips and loans of equipment and materials. And, in *Committee for Public Education and Religious Liberty v. Regan*,[51] decided in 1980, the Supreme Court upheld a New York program of reimbursements to church-related schools for the costs of administering, grading, and reporting the results of standardized tests and for the costs of reporting pupil attendance and other basic data required by the state.

In its 1982–83 term, the Supreme Court returned to the question of tax credits and tax deductions, thought to have been settled in *Nyquist*. Since that case was decided, however, conflicting holdings were made in two lower court cases, *Mueller v. Allen*[52] and *Rhode Island Federation of Teachers v. Norberg*.[53] In *Mueller*, the Court of Appeals for the Eighth Circuit upheld a Minnesota law providing for tax deductions for the cost of tuition, transportation, and secular textbooks on grounds that because all parents could use the deduction, the statute was on its face neutral toward religion.[54] The ruling was made despite a showing that only 79 of the state's 805,000 public school pupils paid tuition in 1978–79 and that since 96 percent of Minnesota's 89,000 nonpublic school students paid tuition to sectarian schools, 71 percent of the tax benefits would go to parents of children in religious schools.[55]

In *Norberg*, on the other hand, the Court of Appeals for the First Circuit struck down a Rhode Island statute virtually identical to the one upheld in *Mueller*. Because 94 percent of private school students in Rhode Island went to religious schools, this court concluded that the tax relief given by the state was distributed "along nearly solid sectarian lines"[56] and was therefore unconstitutional.

The Court resolved the conflict by upholding the ruling in *Mueller*, agreeing with the lower court that the Minnesota law offered benefits to a "broad spectrum of citizens" and not just to those whose children attended sectarian schools.[57] At least five members of the Court saw a distinction between the "neutrality" of Minnesota's policy and the restricted beneficence of the New York statute it struck down in *Nyquist*.[58] Tax breaks designed to help only the users of religious schools are still, therefore, unconstitutional; those working to everyone's potential benefit are not.

Some see confusion and inconsistency in this long series of cases.[59] And indeed, the Supreme Court has not described the constitutional status of every kind of aid to religious schools that one might imagine. Nor has its three-part rule given every citizen in the country an absolutely precise idea of what is and is not permitted. But that is the way of constitutional adjudication. Courts construct rules, and they apply them as cases arrive. Over time, patterns emerge that, while they may not satisfy everyone's needs for mathematical precision, are good enough. In these cases, it seems clear that secular textbook grants or loans are all right, because they do not involve government in the affairs of schools to other than a minimal degree, and that equipment and materials loans are impermissible because they do. Payments by the state of teachers' salaries in religious schools are not allowed for the same reason; to guarantee that the state was paying teachers only for their secular teaching would require government to inquire too deeply into the practices of religious schools, an inquiry government has no business making. So long as they are tied to tuition payments to religious schools and are not allowed to parents of public school children, tax credits, tax deductions, and reimbursements are all intended to aid religion and, at least in the Supreme Court's view, are just as much forbidden by the First Amendment as would be direct grants to the schools themselves.

But if we derive at least that much clarity and consistency in the Court's opinions, we may still have reason for uncertainty about the prospects of federal tax credits for sectarian education. Any such program would be expensive if, as Reagan Administration proposals contemplate, aid were limited to parents of private school children. To satisfy the Supreme Court's reasoning in *Mueller,* tax credits would also have to be made available to public school parents, thus making an aid package even more expensive. At a time when most mainstream politicians are talking about reducing budget deficits, legislation providing so large a package would be quite difficult to adopt.

VOUCHERS INSTEAD OF TAX CREDITS?

Aid for religious schools through tuition tax credits seems fairly remote, then, given current political circumstances, the state of the economy, and the disposition of the Supreme Court. Aid delivered in the form of general grants, so far the closest approximation to which are the educational vouchers we described earlier, may well have a better chance, at least constitutionally. With an improved economy, their chances may be better still.

What may work against vouchers, however, is their limited history in this country and the not altogether favorable experience gained from their use.[60] Responding to initiatives in the Nixon White House, the Office of Economic Opportunity commissioned the Center for the Study of Public Policy to make a report on how feasible an experiment with vouchers might be. The immediate results were a description of eleven voucher systems and a recommendation that an experiment using one of them be tried. At the urging of OEO, six school districts eventually agreed to try a voucher plan, but only one finally put a program in place. This was the Alum Rock district of San Jose, California, a low income, Mexican-American, largely rural school district with serious financial problems. As it turned out, the experiment failed to test a number of fairly critical aspects of the theory supporting the use of vouchers. The California legislature first neglected to allow private schools to participate until the project was under way. When the legislature finally did act, one private school tried to take part but soon closed for lack of interest. The result was that no private schools were involved in the Alum Rock experiment.

Second, teachers were given job security as a condition of their participation, but their salaries were not tied to what they could accomplish with their students. Thus the force of competition, from which the theory would predict some measure of increased quality, was blunted. Third, the school board could not surrender its control of the schools, and, fourth, the participation of parents, a necessary condition according to the theory, was considerably lower than expected. Theoretical conditions that were met, in varying degrees, included minischools (within each of the fourteen participating schools) offering a variety of teaching methods and curricular emphases. On the basis of information supplied to parents each spring choices could be made among any of the minischools with free transportation to accommodate the necessary movement of children from home to school.

The results were mixed. Test scores in reading and mathematics, on the average, did not increase, though their liking for school among children using vouchers did. Some increase in parental interest in curriculum and budget decisions was also noted. At the end of the experiment, parents using the voucher schools seemed to be more satisfied with the public schools than they were at the beginning. But so were the parents using the eleven non-voucher schools. Parents had some difficulty learning how the system worked, and among those with the lowest incomes and least education the information levels were a good deal lower than in other families.[61]

Owing to parental choice, children tended to cluster along lines of ethnicity and religion, as well as family income, parents' education, and parental childrearing values. It also happened that children tended to enroll in neighborhood schools, though this tendency diminished somewhat in the later years of the experiment. Overall, the Alum Rock experience seems to suggest that parents learn in time how the system operates and how to make choices that reinforce already present familial values. In the process, however, they may also reinforce standing class distinctions and the attitudes, beliefs, and interpersonal abilities that attend those distinctions.[62]

Given the deficiencies in the experiment's design, one wonders how much of this evidence can be taken seriously.[63] Perhaps it is fair to say only that the evidence is suggestive and not conclusive and that an educational voucher system and the theory supporting it deserves another try. However that may be, certain other conclusions about Alum Rock can be drawn with some confidence.[64] We might observe, first, that despite the encouragement of a federal agency with sizable amounts of money to spend only six school districts could be found with an interest in a voucher system, and only one of those actually went ahead with it. The problem, as Van Geel points out, is that getting the beneficiaries of a program to work for it is difficult. The benefits lie far in the future, the work entails heavy personal costs, and in such circumstances people would prefer that someone else do the necessary political chores. So, while strong opposition to OEO's plan could be found easily, no cadre of strong supporters ever emerged. As Van Geel writes: "When the costs of a project are perceived by a few active and politically powerful individuals and groups, and when the benefits are diffuse and not sharply perceived by any significant group or individual, a reform effort will fail."[65]

A second observation drawn from Alum Rock is that the teachers were able to tie security in their positions to the conduct of the experiment. One would look far for better evidence of the success of Van Geel's "few active and politically powerful individuals and groups" at turning a reform to their advantage, if not defeating the program altogether. Of course, those few could be neutralized were there enough fervor and commitment on the other side, but for those traits to materialize there must first be substantial benefit at stake and a clear understanding of what those benefits are and to whom they will flow. That no such conditions were present in the efforts of OEO and Alum Rock follows, perhaps primarily, from what Cohen and Farrar have called "a serious overestimate of popular discontent and the demand for change in education."[66]

OEO's failure to get vouchers to take root is not the only one. John Coons and Stephen Sugarman sought—without success—to submit a voucher plan to California voters in 1980. According to a study of this effort,[67] the initiative failed because its proponents lacked the financial base characteristic of recent and more successful initiatives such as Proposition 13. The primary reason for the lack of financial strength was that major interest groups failed to lend the necessary organizational and financial support. This support was not forthcoming for a number of reasons: Interest groups generally avoid positions that place them in opposition to public education; any given group finds it difficult to take a position against an existing system unless its members share a nearly unanimous dissatisfaction, a condition not likely to be met because of members' participation in or identification with other interests that support present arrangements; proposals that do not offer direct and clearly defined benefits to members will not attract support of interest groups until some sense of compensation for effort can be realized; interest groups will not support proposals whose effects are ambiguous, as is the case with voucher systems whose constitutionality or whose legal implementation by a legislature is still in doubt; and interest groups will withhold support from proposals that pose the possibility of conflict with other groups on whom they depend for support on other issues.

East Hartford, Connecticut, considered a proposal for vouchers in 1976. The Board of Education voted the proposal down, however, after serious opposition arose and after it became clear that the public was confused about the proposal. William Weber, who studied this case, concluded that vouchers failed in East Hartford because of controversy over religious schools, resistance by a teachers union, and a lack of full public understanding.[68] And if one wants an example from abroad, there is the failed effort in France of the last century reported by Van Vliet and Smyth.[69] They trace failure in this instance to a lack of public interest and the unfortunate circumstance that the proposal was "submerged under ideological positions concerning religious instruction and the role of the Catholic church."[70]

PROSPECTS FOR AID TO RELIGIOUS SCHOOLS

If we combine the findings from this brief survey with some ideas expressed here much earlier, perhaps we can identify the more important of the conditions that would have to be met for a federal program of tuition tax credits or educational vouchers to have a chance of succeeding. First, of course, the measure must not be unconstitutional; tuition tax credits probably do not meet this test; vouchers may. Second, the national economy must be healthy enough to absorb the additional cost of supporting private education. Third, the support for such a program must be well-organized, politically skillful, and financially able to carry on an intensive campaign. This requires, fourth, that beneficiaries be made aware of the benefits that will accrue to them and that they be convinced the benefits outweigh the political and other costs success will entail. These latter conditions must exist in order to meet the fifth: opposition to the program must be split or weakened by alternative protections for the interests of its members, either as individuals or as groups. That benefits of tuition tax credits and educational vouchers are highly diffuse and often quite abstract, while the threats of such programs are direct, immediate, and easy to grasp suggests that the latter three conditions will be extremely difficult to realize.

Nevertheless, given the support of a popular and effective President, the backing of a powerful Senate or House committee, and the apparent coalition of a number of groups in support of tuition tax credits—as well as possible changes in the membership of the Supreme Court and with them a change in the Court's collective mind about aid to religious schools—several of these conditions have a better likelihood of being met now or in the near future than before. If that is so, one would expect that the opposition would dig in, which it apparently has, and that it would seek to divide the proponents by developing its own solutions to the problems in education that are supposed to exist. Some of these solutions have already been proposed: alternatives within the public schools for those who are serious about having a choice,[71] merit pay to induce some degree of competition for those who worship at that shrine,[72] innercity magnet schools[73] to attract those who have moved to the suburbs to escape poor quality schools but not, by their claim, to run from racial integration. Imaginative minds have and no doubt will continue to invent additional schemes to satisfy parents who might otherwise be attracted to private schools and to support of vouchers and tax credits. Those are matters to be worked out within the public school community, and to the degree that any such efforts result in improvement of public schools the competitive thrust bound up in advocacy for vouchers and tax credits will not have been at all wasted or unproductive. But along the way it should also be noted that improvement of public schooling and broadening of parental choice are not always the same thing. Schools, after all, have social and professional responsibilities that must transcend the will or whim of interested parties, parents included.[74]

And finally, to those who want religion with their schooling, it may have to be said that in a secular society such as ours this is a wish that can be satisfied by government only in part. And the part need not be small. Tax exemptions to churches and tax deductions for those who support churches, textbook loans, transportation, released time, and the delivery of a variety of services already represent a considerable accommodation of religion by government and a not inconsiderable expense of public money.[75] Here, of course, the argument against double taxation cuts both ways. Just as parents of private school children may feel that they are taxed for services they do not use, parents of public school children may be entitled to argue that their tax dollars support religious schools for which they have no use and religious teaching in which they do not believe. The grievance, in any case, does not lie entirely on one side.

The value to a plural society of nonpublic schools is incontestable. To support their existence and to offer some very limited forms of assistance, as is now the case, is wise public policy. But perhaps that is the most we can do without compromising other values just as important as our concern for quality, choice, and equity in education.

NOTES

1. For a succinct discussion of these matters, see Thomas Sowell, "Tuition Tax Credits: A Social Revolution," *Policy Review* 4 (Spring 1978): 79–83; Walter E. Williams, "Tuition Tax Credits: Other Benefits," *Policy Review* 4 (Spring 1978): 85–89; E. G. West, "Tuition Tax Credit Proposals: An Economic Analysis of the 1978 Packwood/Moynihan Bill," *Policy Review* 3 (Winter 1978): 61–75; and "Government Neutrality and Separation of Church and State: Tuition Tax Credits," *Harvard Law Review* 92 (January 1979): 696–717.

2. See, for example, James S. Coleman, *Public and Private Schools* (Washington, D.C.: National Center for Education Statistics, 1981); Donald A. Erickson, "Should *All* the Nation's Schools Compete for Clients and Support?" *Phi Delta Kappan* 61 (September 1979): 14–17, 77; and James S. Coleman, "Private Schools, Public Schools, and the Public Interest," *Public Interest* 64 (Summer 1981): 19–30.

3. Stephen Arons, "The Separation of School and State: *Pierce* Reconsidered," *Harvard Educational Review* 46 (February 1976): 76–104.

4. For a leading example of this argument, see E. G. West, *Education and the State*, 2d ed. (London: Institute of Economic Affairs, 1970).

5. This argument is examined in "Values and Education: Pluralism and Public Policy," *Religious Education* 70 (March 1975): 115–201.

6. This history is reviewed in Daniel J. Sullivan, *Public Aid to Nonpublic Schools* (Lexington, Massachusetts: Lexington Books, 1974); and Norman C. Thomas, *Education in National Politics* (New York: David McKay, 1975).

7. For discussion and analysis of these activities, see Thomas, *Education in National Politics;* American Enterprise Institute, *Tuition Tax Credits and Alternatives* (Washington, D.C.: American Enterprise Institute for Public Policy Research, 1978); Rochelle L. Stanfield, "Political Maneuvering over Tuition Tax Credits," *National Journal* 10 (July 2, 1978), 1157–59; and "Controversy in

Congress over Federal Student Aid Policy," *Congressional Digest* 58 (January 1979): 1–32.

8. Almost all discussions of tuition tax credits advance one policy position or another. One that does not is "A Status Report on Tuition Tax Credits," *Phi Delta Kappan* 60 (September 1978): 46, 66.

9. Voucher systems are described more or less objectively in Charles S. Benson, *The Economics of Public Education*, 3d ed. (Boston: Houghton-Mifflin, 1978), pp. 165–77; and John Lindelow, *Educational Vouchers* (Reston, Virginia: National Association of Secondary School Principals, n.d.).

10. "The Case for Tuition Tax Credits," *Phi Delta Kappan* 60 (December 1978): 274–76.

11. Ibid., p. 275.

12. "Government and the Ruin of Private Education," *Harpers* (April 1978), pp. 28–38.

13. *Education Daily*, 2 April 1982.

14. "The Case against Tuition Tax Credits," *Phi Delta Kappan* 60 (December 1978): 277–79.

15. Ibid., p. 278.

16. *Congressional Quarterly Weekly Report*, 19 February 1983, p. 407.

17. *Congressional Quarterly Weekly Report*, 19 March 1983, p. 590.

18. *Congressional Quarterly Weekly Report*, 24 April 1982, pp. 911–13.

19. 413 U.S. 756 (1973).

20. See, for example, Senator Hollings' comments in "The Case against Tuition Tax Credits," p. 279.

21. 175 U.S. 291 (1899).

22. 281 U.S. 370 (1930).

23. 330 U.S. 1 (1947).

24. Ibid., pp. 15–16.

25. Ibid., p. 18.

26. 268 U.S. 510 (1925).

27. 343 U.S. 306 (1952).

28. Ibid., p. 312.

29. Ibid.

30. 374 U.S. 203 (1963).

31. Ibid., p. 213.

32. Ibid., p. 214.

33. Ibid., p. 222.

34. Ibid.

35. 392 U.S. 236 (1968).

36. 397 U.S. 664 (1970).

37. Ibid., p. 674.

38. 403 U.S. 602 (1971).

39. *Earley v. DiCenso* and *Robinson v. DiCenso*, 403 U.S. 602 (1971).

40. 413 U.S. 756 (1973).

41. Ibid., p. 789.

42. Ibid., p. 793.

43. Ibid.

44. Ibid., p. 794.

45. Ibid., p. 797.

46. Ibid.

47. Ibid., p. 791.

48. 413 U.S. 825 (1973).

49. 421 U.S. 349 (1975).

50. 433 U.S. 229 (1977).

51. 444 U.S. 646 (1980).

52. 676 F. 2d 1195 (1982).

53. 630 F. 2d 855 (1980).

54. 676 F. 2d 1195, 1204 (1982).

55. *Education Daily*, 10 August 1982.

56. 630 F. 2d 855 (1980), p. 860.

57. *Education Week*, 17 August 1983, pp. 12–13.

58. These were Chief Justice Burger and Associate Justices O'Connor, Powell (who wrote the opinion in *Nyquist*), Rehnquist, and White.

59. See, for example, Senator Moynihan's reference to legal authority in "The Case for Tuition Tax Credits," p. 275.

60. The following account is drawn variously from Lindelow, *Educational Vouchers;* Gary Bridge, "Citizen Choice in Public Services: Voucher Systems," in E. S. Savas, ed., *Alternatives for Delivering Public Services: Toward Improved Performance* (Boulder, Colo.: Westview Press, 1977), pp. 51–109, especially pp. 77–88; and L. H. Salganik, "Fall and Rise of Education Vouchers," *Education Digest* 47 (December 1981): 6–10.

61. See Gary Bridge, "Information Imperfections: The Achilles Heel of Entitlement Plans," *School Review* 86 (May 1978): 504–29; and Michael A. Olivas, "Information Access Inequities: A Fatal Flaw in Educational Voucher Plans," *Journal of Law and Education* 10 (October 1981): 441–65.

62. Bridge, "Citizen Choice in Public Services: Voucher Systems," pp. 85–86.

63. For a methodological critique of the Alum Rock experiment, see Paul M. Wortman and Robert G. St. Pierre, "The Educational Voucher Demonstration: A Secondary Analysis," *Education and Urban Society* 9 (August 1977): 471–92.

64. Here again we draw on Lindelow, *Educational Vouchers;* Bridge, "Citizen Choice in Public Services: Voucher Systems"; and Salganik, "Fall and Rise of Education Vouchers."

65. Tyll Van Geel, "Parental Preferences and the Politics of Spending Public Educational Funds," *Teachers College Record* 79 (Fall 1978): 352.

66. David K. Cohen and Eleanor Farrar, "Power to the Parents? The Story of Education Vouchers," *Public Interest* 48 (Summer 1977): 96.

67. The results of the study are summarized in Pauline B. Gough, "Some Hypotheses on Voucher Plan's Failure to Attract Support from Interest Groups," *Phi Delta Kappan* 61 (May 1980): 656–57.

68. "Eclipse of Education Vouchers in America: The East Hartford Case," *Journal of Education* 159 (May 1977): 36–42.

69. W. Van Vliet and J. A. Smyth, "Nineteenth Century French Proposal to Use School Vouchers," *Comparative Education Review* 26 (February 1982): 95–103.

70. Ibid., p. 102.

71. See, for example, the proposals advanced in Mario D. Fantini, *Public Schools of Choice* (New York: Simon and Schuster, 1973); and Evans Clinchy

and Elisabeth Allen Cody, "If Not Public Choice, Then Private Escape," *Phi Delta Kappan* 60 (December 1978): 270–73.

72. See Jack Frymier, "Merit Pay—Yes! Vouchers—No!" *Educational Forum* 46 (February 1981): 4–8.

73. See John Premazon and Philip T. West, "Requiem or Rebirth? From Voucher to Magnet," *Clearing House* 51 (September 1977): 38–40.

74. Compare the comments of R. Freeman Butts in "Educational Vouchers: The Private Pursuit of the Public Purse," *Phi Delta Kappan* 61 (September 1979): 7–9.

75. For descriptions of other services and financial benefits provided by government to religious institutions, see Jean Rosenblatt and Hoyt Gimlin, "Tuition Tax Credits," *Editorial Research Reports*, 14 August 1981, pp. 595–612; and Thomas Vitullo-Martin, "Federal Policies and Private Schools," *Academy of Political Science Proceedings* 33 (1978): 124–35.

Chapter 9

Bad Fences Make Bad Neighbors: A Look at State Regulation of Private Schools

DONALD A. ERICKSON

Before I built a wall I'd ask to know
What I was walling in or walling out . . .

So wrote Robert Frost.[1] The authors of state regulations for private schools seem to feel no similar need to justify their wall-building. Their regulations seldom reflect any defensible rationale, specifying the good things to be walled in and the bad things to be walled out. As one frequent result of this confusion, the regulations encourage what should not be encouraged, discourage what should not be discouraged, punish people who deserve no punishment, and create much avoidable animosity. That is the contention of the present chapter.

To be sure, one can identify a reputable rationale for state regulation of private schools—to ensure that these schools provide children with the preparation they need to be responsible adults in this society, but to do so without unnecessarily hampering the liberty of parents to direct the upbringing of their own children and the freedom of educators to depart from conventional forms of schooling.

This rationale for regulation was enunciated by the U.S. Supreme Court in three early cases. In *Meyer v. State of Nebraska*, the Court said it did not question "the power of the state to compel attendance at some school and to make reasonable regulations for all schools, including a requirement that they shall give instructions in English."[2]

227

The state could prescribe a curriculum "for institutions which it sup-ports," but not in any extensive form (the Court implies) in schools which it does not support. In *Pierce v. Society of Sisters,* the Court referred back to this "doctrine of *Meyer v. Nebraska,*" which con-demned intervention that "unreasonably interferes with the liberty of parents and guardians to direct the upbringing and education of children under their control."[3] Some matters, however, could be reg-ulated in all schools: The state could require "that certain studies plainly essential to good citizenship must be taught, and that nothing be taught that is manifestly inimical to the public welfare." In *Far-rington v. Tokushige,* the Court struck down regulations that "would deprive parents of fair opportunity to procure for their children in-struction which they think is important and we cannot say is harmful. The Japanese parent has the right to direct the education of his child without unreasonable restrictions."[4]

To demand what is plainly essential to good citizenship and forbid what is clearly harmful to the general weal—that objective seems straightforward and defensible. Why, then, is there so much contro-versy over state regulation of private schools? In this writer's experi-ence, most controversy of this nature arises when the regulations in question considerably overreach the limits expressed in the above-discussed rationale. Sometimes the regulations reflect the view that the state's power to regulate private schools is as plenary as its power to regulate public schools. At other times, states acknowledge that their power to regulate private schools is limited, but nevertheless adopt a mode of regulation that unnecessarily intrudes upon the freedom of parents and educators to depart from educational meth-ods which state officials happen to favor. In both instances, the writ-ers and enforcers of the regulations appear to have a particularly jaundiced view of private schools and their patrons.

OVEREXTENDED REGULATIONS

Some state regulations appear to reflect the view that private schools not only must provide an education essential to good citizen-ship, but must follow whatever modus operandi the regulation writers happen to favor. What is favored is arbitrary, differing from time to time and from state to state.[5] Regulations written in the era of Con-ant's pronouncements about high schools demand certain minimal enrollments and physical facilities; regulations written in the era when "community action" programs were popular tend to demand extensive community participation in virtually every phase of school affairs, ignoring the fact that the constituencies of some private schools are scattered over large areas; and regulations written when "behavioral objectives" were in vogue demand their extensive development and use. At times these regulations become ludicrous, as when Ohio demanded that all rooms in a school be entirely free of odors, and that every school have at least one water fountain "with a stream of water coming out on a slant."[6] Iowa, somewhat similarly, threatened to disapprove a Friends boarding school near West Branch because the school chose to teach the "practical arts" by having students participate in every phase of maintaining the school buildings, grounds, cattle, and crops, rather than by taking formal courses.[7]

While this is not the place to consider in detail the motivations of people who write and enforce such overreaching regulations, a few possibilities deserve brief mention. The historical context makes clear that fear of "foreign elements," such as German-speaking ethnic conclaves around the end of World War I, had a lot to do with extreme regulations.[8] More recently, Sol Cohen argued persuasively that the mental health movement was a powerful force behind the spread of the idea that schools should bear responsibility for the global personality development of children.[9] Public officials who assented to that view could easily have slipped into the assumption that the state must require all schools, public and private, to make the same "mental health" contributions to children. (A basic problem here, of course, is widespread disagreement as to the school conditions that are healthful mentally.) This writer suspects that extreme regulations for private schools often come about because, on the one hand, teacher organizations, composed primarily of public school personnel, seek to minimize threats posed by unconventional private schools (through regulations that, in effect, outlaw the truly unconventional), while, on the other hand, opposition to the regulations on the part of politically influential private school groups is often neutralized. The opposition often seems neutralized by the unwillingness of highly reputable (generally expensive) private schools to associate with the unconventional schools currently under attack, and by the tendency of Catholic school leaders to exhibit a "cooperative" stance toward public authority in an effort to secure tax support. These possibilities deserve study by educational historians.

Whatever the causes of extreme, overreaching state regulations, they have been struck down in several cases, beginning as early as the above-discussed *Farrington* case and including rather recent instances.[10] However, the limits of state authority to regulate private schools have not been established unambiguously in case law. There is much inconsistency in the pertinent court decisions.[11]

UNNECESSARILY INTRUSIVE REGULATIONS

Some difficulties arise, as has already been noted, because state regulations reflect the apparent view that government power to regulate private schools is pervasive. Other difficulties arise when state regulations, while ostensibly based on a recognition of limited state power, unnecessarily intrude upon the freedom of parents and educators to adopt methods and goals which public officials do not happen to favor.

A federal case in Maine, in which a court recently ruled that the state could not close "unapproved" Christian schools, is a good example of the latter tendency.[12] In this case the most controversial element of the state's regulatory scheme for private schools was the demand that all teachers be state-certified. The State of Maine acknowledged that its purview over private schools was limited; it was not attempting to assert unlimited power. The state argued, however, that the minimum educational essentials for good citizenship could be ensured only by demanding a certified teacher in every classroom. The alternative, proof-of-the-pudding approach of determining whether every private school product could read, write, cipher, and comprehend the basics of our form of government—this approach was rejected by the state as too costly, bureaucratically complex, and intrusive upon school autonomy.

Testifying in the Maine case, the writer argued that the bugaboos of testing dramatically emphasized by the state's expert witnesses could be avoided if one concentrated on the basic understandings and skills plainly essential to good citizenship, and if testing were kept simple and straightforward. To determine whether a child could read, for instance, one could hand the child a book, say "Please read out loud," and listen to the results. If the results seemed reasonable, one could ask a few questions to test comprehension. It should not be a drastic intrusion upon the autonomy of a school to determine whether its students at some level of instruction could read. Nor should such an approach be bureaucratically and fiscally unmanageable, The judge himself observed in the courtroom that society managed to test everyone licensed to operate a car.

Thus, the assumption that society cannot determine (without overwhelming cost and machinery) whether the fundamental learnings have occurred does seem unwarranted. What, then, of the assumption that these learnings can be assured by putting a state-certified teacher in every classroom?

The idea of requiring teachers to be certified appeals to many people, for they are accustomed to assume that they are protected against incompetent physicians, attorneys, accountants, engineers, architects, and other professionals by similar demands for certification or licensure. Incompetent and unscrupulous professionals slip into these occupations regardless, but some significant screening, at least, has occurred. Physicians, for instance, undergo long periods of formal instruction, and work under the scrutiny of senior colleagues for extended periods of time before practicing on their own. What is generally forgotten is that schoolteaching, as Dan Lortie demonstrates, is characterized by "eased access."[13] Almost anyone can get into the occupation. Many training programs for would-be teachers lack rigor, are often largely irrelevant to the classroom world that teachers later encounter, and lack a reliable knowledge base. There is evidence that such training programs do not "take." Teachers develop instructional strategies in response to exigencies encountered in classrooms, in ways that fit their personal need dispositions. Operating largely in isolation, behind classroom doors, teachers develop pretty much along the lines that appeal to them. Teachers generally exhibit weak career commitment. They are sometimes anti-intellectual. They resist change frequently. Some people who enter teaching do so as a second choice, perhaps because they are incapable of succeeding in their first-choice careers. Recent evidence suggests that the ability level of teachers-in-training is lower than ever and continuing to decline.[14] Consequently, one may demand teacher certification as much as one wishes, but many schools of education, needing students to survive, will continue to admit candidates regardless of their ability; school systems, needing persons to manage classrooms, will continue to hire teachers from the available pool; and many current training programs, lacking a firm knowledge base, will often have negligible effect.

One should acknowledge, in passing, that research is beginning to reveal some teacher behaviors that are rather consistently associated with student learning in *some* contexts (mostly, in the context of basic skills instruction of disadvantaged children in the primary grades).[15] As some scholars have noted, we now seem to be in serious danger of generalizing too broadly from those findings, introducing into training programs new dogmas that will soon prove to be premature and in many situations harmful.[16]

Considering the lack of evidence for teacher certification requirements, one wonders what motives make those requirements increasingly popular. (More and more states are demanding certification in private schools.[17]) One motive may be that teachers know the certification demand will curtail competition by keeping at least some people out of the occupation—the most competent people perhaps, whose active, independent minds will not tolerate some experiences required for certification. Another motive may be to ensure that schools of education remain in business. (Certification requirements are probably the major force channeling students into their classrooms.) In the latter context, the certification demand may force all would-be school teachers to undergo whatever training programs happen to be popular in schools of education at the moment, including, as was observed earlier, some based on hasty, ill-conceived assumptions. This forced standardization of teacher training is exactly what many private school leaders fear when they oppose teacher certification requirements. They do not want their teachers trained exactly as public school teachers are trained. Since there is no evidence that certification is critical to student acquisition of understandings and skills essential to good citizenship, it seems unjustifiable to rob private school leaders of the freedom to use teachers with unconventional backgrounds.

The demand for certified teachers is just one example of a pervasive tendency in state regulations—the tendency to assume that educational quality depends primarily upon the technical aspects of schooling, such as formal teacher qualifications, physical facilities, and pupil-teacher ratios. As will be noted later, school attributes which can readily be bought or prescribed have never been firmly linked to superior student learning. This approach, of attempting to "legislate" learning by demanding this and forbidding that, has been criticized more extensively by Arthur Wise.[18]

UNDULY JAUNDICED ASSUMPTIONS

In recent studies the school characteristics most consistently associated with superior student learning are not of the type emphasized in state regulations. They relate, instead, to the classroom behaviors of teachers and students, especially behaviors reflecting a dedication to learning, an agreed-upon goal, and reasonable discipline. If state regulators were taking this research seriously they would have a much less jaundiced view of private schools than they seem customarily to exhibit. Instead of seeking to make private schools adopt the modus operandi of public schools, they might be asking why public schools cannot approach certain private school norms, for in study after study the private schools have been found superior to public schools in the above-mentioned particulars.[19] It is not likely that these differences occur because private school educators are somehow superior people, but rather because of the different constraints under which the two types of school operate. During recent decades, well-intentioned reformers may have introduced change after change in public schools with primarily negative results, until public school educators are now often confronted with system characteristics that make effective instruction extremely difficult to achieve. As a result of well-intentioned reforms, for example, many public schools have become too large, too disconnected from the homes they serve, too dominated by decisions made far away, and too torn apart by the dissension and hostility of diverse factions.

Another questionable assumption lying beneath much creation and enforcement of regulations for private schools is the assumption that parents in these enterprises are particularly suspect—unlikely, if left on their own, to ensure that their children are properly educated. Some parents will indeed be derelict in providing for their children's education. Society, however, does not need a massive system of legal compulsion to deal with the small minority of parents who will do this, any more than it needs a massive compulsion system to protect the young from bad parental decisions concerning nutrition, clothing, shelter, and medical care. If the current principle of compulsion in education were applied consistently in other areas, society would have public dining rooms for the feeding of children, coupled with regulation of all meals offered to children at home; and it would have public clothing depots, coupled with regulations to ensure that parents who assumed the clothing of their children would do so properly. In other words, the American system of educational compulsion, if consistently applied, would go a long way toward transforming all children into wards of the state. In other areas, society assumes that most parents will be decent, reasonably sensible people (probably far more decent and well motivated vis-à-vis their own children than most state officials will be), and officials are authorized to intervene in behalf of the child only when they encounter the unusual parent who is guilty of serious neglect or abuse.

It may be informative to examine recent evidence about the concern and decision-making behavior of the apparently typical private school parent. The evidence is drawn from one component of a four-and-one-half year study of government aid to private schools in British Columbia, the part of Canada generally regarded as most similar to the United States.[20]

In the component of the study that is pertinent here, structured telephone interviews, consisting mainly of open-ended questions, were conducted with 993 parents. The sample was drawn so almost precisely half of the parents had chosen public schools and half had chosen private schools for their children. The sample was limited to parents whose children had just begun in the first grade of an elementary or secondary school and to parents who had just switched their children from public to private schools, or vice versa. Many questions were asked about reasons for selecting a school, the amount of effort and time put into the decision, the sources of information used, and the members of the family who had been active in the decision. Quite consistently, the reasons most frequently given for choosing a private school rather than a public school were, in the following order of frequency: (a) that the school, teachers, parents, or students were more religious or spiritual; (b) that discipline was superior; and (c) that academic quality was better. These overall trends, however, were heavily influenced by the prevalence of Catholic schools in the sample. A more revealing picture emerged when the private schools were divided into several types.

The reason most often given by public school parents was that the school was closer or more convenient. This does not necessarily mean that the parents were preoccupied with convenience, for many responses thus coded may be interpreted to mean, "Since this was the one public school in our attendance area, we had no choice." The other reasons given by public school parents were exceptionally varied, revealing surprisingly disparate views about what is important in schools. Among the reasons mentioned by at least 15 percent of the public school parents (certainly not a large proportion) were that the choice of the school was beyond the family's control, that the discipline was better, or that the academic quality was high.

Comparisons among private schools of different types revealed a quite logical, predictable pattern. Religion was never given as a reason for attending the nonsectarian private school, but the patrons placed high emphasis on discipline and superior academic quality. In contrast, religion was the most frequently mentioned reason for attending a sectarian school, Catholic or non-Catholic. Religion was stressed far more by patrons for non-Catholic sectarian schools than by Catholic school patrons. In Catholic schools, concern for discipline ran a very close second, followed by academic quality; both were mentioned by many parents. Discipline and academic quality were often mentioned in other sectarian schools as well, though not as often as in Catholic schools. Patrons of non-Catholic sectarian schools surpassed their Catholic peers in emphasizing the importance of the school climate, stressing the need for moral and social values, good relationships among people, and superior student attitudes. Ironically, the concerns of these people have a far closer demonstrated relationship to pedagogical excellence than do the technically oriented concerns of the state officials who seek to regulate them, as evidence discussed below will indicate.

The reasons given by parents for choosing schools of different types were not associated with social class to any marked degree. Both when parents in various social strata were compared and when social class groups and school types were considered simultaneously, the most striking result was the lack of association between parents' reasons and social class. Parents' reasons differed by type of school, but not by social class, except for very minor variations. Although the numbers were too small to be taken very seriously, the lower-class parents mentioned academic quality as a reason for choosing a private school more often (proportionately) than did any other group. This bit of data suggested that private schools attracted the lower-class parents who were the most concerned about their children's education.

It was quite obvious that the private school parents, as a group, had put much more effort and thought into the choice of a school than had the public school parents as a group. Anyone would expect this, since the choice of a public school is automatic for many people. Many people think it only normal to send their children to public schools, and usually the individual schools which their children attend are a matter of school board policy regarding attendance areas, rather than a matter of parental choice. Within the private school group, the amount of time and effort expended on the choice of a school was associated, insofar as several measures were concerned, with the amount of money paid to the school. The higher the fees, the more effort and time the parents had devoted to choosing the school. This bit of data suggests that the schools in which state regulators should be most concerned about uncaring parents are the schools that levy no fees. The founding fathers of the common school thought they had triumphed when they ensured that no fees would be charged at the school door. In the process, they may have ensured that public schools would automatically get a disproportionate share of unconcerned parents.

In this same study, it was intriguing to stumble upon one unanticipated group of parents. These parents, when asked about their choice of a school, said they had not made a choice, or had not given the matter much thought. Several characteristics of these parents suggested that they were alienated and unhappy, dissatisfied with their schools, but incapable of remedial action. These "unthinking" parents were virtually all found in public schools. No one would expect them to make the effort and pay the fees that private schools entail.

In a mailed questionnaire, many of the same parents were asked, several months later, to rate their schools, on a scale running from "excellent" to "very poor," in seventeen areas of performance. Dramatic differences appeared between the ratings of public and private schools. The range of "excellent" ratings for the two types did not even overlap. The proportion of parents in a public school rating the school as "excellent" ran from 7 to 25, while the same proportion started at a low of 33 percent in private schools and ran as high as 66 percent.

One might suspect that the differences were attributable to social class, since public and private school patrons differed somewhat in this regard. Careful analysis, however, uncovered a high degree of consensus among parents from various social classes concerning the relative strengths and weaknesses of schools of different types. Different school types were given different distinctive profiles of relative strength and weakness by the parents patronizing them, almost regardless of social class.

One cannot simply assume, obviously, that the parents' ratings reflect actual school performance. For a variety of possible reasons, private school patrons could be deceiving themselves or attempting to deceive others. For instance, it may be difficult, once a parent has invested fairly heavily in a school, to accept the idea that the investment was a mistake. Or if many parents were choosing private schools to get away from lower-status people, they might not wish that fact to be obvious and thus might describe their schools as superior as a way of voicing a socially acceptable reason for patronizing them. Several trends in the data, however, make it difficult to believe that the private school parents were merely viewing their schools through rose-colored glasses or that the high ratings were produced by higher-status people trying to obscure their own snobbishness. In particular, the parents' responses are too differentiated and systematic across school types to be attributed to a generalized tendency to respond favorably (the halo effect). If the halo effect were prominent, or if parents were merely fabricating, one would not expect the impressive differentiation of responses from one school type to another or the impressive consistency across social classes. There were other indications of validity as well. For instance, in schools which parents rated as very superior academically students had a tendency to complain that academic performance was emphasized too much for their tastes. Also, some parent reports were not of a type that should be produced by mere halo effect or deception. For example, the private schools generally were described as exhibiting a high degree of social cohesion. This is a quality which many parents do not value, wanting, instead, to find schools characterized by a variety of ideas and social backgrounds. Yet the parents agree impressively concerning the presence of this characteristic. Finally, the evidence, taken as a whole, suggests that the choice of a private school is associated with such parent characteristics as (a) intolerance of inferior goods and services; (b) high aspirations for their children's schooling; (c) superior access to information; (d) unusual awareness of educational options; (e) assertiveness; and (f) superior levels of educational attainment. It is difficult to believe that parents with these characteristics not only choose unwisely when seeking superior schools, but deceive themselves to such an overwhelming extent that they rate their schools, not merely as superior, but as vastly superior.

One should not interpret this evidence as condemning the public schools, though it may throw an unflattering light on the conditions under which many public schools are now forced to operate. The evidence does suggest, however, that the view of private school parents apparently adopted by many state regulators is fallacious. In general, private schools do not seem to be likely places to look for naive and neglectful parents.

PREDICTIONS AND CORROBORATING EXAMPLES

When these weaknesses in state regulations for private schools are analyzed, it seems predictable that much relevant legislative, administrative, and litigative action may do more to limit the liberty and happiness of good people than to protect children against substandard instruction. The regulations, when enforced, may often punish the innocent instead of the guilty, inhibit badly needed departures from pedagogical orthodoxy, and foist inferior schooling upon children.

Lacking evidence from any systematic investigation of these possibilities, one can only speculate as to their frequency and severity on a national scale. Nevertheless, some fairly startling examples can readily be found. They may be sufficient to underline the need for serious reassessment of public policy in this area.

Example 1: The Persecution of LeRoy Garber

A few days before Christmas, 1968, the writer sat in a rented car in front of LeRoy Garber's abandoned farmhouse at the top of a small Kansas hill.[21] The wind howled through the fence, covering a toy wagon with snow. Two cats meandered in confusion, complaining that no one was home.

A few weeks earlier, the writer met the Garber family in that same farmhouse. The place was a mess, Mrs. Garber had apologized, with these stacks of boxes waiting for the truck. The farm and its equipment had been sold, and the family was leaving Kansas in search of peace. LeRoy Garber had been prosecuted as a criminal for educating his daughter Sharon during the high-school years in an unconventional, though apparently effective, manner. After years of agony and expense, Garber had lost his case in the Kansas Supreme Court. His son Galen was now ready for high school. Rather than facing another legal fight or compromising conscience, Garber sold out and left.

It turned out later that Garber did not derive enough money from the sale of his Kansas farm to reestablish himself in a farm in his new location. He lost the way of life that the Old Order Amish consider virtually essential to their faith. His daughter Sharon, who had been working in a nearby Kansas greenhouse and hoping to establish a greenhouse of her own, lost her employment and her dream. The family lost many friends, even before moving, because of the controversy over the case (many Amish felt Garber was wrong to defend himself in court).

Investigation revealed that the prosecution and long court battle had nothing to do with the adequacy of Sharon Garber's education. She had successfully completed all high school subjects required by Kansas law and more. Records in the local public library suggested that she was a voracious reader. Her greenhouse employer called her "the best help we've had yet." Her acquaintances described her as a superb cook, excellent seamstress, unfailing green thumb. Later, she published her own article on her experiences during the litigation. Encounters with the local prosecuting officials suggested to the writer that she was educated more adequately than some of them.

Sharon was self-sufficient and productive, able to participate in the political process, literate, and successful socially in Amish circles. Her father was prosecuted, not because she was deemed inadequate in any of these particulars, but because Sharon had developed these competencies in a manner which state officials did not approve. She had taken her high-school courses by correspondence courses, supplementing this work by attendance on Saturdays at an odd institution known as an Amish vocational high school. Neither of these activities qualified as a school for compulsory attendance purposes, a lower Kansas court asserted, because the statute, if properly interpreted, demanded attendance at "a private or parochial school having a school month consisting of four weeks of five days each of six hours per day during which pupils are under direct supervision of its teacher while they are engaged together in educational activities." When the Kansas Supreme Court reached the same conclusion, the *Wichita Eagle* editorialized, "The law is a ass, a idiot."

It is true, of course, that a decision exactly like this one could not now occur, since the Supreme Court of the United States reached a dramatically different conclusion in the celebrated case of *Wisconsin v. Yoder*, discussed below. But the same Old Order Amish people were later harassed by the State of Nebraska, whose officials apparently thought the *Yoder* logic, which dealt with the high-school years, had no bearing in Amish elementary schools. Furthermore, other religious groups are not clearly protected by the *Yoder* decision.

Example 2: A Showdown at an Iowa Schoolhouse

In Iowa public officials descended upon an Amish schoolhouse one cold November morning to defy the parents' wishes by forcibly removing all the children and transporting them to a public school in the nearby town.[22] Since the Amish are pacifists, the officials knew they would encounter no physical resistance and thought the plan would work well. Entering the school building, the truant officer told the children he was their friend, wanting only to take them to the town school where they would be properly educated and asked them to please file quietly into the school bus outside. The sheriff, gun on hip, led the procession toward the bus. When the first children were about to enter the bus, somebody shouted in German, "Run!" The pupils bolted for the field behind the schoolhouse, scrambled through the barbed wire fence, and ran through the adjoining cornfield into the woods beyond. Some never stopped running until they reached their homes. Emanuel, a portly boy of thirteen, could not keep up with his peers, waddled confusedly into an official's grasp, and was led weeping to the bus. Sara, a tiny six-year-old, was left behind in the cornfield, shivering in the bitter cold and screaming distractedly.

Sensing the bedlam they had caused, the officials gave up and left but made plans to return on the following school day. This time many Amish parents were present. The school entry-room was full of weeping mothers. Stern-faced fathers stood outside, blocking the door. The truant officer forced the men aside (quite easily, since they would not fight back) and brushed off the mothers, who pulled at his clothing and begged him not to proceed. The gun-toting sheriff followed into the classroom. The pupils began singing, half-hysterically, chorus after chorus of "Jesus Loves Me," led by a teacher who circled the room in agitation. Mothers rushed in to hug their youngsters protectively. The truant officer attempted to pry a screaming schoolboy from his desk. Several boys huddled in a corner. Fathers burst in to protest. The county attorney shouted his disgust at the behavior of the Amish. Newsmen entered, scribbling madly. Children wailed, women whimpered, flashbulbs popped, officials barked orders, and tides of emotion swept the room. Sensing another disaster, the officials gave up again. This time they flew to the governor's office in Des Moines, demanding that the national guard help them round up the Amish children.

In this situation it was particularly clear that state officials did not take action because they believed the children were being deprived of a decent education. Rather, Amish educational practices which had been tolerated for many years were suddenly made the basis for these attacks because of an episode that inflamed local prejudice against the Plain People. It had become evident that a local school was closed because the Amish registered the decisive votes in favor of school district consolidation. In response, local people had vowed to make the Amish pay dearly for the loss of the school.

The action against the Amish had begun in the courtroom of the local justice of the peace. Offending parents had been fined in that courtroom each school day over a period of many weeks for failing to send their children to a state-recognized school. As the fines mounted, Amish properties were seized and sold at auction. When the financial ruin of the Amish community seemed imminent (a development that would embarrass the prosecuting authorities), the strategy was devised of transporting all the children to the public school in the nearby town in defiance of their parents' objections, instead of continuing to levy fines. Thus the Iowa compulsory attendance law, coupled with state regulations for private schools, proved a handy instrument for the persecution of an unpopular minority, harnessing public power to the wagon of local prejudice.

Example 3: Wisconsin v. Yoder

The now-famous Supreme Court case of *Wisconsin v. Yoder* began in the picturesque district court building in the Swiss-American town of New Glarus, Wisconsin.[23] Here, a group of Amish, including poor Adin Yutzy who had fled Iowa to escape the trouble described earlier, was prosecuted for failing to send their children to regular high schools. The local superintendent of public schools took the stand to explain why it was necessary, in his view, to force all Amish children into regular high schools when they reached the proper age. It was necessary, he asserted, because many youngsters would otherwise grow up to be unemployed and go on welfare, and quite a few might become juvenile delinquents and later engage in criminal activity. This assertion was dramatically counteracted by the testimony of a parade of other local officials, all of whom testified that, of all the people on record in the county for delinquency, unemployment, indigence, and crime, not one was an Old Order Amish. John Hostetler of Temple University, the nation's leading authority on Amish culture, testified that the culture would be destroyed if all Amish youngsters were forced into regular public high schools. The writer testified that if an education was to be judged by its results in adult life, then the extraordinary record of self-sufficiency in Amish communities suggested that Amish educational methods, unconventional though they were, were probably more effective than the methods followed by the public authorities who were prosecuting the Amish. Testimony was introduced to indicate that one reason for prosecuting the Amish was the desire of local public school officials to qualify for more state money by adding all the Amish children to their attendance rolls. The local superintendent reportedly had told the Amish that if their children would attend long enough to be counted in the state-aid formula, he would turn a blind eye on whatever happened later.

Example 4: Repeated Prosecution of Fundamentalists

In recent years in Ohio, Kentucky, North Carolina, Michigan, and Maine the writer has testified in defense of fundamentalist parents under legal attack, directly or indirectly (through action against their schools), for failing to send their children to schools which the state was willing to recognize as adequate.[24] In case after case the prosecutions were based, not upon any contention that children were failing to learn properly (in fact, evidence was usually introduced to the contrary), but upon the fact that some state regulation(s) for schools had been violated. The regulations in question often seemed arbitrary, sometimes to a ludicrous degree. There was never any empirical evidence that if they were followed the schools would be better rather than worse. It is far from pleasant to be prosecuted as criminals, as most parents in these cases were. Erecting a legal defense was expensive. There was the constant threat that the defense would prove futile and court sentences would follow. The parents lived for months, and sometimes years, under the menace of the state's contention that they were lawbreakers. Some courtroom scenes were marked by anxiety-lined faces and tears. What made the situation particularly ironic was the obvious fact that these parents were being prosecuted, not because they were neglecting their children (as thousands of American parents do without incurring the slightest legal repercussion), but because they sought to give their children a superior education in ways that contradicted the state's official view of what was best. It appeared that one could with impunity deprive one's child of adequate affection, mental stimulation, nutrition, clothing, and medical care. One could even handicap a child educationally by discouraging regular school attendance, homework, and respect for school authorities. What one could *not* do without risking loss of liberty, substance, and in some cases the custody of one's own children, was go to the extra trouble and expense of educating one's child in a manner or setting which state officials regarded as unorthodox, even when there was no evidence that the state's view was right and the parents' view, wrong.

IMPLICATIONS

In the instances described in this essay, it seems clear that state regulations for private schools have had the effect, not of enhancing the probability that the children in question will receive at least a minimally adequate preparation for good citizenship, but that schools will hew more closely to whatever line of thought the regulators currently favor, that prejudiced local people will more easily persecute unpopular minorities, that some of the parents who are the most concerned about their children's schooling will be prosecuted and harassed as if they were the parents who were the least concerned, and that the freedom of parents to govern the upbringing of their own offspring will be curtailed unnecessarily.

The solution to this problem also seems clear. If the state is to avoid the kind of thought control that the First Amendment to the U.S. Constitution seems to forbid, it must cease hampering the operation of schools which state officials do not happen to like, at the very least. The state should explicitly and systematically recognize that its right to regulate is limited to the agreed-upon essentials of good citizenship. It should insure the acquisition of these essentials by the most straightforward method available—by using simple, direct testing methods to see whether those essentials are being acquired. Beyond matters of health and safety, the state should never dictate the manner in which children are to acquire those essentials, especially in this era when favored methods of instruction and school organization continue to shift and continue to be based far more on opinion than upon firm empirical evidence.

NOTES

1. Robert Frost, "Mending Wall."
2. 262 U.S. 390 (1923).
3. 268 U.S. 510 (1925).
4. 273 U.S. 284 (1927).
5. Most of the discussion in this paragraph is based upon study of state regulations in connection with the author's testimony in cases discussed later, in addition to study in preparation for the national conference whose proceedings appear in Donald A. Erickson, ed., *Public Controls for Nonpublic Schools* (Chicago: University of Chicago Press, 1969).
6. Considerable evidence concerning the Ohio regulations was introduced in *State v. Whisner*, 351 NE 2d 750, 45 Ohio St. 2d 181 (1976).
7. The author investigated this situation firsthand (at the Scattergood School, West Branch, Iowa) as part of his preparation for the above-mentioned national conference.
8. Donald A. Erickson, "On the Role of Non-public Schools," *School Review* 69 (Autumn 1961): 338–353.
9. Sol Cohen, "The School and Personality Development: Intellectual History," in *Historical Inquiry in Education*, ed. John H. Best (Washington, D.C.: American Educational Research Association, 1983), pp. 109–37.
10. For example, *Farrington v. Tokushige*, 273 U.S. 284 (1927); *State v. Whisner*, 351 NE 2d 750, 45 Ohio St. 2d 181 (1976); and *Kentucky State Board of Education v. Rudasill*, 589 S. W. 2d 877 (Ky., 1979).
11. In contrast to the decisions cited in note 10, above, which declared certain state regulations unconstitutional, the following cases were decided basically in favor of somewhat similar regulations: *Prettyman v. State of*

Nebraska, 537 F. Supp. 712 (D. Neb. 1982); and *State v. Shaver*, 294 N. W. 2d 883 (N. D. 1980).

12. *Bangor Baptist Church v. State of Maine*, 549 F. Supp. 1208 (D. Me. 1982).

13. Except when other sources are noted, the evidence on which this paragraph is based is derived principally from Dan C. Lortie, *School Teacher: A Sociological Study* (Chicago: University of Chicago Press, 1975).

14. For example, Sandra D. Roberson, Timothy Z. Keith, and Ellis B. Page, "Who Aspires to Teach?" *Educational Researcher* 12 (June–July 1983): 13–21.

15. One of the best recent summaries of this body of research, relating not only to the most consistent findings, but also to their serious limitations, is found in Penelope L. Peterson and Herbert J. Walberg, eds., *Research on Teaching: Concepts, Findings, and Implications* (Berkeley, Calif.: McCutchan Publishing Corp., 1979).

16. John I. Goodlad, *A Place Called School* (New York: McGraw Hill, 1983).

17. Patricia M. Lines, "Private Education Alternatives and State Regulation," paper distributed by Law and Education Center, Education Commission of the States, 1860 Lincoln St., Denver, Colo. 80295, March, 1982; for a more readily available, abbreviated version, see: Lines, "State Regulation of Private Education," *Phi Delta Kappan* 64 (October 1982): 119–123.

18. Arthur M. Wise, *Legislated Learning* (Berkeley, Calif.: University of California Press, 1979).

19. For example, J. S. Coleman, T. Hoffer, and S. Kilgore, *Public and Private Schools*, a report to the National Center for Education Statistics (Chicago: National Opinion Research Center, 1981); and Gerald Grant, "The Character of Education and the Education of Character," *Daedalus* 110 (Summer 1981): 135–149.

20. Donald A. Erickson, *The British Columbia Story: Antecedents and Consequences of Aid to Private Schools* (Los Angeles: Institute for the Study of Private Schools, 1982).

21. Donald A. Erickson, "The Persecution of LeRoy Garber," *School Review* 78 (November 1969): 81–90.

22. Donald A. Erickson, "The 'Plain People' and American Democracy," *Commentary* 45 (January 1968): 36–44.

23. *Wisconsin v. Yoder*, 406 U.S. 205 (1972).

24. In addition to *State v. Whisner, Kentucky State Board of Education v. Rudasill;* and *Bangor Baptist Church v. State of Maine*, cited above, see *Sheridan Road Baptist Church v. State of Michigan* (Ingham Circuit Court, Docket No. 80-26205-AZ, December 29, 1982); and *Organized Christian Schools of North Carolina et al. v. North Carolina State Board of Education and A. Craig Phillips et al.* (United States District Court, Eastern District of North Carolina, Docket No. 78-654-CIV-5, 1979).

Contributors

JAMES C. CARPER (Ph.D., Kansas State University) is Assistant Professor of Foundations of Education at Mississippi State University. His scholarly interests include history of American education and church-affiliated schools, particularly Christian day schools. He has contributed articles to *Kansas History, Mid-America, Educational Forum, Journal of Church and State, High School Journal,* and *Review Journal of Philosophy and Social Science.*

JON DIEFENTHALER (Ph.D., University of Iowa) is Pastor of Bethany-Trinity Evangelical Lutheran Church, Waynesboro, Virginia. He recently completed a postdoctoral fellowship in American religious history at Johns Hopkins under the direction of Timothy L. Smith. His first book, *H. Richard Niebuhr: Perspectives on Christ and Culture,* will be published by Pilgrim Press.

PETER P. DEBOER (Ph.D., University of Chicago) is Professor of Education at Calvin College. His areas of special interest include Protestant schools in North America, curriculum theory, and Christian philosophy of education. He has contributed articles to *History of Education Quarterly, Reformed Journal, Viewpoint,* and *The Encyclopedia of Education.*

DONALD A. ERICKSON (Ph.D., University of Chicago) is Professor of Education at the UCLA Graduate School of Education and Director of the Institute for the Study of Private Schools. For more than four years he has been studying longitudinally the effects of government aid to private schools in British Columbia. He has authored numerous reports on private school enrollment patterns and characteristics, and has contributed articles to *School Review, Commentary, Educational Researcher,* and *Phi Delta Kappan.*

JAMES F. HERNDON (Ph.D., University of Michigan) is Professor of

245

Political Science at Virginia Tech. He has published extensively on Congress, interest groups, constitutional law, and issues of church and state. He has also served on the staff of the Senate subcommittee on constitutional rights.

THOMAS C. HUNT (Ph.D., University of Wisconsin) is Professor of Foundations of Education at Virginia Tech. His major interest is history of American education with an emphasis on religion and schooling. He has coedited *The American School in Its Social Setting* (1974) and *Religion and Morality in American Schooling* (1981), and his articles have appeared in *Journal of General Education, Religious Education, Review Journal of Philosophy and Social Science,* and *Journal of Church and State.*

GEORGE R. KNIGHT (Ed.D., University of Houston) is Associate Professor of Educational Foundations at Andrews University. His books include *Philosophy and Education: An Introduction in Christian Perspective* (1980) and *Issues and Alternatives in Educational Philosophy* (1982). He has also contributed articles on history and philosophy of education to various publications, including *Phi Delta Kappan, Journal of Adventist Education,* and *Adventist Heritage.*

CHARLES R. KNIKER (Ed.D., Teachers College, Columbia University) is Professor of Education at Iowa State University. He has published extensively on values education and religion and education. His books include *You and Values Education* (1977) and, with Natalie A. Naylor, *Teaching Today and Tomorrow* (1981).

NORLENE M. KUNKEL (Ph.D., University of Notre Dame) is Assistant Professor of Education at St. Mary's College in Winona, Minnesota. Her interests include history and philosophy of education. She has contributed several articles to the *Notre Dame Journal of Education.*

DONALD OPPEWAL (Ph.D., University of Illinois) is Professor of Education at Calvin College. His current research interests are vouchers and secular humanism. He has contributed numerous articles to various publications, including *Educational Forum, Reformed Journal,* and *Christian Legal Society Quarterly.*

EDUARDO RAUCH (Ed.D., Harvard University) is Co-director of the Melton Research Center for Jewish Education and Visiting Assistant

Professor of Education at the Jewish Theological Seminary of America in New York City. He has published extensively in a number of Jewish periodicals, and is coeditor of *The Melton Journal: Issues and Themes in Jewish Education.*

Index of Names

Index of Subjects